Controversies in Monetary Economics, Revised Edition

Controversies in Monetary Economics, Revised Edition

John Smithin

Professor of Economics, Department of Economics and the Schulich School of Business, York University, Toronto, Canada

Edward Elgar
Cheltenham, UK • Northampton, MA, USA

Published by
Edward Elgar Publishing Limited
Glensanda House
Montpellier Parade
Cheltenham
Glos GL50 1UA
UK

Edward Elgar Publishing, Inc.
136 West Street
Suite 202
Northampton
Massachusetts 01060
USA

First published 1994
Revised edition 2003

A catalogue record for this book
is available from the British Library

Library of Congress Cataloguing in Publication Data

Smithin, John N.
  Controversies in monetary economics / by John Smithin. – revised ed.
    p.   cm.
  Includes index.
  1. Money. 2. Monetary policy. I. Title.
HG221 .S643 2003
332.4–dc21   2002037922

ISBN 1 84064 829 5 (Revised edition, cased)
ISBN 1 85278 399 0 (First edition)

Printed and bound in Great Britain by MPG Books Ltd, Bodmin, Cornwall

Contents

Preface to the revised edition (2003)

After nine years and the start of a new century, the time seems right for a second edition of this book, first published in 1994. From my own point of view, I would like this revision to be seen as superceding or replacing the previous volume. This is not because of any radical change in the basic argument, which remains the same, but simply because I think that the exposition has been improved in this version, and also I have been able to develop some of the original ideas much further than the point I had reached earlier.

Five of the 10 chapters, Chapters 1, 2, 3, 6 and 10, correspond fairly closely to their counterparts in the first edition, although with appropriate emendation and updating. The original Chapters 7, 8 and 9 can also be recognized in the present work, although the order is changed. The 'alternative monetary model' is now the first of these, rather than the last (Chapter 7 rather than Chapter 9), with the chapters on the international economy and the costs of inflation pushed back correspondingly. Chapter 7 is also the place where the model has been most developed from the earlier discussion. One chapter, Chapter 5 of the first edition, has been eliminated entirely, although much of the material from that chapter, which dealt with 'the power of the central bank', has been retained in the appropriate places elsewhere in the book. The old Chapter 4, on the 'real bills doctrine' (etc.) has now become Chapter 5, and there is a new Chapter 4, which is really just an exposition of textbook-type material in macroeconomics. Although I approach this material in a sceptical manner, I felt that it should be set out in more detail, rather than simply discussed verbally, as was done in the first edition.

In the acknowledgments section to the first edition (reproduced below) I thanked a number of individuals for help, not so much with the specifics of the book, but with the various topics that arise in monetary economics generally. To that list I would like to add the following names, with the same disclaimer, Geoff Ingham, Markus Marterbauer, Jeff Lau, Eric Kam, Geoff Harcourt, Otto Steiger, Louis-Phillipe Rochon, Tom Palley, Ric Holt, Per-Gunnar Berglund, Alain Parguez, Peter Howells, Hassan Bougrine, Steve Pressman, John Grieve-Smith, Chris Paraskevopoulos, Gilles Dostaler and Nick Falvo.

As I said before, the one debt I shall never be able adequately to repay is to Hana Smithin.

Acknowledgments (first edition 1994)

In writing this book, my working method has been such that nobody except myself, my wife Hana, the readers commissioned by the publisher, and the editorial and production staff at Aldershot, will have seen the complete manuscript before production. Nonetheless, I have received a great deal of help from others in preparing the individual chapters, often in the form of comments or criticisms on draft papers dealing with topics later reworked for inclusion in the book.

In particular, I have greatly benefited from the opportunity for detailed collaborative work with Sheila Dow, Keith MacKinnon, John Paschakis and Bernard Wolf in earlier papers (both published and unpublished) dealing with issues which I also treat in these pages.

In addition, the following colleagues have made helpful comments and criticisms, either in correspondence or conversation, on draft papers relevant to this volume which have either been circulated or presented at conferences. Thanks are due to Meyer Burstein, Victoria Chick, Paul Davidson, Peter Gray, David Laidler, Marc Lavoie, Basil Moore, Ingrid Rima, Thomas Rymes, Mario Seccareccia, Hans-Michael Trautwein and Randall Wray. I suspect that some of those mentioned will not remember the precise conversation or letter that I have in mind (some of which were a number of years ago) but I assure them all that they have had an influence. I am sure also that I have forgotten to mention a number of individuals from whom I have learned about monetary economics, and, if so, I hope that they will forgive me.

I owe a particular debt to the late Sir John Hicks, who was kind enough to initiate a correspondence with me after the publication of one of my earliest papers in monetary economics a decade ago, and whose later work on money has, of course, been a great inspiration.

Needless to say, none of the economists mentioned are in any way responsible for the remaining shortcomings of this book, all of which are entirely of my own making.

As always, the greatest debt of all is to my wife, Hana, without whose support and encouragement literally nothing would be possible.

Finally, I would like to thank Julie Leppard and the editorial and production staff at Edward Elgar Publishing for their highly efficient and professional work on this volume.

Partial list of symbols

One of the disadvantages of using algebraic-type formulations of economic propositions, as we are more or less obliged to do, is that there are never enough letters in the English and Greek alphabets to go round. In what follows the same symbols are therefore sometimes used for different concepts in different chapters (never within the same chapter). For the convenience of the reader the following list records those symbols that are, in fact, used more than once.

Chapter 3
C = currency in the hands of the non-bank public
D = bank deposits
H = the monetary base ('high-powered money')
R = bank reserves
w = the ratio of 'human to non-human wealth'

Chapter 4
a = responsiveness of the 'natural' unemployment rate to past actual unemployment
b = coefficient relating a 'vector' of supply side variables to the 'natural rate' of unemployment
β = coefficient in the equation for the 'Lucas supply curve'
λ = speed of adjustment coefficient in an 'adaptive expectations' mechanism
w = log of the nominal wage rate

Chapter 5
a = responsiveness of the rate of growth of bank lending and the money supply to the interest differential
c = propensity to consume
C = consumption spending
e = proportion of production costs that are financed by bank loans
k = 'mark-up factor'
θ = coefficients in the 'Taylor rule'
s = propensity to save
S = savings

Chapter 6
a = total real value of assets
c = real consumption
k = real capital stock
H = value of 'Hamiltonian' function
λ = 'co-state' variable
ρ = rate of time preference
v = real value of money transfers

Chapter 7
a = log of the average product of labour
b = log of B (a parameter of the demand for money function)
β = negative of b above
c = propensity to consume
D = real aggregate demand
e = responsiveness of demand growth to an increase in the profit share
h = responsiveness of real wages to an increase in growth
k = aggregate profit share
θ = rate of growth of autonomous demand
v = responsiveness of productivity to an increase in growth
w = log of the nominal wage rate

Chapter 8
C = consumption spending
D = real foreign debt position
R = foreign investment income
ρ = coefficients in the equation relating the currency risk premium to real foreign debt position
s = log of the nominal spot exchange rate
S = the nominal spot exchange rate

1. Money and economic theory and policy

INTRODUCTION

The role of money in the economy and the impact, if any, of monetary changes on overall economic performance have always been a matter of intense controversy and dispute within economics.

A substantial proportion of economic theory and thinking about economic policy actually assigns no role to money, or at least a very minor role, in the determination of the 'real' economic variables that are thought to be of primary interest. This was certainly true, for example, of neo-Walrasian general equilibrium theory, which at one time had claims to be the apex of 'high theory' (Hahn, 1983). Within macroeconomics a popular area of research towards the end of the twentieth century was the so-called 'real business cycle' (RBC) model (Kydland and Prescott, 1982; Snowdon and Vane, 1997; Ryan and Mullineux, 1997) whose name is self-explanatory. Similarly, neoclassical long-run growth models (Jones, 1998; Snowdon and Vane, 1997), whether or not they allow for 'endogenous growth' (Romer, 1986), have also tended to focus almost exclusively on non-monetary factors, such as the accumulation of physical capital, technological innovations and the growth of 'knowledge' (that is, technical expertise). Finally, there have even been several versions of so-called 'Keynesian economics', which have interpreted Keynes as asserting that money does not matter, in spite of the fact that the full title of Keynes's most famous work was *The General Theory of Employment Interest and Money* (1936).

As noted by Smithin (2000), this apparent neglect of the role of money in the socioeconomic system cannot be seen primarily as a response to recent technological innovations in the financial and payments system. It is true that changes in computer technology have led on to discussions of a 'cashless society', 'virtual money', and so forth. However, it seems fairly obvious that this is a change of form rather than substance. All that is implied by talk of a cashless society is that it is possible to envisage an electronic payments technology that makes no use of bits of paper and small metal disks. However the cashless society is hardly 'moneyless', far from it. The purpose of 'e-business', or 'e-commerce', is also to 'make money', exactly as before. Indeed, under capitalism new technology would not be introduced at all if it could not be made to pay in the traditional sense.

A far more serious issue, from the perspective of arriving at an understanding of how the economic system actually operates, is that orthodox economic theory, the theory on which we were all 'brought up' (Keynes, 1936), has always had a tendency to deny the importance of money and monetary factors in determining economic outcomes. This goes back to a time long before anybody had thought of computers. The essence of the economic thought of the classical economists, such as Smith (1776), Ricardo (1817) and Mill (1848) was precisely their indignation at what they perceived to be the errors of their mercantilist predecessors, including the idea 'that wealth consists in . . . gold and silver' (Smith, 1776), in other words the money of their era. And this attitude has persisted to the present day. As stated by Dostaler and Maris (2000), 'orthodox economics wanted to create a science that ignored money', and every economist is familiar with the catchphrases and slogans which express this point of view, such as 'money is neutral' or 'money is a veil'. Underlying these notions is the view that economics deals fundamentally with the so-called 'real' exchange of goods and services, as opposed to the accumulation of financial resources. As Yeager (1997) has expressed it, in a volume which nonetheless stresses the importance of monetary *disequilibrium*, '(F)undamentally, behind the veil of money, people specialize in producing particular goods and services to exchange them for the specialized outputs of other people.' This a proposition which is more or less unchallenged in the textbooks and journal articles of current neoclassical economic analysis, and quite naturally leads on to a point of view which de-emphasizes the importance of money in the evolution of actual economic outcomes, except precisely in disequilibrium situations. The latter, however, no matter how serious the consequences may be in the short run, are held not to permanently affect the underlying real economic equilibrium.

At a more formal level, and as discussed in detail by Rogers (1989), Schumpeter, in his classic *History of Economic Analysis* (1954) made the important distinction between 'real analysis' and 'monetary analysis' in the history of economic thought. Real analysis operates on the above assumption that all the important features of the economic process can be understood in terms of the barter exchange of real goods and services, and their cooperation in production. In monetary analysis, however, the fact that employment and production outcomes depend upon calculations made in monetary terms, and that, in general, the reward structure of the whole society depends ultimately on monetary receipts and monetary disbursements, is taken seriously. In short, money, credit creation and the cost of acquiring financial resources are an integral part of the economic process.

For our purposes, the significance of the Schumpeterian distinctions is that almost all mainstream economic theory, from the time of Adam Smith onwards, has been oriented to real rather than monetary analysis.

THE KEYNESIAN CONCEPT OF 'MONETARY PRODUCTION'

The most prominent exception to the tradition of real analysis during the twentieth century was obviously Keynes's 'monetary theory of production' (Dillard, 1988; Dimand, 1988; Rotheim, 1999), which, however, was ultimately only a partial success in challenging traditional views on economic theory and policy (Smithin, 1990, 1996).

The general idea of monetary production is that the economic system under which we live, variously described as capitalism or the market economy, and which has existed in one form or another since the industrial revolution is, in fact, pre-eminently a *monetary* system. Those responsible for setting production in train, whether they are entrepreneurs or corporations, must first acquire monetary resources by borrowing, selling equity, or previous (financial) accumulation before they can do so. The ultimate proceeds of productive activity from the subsequent sale of goods and services are also sums of money. Intuitively therefore in such an environment, and contrary to the point of view that money does not matter, the functioning of the monetary system takes on major significance. In particular, the 'terms on which' (Keynes, 1936) the monetary resources necessary for production are obtainable (that is, the rate of interest) would seem to be of vital importance.

As described by Asimakopoulos (1988), Keynes (in a draft chapter of the *General Theory*, which unfortunately did not survive in the final version), once made the useful distinction between what he called 'a cooperative economy' and a 'money wage or entrepreneur economy'. The former would essentially involve barter in the sphere of production as well as of exchange, the factors of production cooperating in the productive process agreeing to receive their reward in terms of a predetermined share of the actual output produced. According to Keynes, the orthodox economic theory of his day, what he called the 'classical' theory,[1] basically confined itself to the study of a system of this kind, or at least a system which replicates the properties of the cooperative economy, even if money could be included in a token fashion. Modern theories which assert the unimportance of money are operating under basically the same assumptions. In the entrepreneur economy, however, the point is that production and employment decisions are made by those who must hire the factors of production by making monetary payments, and whose receipts from the eventual sale of output will also be in terms of money. According to Keynes, this was a better description of the actual economy than the barter-oriented world of the cooperative economy. In the entrepreneur economy, output and employment outcomes will depend upon expectations of money receipts relative to money cost. More generally, monetary conditions will matter in an essential way for overall economic performance. As Keynes himself remarked in the *General Theory*, monetary factors must enter 'as a real determinant into the economic scheme'.

As with the issue of the computerization of the payments system, touched on above, it obviously is reasonable to inquire to what extent these insights from three-quarters of a century ago would still be relevant to the economy of the twenty-first century. After all, one of the favourite themes of present-day economic commentators is one version or another of the 'new economy' (one of which seems to appear every three or four years). Incessant technical change has indeed been a feature of the capitalist economic system from the beginning, and is itself one of its 'permanent' characteristics. Hence it is true that the tangible structure of the economy, in terms of methods of production, technology, the range of goods and services offered, and so on, is always in flux. Nevertheless, the basic *social* structure identified by Keynes, that is of production, sales and accumulation in money terms, is clearly still instantly recognizable in the contemporary economic scene, as it was for centuries before Keynes's time. In other words, it seems to be the *monetary aspect itself* that provides the element of historical continuity, and makes possible a genuinely macroeconomic theory as such (Fletcher, 2000; Smithin, forthcoming), which retains its broad relevance across a number of different epochs.

THE LESSONS OF HISTORY

In spite of the eclipse of Keynesian thought, and the ubiquitous influence of current orthodoxy, the historical record does in fact suggest a number of seemingly compelling reasons for questioning the validity of the underlying neutral money assumption. The most obvious of these is the frequency with which problems in the real economy have been accompanied by, or coincided with, similar disruptions and crises in monetary conditions, and the twists and turns of monetary policy. Also, a number of the important political debates in each era seem to have had a monetary connection or monetary aspects, illustrating the significance that politicians and commentators have instinctively ascribed to monetary matters. More than a hundred years ago, for example, depressed economic conditions in the US economy at the end of the nineteenth century (the original Great

Depression) were blamed on the gold standard, in the celebrated 'cross of gold' speech by the presidential candidate William Jennings Bryan in 1896 (Galbraith, 1987; Mankiw, 1992).[2] The debate over the role of monetary policy and the banking crisis in the still more catastrophic Great Depression of the 1930s provides a probably more familiar example (Friedman and Schwartz, 1963; Friedman and Friedman, 1980; Temin, 1976, 1989). Monetary questions likewise seem to have been central in disputes over the stagflationary conditions of the 1970s, the 'monetarist experiments' and the re-emergence of mass unemployment in the 1980s (Smithin, 1990, 1996), and recurrent international currency crises during the 1990s (Grieve-Smith and Michie, 1999; Soros, 1998). Moreover, if it were really true that money does not matter it would be extremely difficult to explain why the social control and production of money is continuously the subject of such ferocious political debate. Why (at the time of writing) does it seem to be such an important issue to the financial interests that central banks should be 'independent' (that is, not subject to control by elected legislatures)? Why do participants in financial markets in Wall Street, and elsewhere, hang on every word uttered by the chair of the Board of Governors of the Federal Reserve System in congressional testimony? What is the significance of the contentious social experiment currently under way in Europe, of a 'single currency', the Euro, for most of the member states of the European Union (Smithin and Smithin, 1998; Parguez, 1999), and analogous discussions of currency union or 'dollarization' elsewhere around the globe?

It is presumably this type of consideration that led Hicks (1967) to remark that 'monetary theory . . . cannot avoid a relation to reality which in other economic theory is sometimes missing. It belongs to monetary history in a way that economic theory does not always belong to economic history . . . monetary theories arise out of monetary disturbances'. Referring specifically to the work of Keynes, Hicks (1983) also characterized that body of theoretical work as 'the intellectual counterpart to the monetary revolution of our times' (that is Hicks's times) by which he meant the collapse of the international gold standard after World War I, and the subsequent struggle to find some alternative monetary constitution, which eventually occupied the entire twentieth century and still continues.

Moreover, it is this sense of how frequently monetary matters seem to be at the heart of real world economic and political problems which has instinctively led many of the most famous names in economics, including, for example, Keynes, Hicks, Hayek and Friedman during the twentieth century, to devote such a large proportion of their energies to money and monetary matters. This point remains valid even if a number of those devoting themselves to money eventually arrived at a real, rather than a monetary, analysis, in the sense defined above. The intellectual effort that such thinkers were prepared to devote to understanding the role of money would hardly have been necessary if the economy could indeed function on a cooperative barter basis.

Somewhat similar instincts have presumably also motivated generations of 'monetary reformers' outside the ranks of professional economists, and outright 'monetary cranks' (Clark, 1989) who have put forward panaceas and nostrums of one sort or another. It might also be remarked that one person's crank is another's 'brave heretic' (Keynes, 1936). On this topic, Robertson (1940), a determined, but sophisticated and informed, critic of Keynes, had this to say about the self-styled monetary reformers:

> It is easy to scoff at these productions: it is not always so easy to see exactly where they go wrong. It is natural that practical bankers, vaguely conscious that the projects of monetary cranks are dangerous to society, should cling in self-defence to the solid rock, or what they believe to be so, of tradition and accepted practice. But it is not open to the detached student of economics to take refuge from dangerous innovation in blind conservatism. [Such a student] . . . must assess with an equal eye the projects of reformers and the claims of the established order; and to this end must build up . . . a theory of money – a critical analysis of the nature and results of the processes by which, under a modern system of banking, money is manufactured.

This in itself seems to be quite a reasonable motto, regardless of the views on money ultimately arrived at by Robertson himself (Fletcher, 2000),[3] but it sets out a task for monetary economists which remains to be completed to this day.

THE INFLUENCE OF MONETARISM

In the third quarter of the twentieth century, one of the most influential academic schools of thought, which came in time also to have considerable political influence in many of the advanced industrialized nations, did seem to place monetary policy and monetary theory at the very centre of their concerns. The reference is to so-called *monetarism*, which was associated particularly with the name of Milton Friedman of the University of Chicago. As discussed in Chapter 3 below, the achievement of this school was to draw the attention of the economics profession to issues of monetary theory and monetary policy at a time when interest in such concerns was at a low ebb. However, as also discussed in more detail in that chapter, it is doubtful whether in the final analysis monetarism itself did much to re-establish the view that money matters. In Schumpeterian terminology, although the subject of monetarism obviously was money, it nonetheless approached that subject from the standpoint of real analysis rather than monetary analysis.

In the monetarist model, the quantity of money was taken to be of a given magnitude capable, in principle, of being exogenously determined by a central bank or some other 'monetary authority'. Changes in the quantity of money might have a temporary or short-run impact on real economic variables, but the only lasting effect would be on nominal prices. Recognition of the short-run non-neutrality of money (due, for example, to nominal rigidities or mistaken expectations) was nonetheless significant, as this would provide some explanation of those real-world episodes in which monetary disturbances did after all apparently play a decisive role. In the long run, however, and at the level of pure theory, the economy described by the monetarists was simply a version of Keynes's cooperative barter economy, in which the real economic outcomes would be the same regardless of whether the monetary system existed or not. In particular, the model assumed the existence of 'natural rates' of both interest and unemployment, which in the long run were determined only by real factors and were impervious to monetary manipulation.

The combination of short-run monetary non-neutrality and long-run neutrality certainly enabled economists such as Friedman and Schwartz (1963, 1982) to put forward a consistent interpretation of both inflationary and deflationary episodes. In effect, they were able to blame the US central bank for *both* the mass unemployment of the 1930s *and* the problems of inflation in the post-World War II era. Nonetheless, the underlying model of the economy was still one in which over the long haul the most important economic variables, such as real interest rates and real economic growth, were determined independently of any monetary influence.

SOME IMPORTANT THEMES IN MONETARY ECONOMICS

The foregoing brief discussion of the reasons why the monetarist model did not provide a genuine monetary theory of production helps to illustrate a number of important themes that seem to have been present throughout most of the controversies in monetary economics, which have arisen both historically and in the modern era. It will be worthwhile to identify explicitly each of these themes at the outset.

The first question to be asked, presumably, is the basic one of how the social constructs of money and credit came into existence in the first place, and how they are reproduced and maintained. This is bound up with the entire logical/historical question of how the capitalist institutions, in particular the basic concept of production for sale in the market, specifically for monetary reward, came to exert such a dominating influence in our social life. The answer to this tends to be taken for granted in the orthodox economic literature, which espouses one version or another of the view of Menger (1892) that the 'market' itself is the primary concept, and that money must logically emerge from the market. However, another view is possible, namely that it is money (the idea or concept of money) which is the starting point and, rather than money emerging from the market, the market emerges from money. In other words, 'money is a social relation' (Ingham, 1996, 2000, 2001), involving a money of account, price lists, credit, and so on, and is itself the precondition for market exchange and monetary production. It can immediately be seen that the (apparently) purely analytical questions in dispute are in fact closely related to the positions taken in this logically prior debate. As remarked by Bougrine and Seccareccia (2001), 'the . . . policy divide in macroeconomics is provided by competing conceptions of money'. Hence these fundamental issues deserve more attention here than is usually given to them in textbook treatments.

One of the most important of the subsequent analytical questions which then arise is that of how money is injected into the economy, or rather how it is created and destroyed. In the contemporary jargon this is the debate over 'exogenous' versus 'endogenous' money. Should the quantity of money be treated as a fixed amount, capable of being determined exogenously by some such agency as a central bank? Or should it rather be treated as an endogenous variable, which expands residually whenever the volume of credit granted by financial institutions increases, and contracts when the volume of credit contracts? In the modern 'credit economy', after all, the statistically defined money supply consists mainly of the liabilities of financial institutions such as 'banks'. This debate has been on going as long as banking institutions have been in existence, up to the present day. The monetarists took the former point of view, arguing that, even in a developed credit economy, the central bank could control the money supply quantitatively via the so-called 'money multiplier' linking the monetary base to the statistically defined monetary aggregates. More recently, however, there has been a considerable revival of the endogenous money approach, particularly among heterodox economists such as Post Keynesians, members of the circuit school, and neo-chartalists (Kaldor, 1986; Moore, 1988; Graziani, 1990; Lavoie, 1992; Nell and Deleplace, 1996; Rochon, 1999; Parguez and Seccareccia, 2000; Wray 1998, 2000). Monetary control on this view could only be indirect, by interest rate changes, for example.

Another ubiquitous analytical theme, then, is the question of interest rate determination, an equally contentious issue in monetary economics, and which, from some points of view, may well be considered *the* key issue.

The most popular assumption among professional economists (as was the case with monetarist theory) has been that the rate of interest is determined fundamentally by real forces *outside* the monetary system, such as the demand for and supply of (physical) capital. This is the doctrine of the natural rate of interest, which has appeared in one guise or another throughout the whole history of discussion of monetary topics. Once such an assumption is made, however, this immediately forecloses the debate over whether monetary changes can have any lasting significance for the real economy. By definition, they will not. If money does affect inflation, then it might well be accepted that monetary changes can affect the nominal interest rate (which is simply the quoted interest rate including an inflation premium). However, by assumption, monetary changes will not affect the 'real' (inflation-adjusted) interest rate, and there is therefore no question of any long-lasting impact of monetary changes on any of the most important real economic variables. Indeed, if a natural rate of interest exists in the model the implication is that there cannot be any monetary analysis at all in the sense defined above, only a real analysis. An alternative point of view, however, is that the real rate of interest itself is essentially a *monetary* phenomenon and that the economy must adjust to the rate of interest established by the monetary system, rather than the reverse. In this case, the outcome of the debate over monetary policy is no longer a foregone conclusion. Money and monetary policy will be fundamentally non-neutral and a genuine monetary analysis will be possible. There have been basically two versions of the argument. The first of these was Keynes's notion of liquidity preference, which should properly be regarded precisely as an alternative theory of interest rate determination, rather than simply as a theory of money demand, as in the textbooks. The second 'monetary theory of interest' is simply the view that the rate of interest is determined administratively or politically by the policy decisions of the central bank. The latter point of view, in turn, has been associated with the revival of the concept of endogenous money mentioned above.

Clearly, the position reached on the question of interest rate determination is highly relevant to the debate about the appropriate monetary control variable, and what are the most appropriate 'monetary policy rules' (Walsh, 1998; Taylor, 1993, 1999). This topic is therefore another of our continuing themes. As mentioned, the monetarist school was in favour of directly controlling the rate of growth of some statistically defined measure of the money supply, or of the monetary base. In the economics textbooks, moreover, the assumption is still frequently made that there is some unique 'M', the 'money supply', which is the exogenous monetary policy variable. As a practical matter, however, both before and after the period of monetarist ascendancy in the late twentieth century, the actual monetary control instrument typically employed by central banks is a short-term interest rate of some kind (Goodhart, 1989; 2002, B. Friedman, 2000).[4] But this, in turn, raises a number of awkward questions in trying to reconcile this fact with both the orthodox literature and the various preconceptions of the way interest rates would theoretically be determined in a barter economy. Some of these questions were prefigured by Keynes (1930) in his well-known discussion of the 'three strands of thought' on bank rate policy. Are the interest rate changes just an indirect method of controlling the money supply or the exchange rate, or are they important in their own right? What is the relationship between those interest rates directly under the control of the central bank and the whole complex of other interest rates in the system? Is the central bank influencing real interest rates or just nominal rates? And so on. As pointed out above, if we have already decided that 'true' interest rates are determined otherwise than by central bank policy we must then differentiate between the interest rate set by the central bank and the hypothesized natural rate, and ultimately make the outcome of economic policy decisions hinge on that discrepancy. Otherwise, taking the contrary view, Keynes's idea of interest rate policy becoming an 'independent influence' becomes a real possibility.

The last of the major monetary themes under discussion is then the various competing views about the impact, if any, of changes in the monetary variables (however these may be defined) on the other important economic variables. How do such changes affect output and employment, their rates of growth, inflation, real wages, profits, the exchange rate, the balance of payments, and so on? The views taken on these issues will (again) depend on the positions that are adopted about whether money is exogenous or endogenous, whether or not there is a natural rate of interest, and whether the interest rate or the monetary base should be regarded as the relevant monetary control variable. The major dividing line on most of these issues will arise from a presupposition about whether or not monetary factors can *permanently* affect real variables, as opposed to some short-run or temporary impact. The latter is usually, if not always, conceded.

If the initial presumption is that, almost by definition, monetary factors cannot permanently affect other economic variables, then evidently the most basic question has been decided without the need for any further analysis. As suggested, something of the kind has almost always been the orthodox view. If this is the case, however, a major difficulty arises in the need to explain why monetary issues and problems have so often been at the forefront of real-world political debate, and not only in the context of the relationship between money and inflation. If eventual monetary neutrality is taken for granted, the only remaining avenue for a coherent explanation of actual monetary problems would be a highly elastic framework along the lines of the monetarist (or Marshallian) distinction between the 'short run' and the 'long run'. The actual calendar length of this short run must then be flexible enough to encompass whatever economic events need to be explained in any particular historical episode.

Each of the major themes identified here will be explored in more detail throughout the book.

PLAN OF THE BOOK

In what follows, Chapter 2, 'The nature and functions of money: a re-examination', corresponds to the textbook chapters on this topic. However, a renewed attention to this issue is required, in particular in the light of the fundamental debate over the role of money alluded to above. The view that ongoing changes in technology imply that production and exchange in a 'market economy' could be carried out via a 'sophisticated barter system', without resort to monetary exchange, is rejected, as is the position that any such non-monetary barter system ever existed in the past. On the contrary, it is suggested that the logic of monetary production does require the existence of some unique monetary asset that represents both the standard of value (unit of account) and the ultimate means of payment (means of final settlement). However, this does not have to be an asset that corresponds to any physical commodity, or one whose supply is exogenously fixed. From these considerations flow most of the distinctive characteristics of the monetary economy.

Chapter 3 then goes on to a discussion and critique of 'Monetarism and the quantity theory of money' as the leading illustration of one of the main existing approaches to monetary issues and problems, while Chapter 4, on 'Short-run non-neutralities, nominal rigidities, misperceptions and the concept of the Phillips curve', takes a similar critical approach to the type of material which frequently appears in mainstream textbooks dealing with the relationship between monetary changes and the real economy. Chapter 5 deals with 'The real bills doctrine, interest rate pegging and endogenous money', and discusses a number of alternatives to, or modifications of, quantity-theoretic reasoning that have been put forward over the years.

Chapter 6, 'Money, interest rates and output', directly addresses the debates about interest rate determination, and in particular whether the (real) interest rate is a 'real' or monetary phenomenon, and the extent to which is can be treated as a policy variable under the control of the monetary authorities. The purpose of Chapter 7 'An alternative monetary model of inflation and economic growth', is then to present an outline of what an alternative approach to some of these key issues in monetary economics might entail. The policy of the central bank is seen as setting the tone for *real* interest rates throughout the system, with the money supply adjusting endogenously to the demand for credit at those interest rates. Changes in central bank policy are therefore seen to affect both output growth and inflation, and the idea of the 'vertical Phillips curve', suggesting that central banks can achieve any inflation rate they want without affecting the real growth prospects of the economy, seems to be a chimera. The same framework suggests that aggregate demand management 'matters', and not only for short-run economic outcomes as the contemporary macroeconomic orthodoxy would have it, but also for economic growth and development.

Chapter 8 broadens the analysis to include a discussion of 'The international economy and alternative exchange rate regimes'. This deals with the relationship between the various competing monetary networks in the international economy. The chapter addresses such questions as which exchange rate regime best serves the interests of the individual national jurisdictions, whether or not an 'independent' monetary policy is possible for such a jurisdiction in the contemporary global economy, and conversely, whether it would be better to adopt fixed exchange rates, or for the individual nation states to relinquish their monetary sovereignty altogether in favour of a common currency at either a regional or global level. Chapter 9, on 'Inflation and the economy', discusses the reasoning behind the seemingly obsessive concern with inflation that appears to have driven so many real-world monetary policy initiatives. It finds that the costs of inflation have not been well articulated by the economics profession and that therefore the basis of the great 'fear' of inflation, which seems to motivate many central bankers, and policy makers in general, is not at all clear. This impression is certainly heightened when those ill-defined costs are compared with the damage to the real economy, which frequently seems to ensue in the wake of monetary policy actions designed to cure inflation.

The final chapter of the book, Chapter 10, contains some 'Concluding remarks'.

NOTES

1. Keynes (1936) admitted that this terminology was a 'solecism' as he included the marginalist neoclassical economists (such as Menger, Jevons, Marshall and Walras) as well as the genuine classical economists (Smith, Ricardo, Mill *et al.*) under this rubric. Keynes's procedure, however, is more defensible in the context of monetary economics than it would be in terms of general economic theory. In the monetary field there is substantial continuity between these groups, particularly in variations on the theme of the natural rate of interest.
2. Mankiw (1992), in an intermediate-level macroeconomics text, makes the fascinating observation that the famous 'children's story' *The Wizard of Oz* was originally a political

allegory about this episode in US monetary history, the 'yellow brick road' representing the gold standard.
3. Fletcher (2000) concludes that Robertson's own position was ultimately far closer to modern real business cycle theory than to Keynesian monetary economics.
4. The IMF (2001) in its annual *World Economic Outlook* explicitly identifies the 'policy-related' interest rate in each jurisdiction. It is striking how closely short-term rates in general mirror the policy-related rates.

REFERENCES

Asimakopoulos, A. (1988), 'The aggregate supply function and the share economy: some early drafts of the *General Theory*', in O.F. Hamouda and J. Smithin (eds), *Keynes and Public Policy after Fifty Years*, vol. 2, *Theories and Method*, Aldershot, UK and Brookfield, US: Edward Elgar.

Bougrine, H. and M. Seccareccia (2001), 'The monetary role of taxes in the national economy', paper presented at the annual meetings of the Canadian Economics Association, Montreal, June.

Clark, D. (1989), 'Monetary cranks', in J. Eatwell, M. Milgate and P. Newman (eds), *The New Palgrave: Money*, London: Macmillan.

Dillard, D. (1988), 'The barter illusion in classical and neoclassical economics', *Eastern Economic Journal*, 14, 299–318.

Dimand, R.W. (1988), 'The development of Keynes's theory of employment', in O.F. Hamouda and J. Smithin (eds), *Keynes and Public Policy after Fifty Years*, vol. 1, *Economics and Policy*, Aldershot, UK and Brookfield, US: Edward Elgar.

Dostaler, G. and B. Maris (2000), 'Dr. Freud and Mr. Keynes on money and capitalism', in J. Smithin (ed.), *What is Money?*, London: Routledge.

Fletcher, G. (2000), *Understanding Dennis Robertson: The Man and his Work*, Cheltenham, UK and Northampton, MA, USA: Edward Elgar.

Friedman, B.M. (2000), 'The role of interest rates in Federal Reserve policymaking', NBER Working Paper 8047, December.

Friedman, M. and R. Friedman (1980), *Free to Choose*, New York: Harcourt Brace Jovanovich.

Friedman, M. and A.J. Schwartz (1963), *A Monetary History of the United States, 1867–1960*, Princeton: Princeton University Press.

—— (1982), *Monetary Trends in the United States and United Kingdom: Their Relation to Income, Prices and Interest Rates, 1867–1975*, Chicago: University of Chicago Press.

Galbraith, J.K. (1987), *Economics in Perspective: A Critical History*, Boston: Houghton Mifflin.

Goodhart, C.A.E. (1989), 'Monetary base', in J. Eatwell, M. Milgate and P. Newman (eds), *The New Palgrave: Money*, London: Macmillan.

—— (2002), 'The endogeneity of money', in P. Arestis, M. Desai and S. Dow (eds), *Money, Macroeconomics and Keynes: Essays in Honour of Victoria Chick*, London; Routledge.

Graziani, A. (1990), 'The theory of the monetary circuit', *Economies et Sociétés*, 24, 7–36.

Grieve-Smith, J. and J. Michie (eds) (1999), *Global Instability: The Political Economy of World Economic Governance*, London: Routledge.

Hahn, F. (1983), *Money and Inflation*, Cambridge, MA: MIT Press.

Hicks, J.R. (1967), 'Monetary theory and history: an attempt at perspective', in *Critical Essays in Monetary Theory*, Oxford: Clarendon Press.

—— (1983), 'The Keynes centenary: a skeptical follower', *The Economist*, 18 June.

IMF (2001), *World Economic Outlook*, Washington, DC, May.

Ingham, G. (1996), 'Money is a social relation', *Review of Social Economy*, 54, 243–75.

—— (2000), 'Babylonian madness: on the historical and sociological origins of money', in J. Smithin (ed.) *What is Money?*, London: Routledge.

—— (2001), 'New monetary spaces?', paper presented at the OECD conference, 'The Future of Money', Luxembourg, July.

Jones, C.I. (1998), *An Introduction to Economic Growth*, New York: W.W. Norton.

Kaldor, N. (1986), *The Scourge of Monetarism*, 2nd edn, Oxford: Oxford University Press.

Keynes, J.M. (1930), *A Treatise on Money* (2 vols), London: Macmillan.

—— (1936), *The General Theory of Employment Interest and Money*, London: Macmillan.

Kydland, F.E. and E.C. Prescott (1982), 'Time to build and aggregate fluctuations', *Econometrica*, 50, 1345–70.

Lavoie, M. (1992), *Foundations of Post-Keynesian Economic Analysis*, Aldershot, UK and Brookfield, US: Edward Elgar.

Mankiw, N.G. (1992), *Macroeconomics*, New York: Worth Publishers.

Menger, C. (1892), 'On the origin of money', *Economic Journal*, 2, 239–55.

Mill, J.S. (1987 [1848]), *Principles of Political Economy*, ed. W. Ashley, New York: Augustus M. Kelley.

Moore, B.J. (1988), *Horizontalists and Verticalists: The Macroeconomics of Credit Money*, Cambridge: Cambridge University Press.

Nell, E.J. and G. Deleplace (eds) (1996), *Money in Motion: The Post Keynesian and Circulation Approaches*, London: Macmillan.

Parguez, A. (1999), 'The expected failure of the European Monetary and Economic Union: a false money against the real economy', *Eastern Economic Journal*, 25, 63–76.

—— and M. Seccareccia (2000), 'The credit theory of money: the monetary circuit approach', in J. Smithin (ed.) *What is Money?*, London: Routledge.

Ricardo, D. (1973 [1817]), *The Principles of Political Economy and Taxation*, ed. D. Winch, London: J.M. Dent & Sons.

Robertson, D. (1940), *Essays in Monetary Theory*, London: P.S. King & Son.

Rochon, L-P. (1999), *Credit, Money and Production*, Cheltenham, UK and Northampton, MA, USA: Edward Elgar.

Rogers, C. (1989), *Money, Interest and Capital: A Study in the Foundations of Monetary Theory*, Cambridge: Cambridge University Press.

Romer, P.M. (1986), 'Increasing returns and long-run growth', *Journal of Political Economy*, 94, 1002–37.

Rotheim, R. (1999), 'Post Keynesian economics and realist philosophy', *Journal of Post Keynesian Economics*, 22, 71–103.

Ryan, C. and A.W. Mullineux (1997), 'The ups and downs of modern business cycle theory', in B. Snowdon and H.R. Vane (eds), *Reflections on the Development of Modern Macroeconomics*, Cheltenham, UK and Lyme, US: Edward Elgar.

Schumpeter, J.A. (1994 [1954]), *A History of Economic Analysis*, London: Routledge.

Smith, A. (1981 [1776]), *An Inquiry into the Nature and Causes of the Wealth of*

Nations (2 vols), R.H. Campbell and A.S. Skinner (eds), Indianapolis: Liberty Fund.

Smithin, H. and J. Smithin (1998), 'Spolecna mena: nove moznosti, nebo hrozba?' (The single currency: new opportunities or a threat?), *Novy domov* (Toronto), 25, August.

Smithin, J. (1990), *Macroeconomics After Thatcher and Reagan: The Conservative Policy Revolution in Retrospect*, Aldershot, UK and Brookfield, US: Edward Elgar.

—— (1996), *Macroeconomic Policy and the Future of Capitalism: The Revenge of the Rentiers and the Threat to Prosperity*, Cheltenham, UK and Brookfield, US: Edward Elgar.

—— (2000), 'What is money? Introduction', in J. Smithin (ed.), *What is Money?*, London: Routledge.

—— (forthcoming), 'Macroeconomic theory, (critical) realism, and capitalism', in P.A. Lewis (ed.), *Transforming Economics: Perspectives on the Critical Realist Project*, London: Routledge.

Snowdon, B. and H.R. Vane (1997), 'To stabilize or not to stabilize: is that the question?', in B. Snowdon and H.R. Vane (eds), *Reflections on the Development of Modern Macroeconomics*, Cheltenham, UK and Lyme, US: Edward Elgar.

Soros, G. (1998), *The Crisis of Global Capitalism: Open Society Endangered*, New York: Public Affairs.

Taylor, J.B. (1993), 'Discretion versus policy rules in practice', *Carnegie-Rochester Conference Series on Public Policy*, 39, 195–214.

—— (ed.)(1999), *Monetary Policy Rules*, Chicago: University of Chicago Press.

Temin, P. (1976), *Did Monetary Forces Cause the Great Depression?*, New York: Norton.

—— (1989), *Lessons from the Great Depression*, Cambridge, MA: MIT Press.

Walsh, C.E. (1998), *Monetary Theory and Policy*, Cambridge, MA: MIT Press.

Wray, L.R. (1998), *Understanding Modern Money: The Key to Full Employment and Price Stability*, Cheltenham, UK and Lyme, US: Edward Elgar.

—— (2000), 'Modern money', in J. Smithin (ed.), *What is Money?*, London: Routledge.

Yeager, L.B. (1997), *The Fluttering Veil: Essays on Monetary Disequilibrium*, ed. G. Selgin, Indianapolis: Liberty Fund.

2. The nature and functions of money: a re-examination

INTRODUCTION

Standard textbooks on money and banking invariably include a chapter with a title similar to that above, in which the objective is to define money at a conceptual level, primarily with reference to the functions it is supposed to perform in the market economy. This is thought necessary because of the difficulties standing in the way of any comprehensive empirical definition. Historically, a very broad range of physical commodities and financial assets has been acceptable as money at different times and places. In an era of rapid financial innovation, such as the present, the evolution of the payments system becomes apparent even to the most casual participant in the process, to the embarrassment of econometricians estimating demand for money functions, or policy makers inclined to conduct monetary policy with reference to one or other of the arbitrarily defined monetary aggregates. The same textbooks provide long lists of the different items which have (actually or reputedly) served as money at one time or another, ranging from the ubiquitous cattle and cowry shells of ancient times, tobacco in colonial America, the stone money of Uap, coins minted from the precious metals such as gold and silver, bank notes and bank deposits, inconvertible paper money, deposits at non-bank financial institutions, and so on, up to and including the 'e-money' (electronic money) of the present day.[1]

The point of defining money in terms of the functions it performs is (presumably) to cut through the problems posed by this continuing evolutionary process. In a given society at any point in time money can then be defined in principle simply as the subset of total financial assets and commodities which are actually performing monetary functions. Three main monetary functions are usually suggested. Money is thought to be that which serves as a *medium of exchange*, *store of value* and *unit of account*. To identify money empirically in a particular context would then simply involve a judgment as to which items currently possess these properties to a greater or lesser extent.

It is apparent, however, that posing the question in these terms really only scratches the surface of the difficult problems involved in defining the role played by money. It immediately invites a debate, for example, about which of these functions should be taken as substantively the most significant and (perhaps even more important to contemporary mathematical economic theorists), which is the most capable of being modelled with the requisite degree of formalism. For example, in the traditional demand for money literature surveyed by Laidler (1993), some of the familiar theories focus exclusively on the medium of exchange function (Baumol, 1952), while others concentrate on money in the context of portfolio choice (Tobin, 1958), and therefore on the store of value aspect. The differences between the alternative approaches, and the issues thought to be important within each, seem to boil down simply to the choice of the analyst about which of the functions to stress. The case is similar with the various methods that have been employed to introduce money formally into the popular neoclassical models that are currently dominant in mainstream economics. These models are based ultimately on barter and, unless some such analytical device can be found, would actually have no role for money (Hahn, 1983). This question is therefore a prominent topic in the graduate-level textbooks in both monetary economics and macroeconomics (Blanchard and Fischer, 1989; Walsh, 1998; Turnovsky, 1999). For example, the 'cash in advance' (CIA) model, based originally on a suggestion of Clower (1967), attempts to model formally the medium of exchange function, while 'overlapping generations' (OLG) models following Samuelson (1958) treat money solely as an intertemporal store of value or wealth. Again, the reasons for potential disagreement between adherents of the rival approaches are easily apparent, and amount to the assertion that each emphasizes one of the monetary functions at the expense of the others. A significant feature, moreover, of the mainstream discussion of money, and as noted by Hoover (1996), is that the unit of account function, although identified by Keynes (1930) as the 'primary concept of a theory of money'[2] seems invariably to be on the back burner.

A further temptation that seems to be suggested by the textbook 'triad' is to raise the question of whether the different functions logically *need* to be bundled together in the same asset or set of assets. Would it be possible to design a coherent system in which the monetary functions are separated? From this viewpoint, it then seems relevant also to ask whether such a system would function more efficiently than the one currently in place, or which of these alternatives might have evolved in some imagined and ideal 'natural economy'. As discussed by Hoover (1988), Trautwein (1993) and Cowen and Kroszner (1994), during the 1980s and 1990s such an approach was debated and advocated by a number of authors whose work, collectively, was labelled the 'New Monetary Economics' (NME). This type of work might be interpreted as having been motivated, on the one hand, by a continuing commitment to a vision of the economic system operating on essentially Walrasian barter-oriented lines, and, on the other, by the idea that modern technological advances finally do make feasible a purely accounting system of exchange in which the only necessary counterpart to 'real' transactions is some form of computerized book-keeping to record wealth transfers (McCallum, 1985). But, clearly, in terms of the effort to identify the key characteristics of a monetary economy, all this *already* pre-supposes a particular answer to the broader question of the role which money plays in economic life.

Another (related) weakness of the textbook triad approach is that it draws attention away from the hierarchical nature of monetary systems in practice (Bell, 2001). Even if there is a multiplicity of media of exchange in any given monetary system, there invariably seems to be a unique asset, which constitutes the unambiguously *final* means of settlement in the given social setting. This corresponds to what is described as *base money* in the mainstream literature or *valuata* money (Wray, 1998) in the chartalist or state money approach. Dow and Smithin (1999), among others, have argued that a hierarchical system is in some sense fundamental, and that a logical prerequisite for a functioning system of monetary production is that the means of final settlement and the unit of account are unambiguously united in the same asset, even in the presence of a multiplicity of actual exchange media. Only in these circumstances, it can be argued, does taking a long position in the production of goods for sale in the market become a feasible or viable proposition.

Given each of these difficulties, it therefore does seem that at the most fundamental level the mere classification of the monetary functions does not go very far in explaining how the operation of a 'monetary economy' (Keynes, 1936) differs from that of other conceivable economic arrangements. It does not tell us, in short, whether money makes any difference.

With regard to these more basic issues, there are broadly speaking two alternative points of view which can be identified (Schumpeter, 1954; Goodhart, 1998; Ingham, 1996, 2000, 2001; Smithin, 2000). The first of these would be one version or another of the 'implicit mainstream view' (see below), which focuses on the medium of exchange function *per se*, and asserts that money arises as an optimizing response to the technical inefficiencies of barter. The classic account usually cited is that of Menger (1892), but the tradition has persisted to the present day, in such contributions as Jones (1976), Kiyotaki and Wright (1989, 1993) and more or less every textbook. On such a view, the introduction of money must (presumably) make some difference to the economic system when it first appears, in terms of reducing transactions costs and improving inefficiency. However, once the concept is firmly established, the implication is that subsequent changes in the monetary variables do not impinge on the underlying barter exchange ratios. The whole approach is therefore consonant with, and leads to, concepts of neutral money, money as a veil, natural rates of interest, fixed quantities of money, and so forth. In short, it would lead directly to an essentially 'real' rather than a 'monetary' analysis in Schumpeter's sense.

The second main line of approach, however, would be a more genuinely sociohistorical approach to the question of the development of monetary institutions. This would focus on what Ingham (1996) has called the 'social relation' of money. From this point of view, the textbook story about money emerging spontaneously from some pre-existing natural economy based on barter is rejected as being both logically and historically inaccurate, and one feature of the alternative approach is therefore to investigate the actual historical origins of money, drawing on evidence from the other social sciences, such as history, anthropology, numismatics and sociology. A counter-manifesto to that of Menger, from around the same time period, can be found in the work of Innes (1913), which has recently been studied and quoted by such writers as Wray (1998, 2000) and Ingham (2001). In the most general terms, monetary concepts and practices are seen as socially constructed and constituted categories. Moreover, in effect, monetary constructs such as price lists, debt, book-keeping and so on are regarded as the precondition for the emergence of market exchange and production for sale in the market, rather than vice versa. The most prominent version of this type of approach to money is perhaps the so-called 'chartalism' of Knapp (1924), which was endorsed by Keynes (1930), and has been revived in the contemporary era by a group which Parguez and Seccareccia (2000) have called the 'neo-chartalist' school (for example, Mosler, 1997–8; Wray, 1998; Bell, 2001). This is the view that money is peculiarly a 'creature of the state' (Lerner, 1947) and, in particular, that the power to levy taxes in money terms gives governments the ability thereby to define the base money of the system. According to Goodhart (1998), this view has considerably more historical and empirical verisimilitude than the rival Mengerian view.

THE IMPLICIT MAINSTREAM VIEW

In terms of the textbook monetary functions, the 'implicit mainstream view' is obviously that the first, the medium of exchange function, is predominant. What supposedly distinguishes a monetary economy from a barter economy is precisely the existence of a generally acceptable means of payment. This is said to eliminate the necessity of a 'double coincidence of wants' as a precondition of mutually profitable trade, and hence the various practical inefficiencies of barter. From this point of view, the role of money as a store of value would actually follow from that of the medium of exchange. Anything that could not serve as a vehicle for storing purchasing power through time would not be acceptable as an exchange medium. However, this need not imply that money is the *best* store of value available in the society. There could well be stores of value that yield higher rates of return but are less generally acceptable in trade for goods and services. In the terminology introduced by Keynes and Hicks in the 1930s, these assets would be less 'liquid'. The supremacy of the medium of exchange function would also tend to imply that the unit of account, that is the unit in which price lists are expressed and accounts are kept, would be equivalent to units of the actual medium of exchange. Pressure to minimize calculation and negotiation costs would tend to push the system in this direction.

This standard view of money, that is as primarily a technical device for overcoming the inefficiency of barter, leads on naturally to the characteristic dual perspective on the relationship between money and real economic activity, which is found in most mainstream monetary and macroeconomic theory. Although the existence of money is accepted (seemingly somewhat grudgingly) as part of the background of economic institutions, monetary changes *within* a given framework are still regarded as essentially neutral. The 'invention' of money must at one time have had some sort of impact in moving the economy away from the original state of barter, but there is no further or ongoing relationship between money and real economic activity. In particular, once society possesses the concept of money, changes in the number of units of the item or item(s) designated as money can have no permanent impact on the level of real activity. At most such changes can have a temporary effect in the presence of (similarly temporary) rigidities in the nominal prices of either goods or labour. Money is therefore at once very important and yet unimportant. Trautwein (1993) puts this nicely when discussing 'the standard view of money as a requisite but essentially neutral lubricant of economic activity'.

Note, however, that the mainstream view is described here as 'implicit' because, although the concept of money as a generally accepted medium of exchange certainly does seem to underlie both textbook discussions about the elimination of barter and the heuristic notions of most economists about the role of money in economic life, it has been notoriously difficult to incorporate this feature into formal monetary theory and make it operational in economic models. On the contrary, and as pointed out by Laidler (1990), the mainstream monetary theory of the mid-twentieth century which developed after the famous contributions of Hicks (1935, 1937), Modigliani (1944), Friedman (1956), Patinkin (1965) and Tobin (1958) actually paid little or no attention to money in its medium of exchange guise and basically treated money as simply one among a number of alternative assets which can be held. In spite of repeated reference to such things as 'transactions demand' and 'precautionary demand', in a terminology derived from Keynes's (1936) three 'motives' for holding money, the actual substance of this strand of development of mainstream monetary theory has been concerned primarily with portfolio choice or, in other words, with the store of value function.

The reason for this emphasis is not difficult to find. The orthodox economic theory of the latter part of the twentieth century was essentially *Walrasian* in the sense that a framework was adopted in which the coordination of exchange activities in a general equilibrium setting was seen as unproblematic. Models based explicitly or implicitly on Walrasian 'microfoundations' therefore have no real role for money to play (Hahn, 1983; Rogers, 1989; Laidler, 1990). The Walrasian auctioneer provides a (fictitious) method of coordinating activities in a market economy without the need for any other agency, and it is hardly surprising that models that easily solve problems of information and coordination in this way can find no role for money. It was because of the widespread acceptance of Walrasian models as the relevant depiction of the real economy that the *implicit* mainstream vision of money as coordinating exchange activities was difficult to make *explicit*. The familiar, but essentially spurious, difficulty of providing an adequate rationale for the holding of monetary assets when they are dominated in terms of their rate of return by other (non-monetary) assets is one consequence of this. The relevant literature was forced to consider money as simply one among many potential stores of value, with no other outstanding characteristic to recommend it, and hence no reason why any higher yielding asset should not always be chosen.

More recent modelling efforts involving CIA, 'shopping time', search, transactions costs and so on, obviously do intend to remedy this particular defect (Hoover, 1996), but again fit awkwardly into a structure which originally presumed to solve all such problems *a priori* via relative price signals.

THE NEW MONETARY ECONOMICS

One potential response to the above difficulty of providing a 'microeconomic' rationale for the existence of money in the market economy is actually to push on a little further beyond the implicit mainstream view and to conclude that, after all, money is *not* necessary for the efficient functioning of the system. It is possible to interpret some of the scenarios presented by contributors to NME, mentioned earlier, as attempts to make this sort of case.

Among the most widely-cited contributors to the NME literature have been Black (1970), Cowen and Kroszner (1987, 1994), Fama (1980, 1983), Hall (1982a, 1982b) and Greenfield and Yeager (1983, 1989).[3] A distinction is sometimes made between work in this tradition and that of the so-called 'legal restrictions theorists' (LRT) whose leading figure is Wallace (1983, 1988), but more commonly the similarities between the two groups are stressed, as in Cowen and Kroszner (1989), who explicitly treat the NME–LRT contributors as presenting a united front against other approaches to monetary economics.

Although each of the authors cited has put forward a distinctive point of view, the common theme is that they have all considered the feasibility and/or desirability of deregulated and technologically sophisticated competitive payments systems which are 'cashless' in the sense of lacking an outside or base money, and in which the media of exchange in circulation are separated from the unit of account. The latter is either a single physical commodity chosen as a *numéraire* or some composite commodity bundle chosen such that prices quoted in it can be expected to be relatively stable. The separation of the monetary functions means that the choice of the unit of account is somewhat arbitrary, but it is nonetheless neutral. The unit of account is intended to play a role in the financial system analogous to that of weights and measures in the physical world, and specifically does not represent units of a reserve asset into which promises to pay are ultimately redeemable. The exchange media themselves, however, can be many and varied, and the unit of account value of these media may well vary with market conditions. They need not be restricted to the fixed nominal value liabilities of institutions similar to banks but could also include, for example, transferable claims to shares of an equity-based portfolio. All exchange media would bear competitively determined yields. Given the existence of numerous alternative exchange media in a competitive, deregulated and technologically advanced financial environment, there would be no well-defined concept of the money supply, and the preconditions for the conduct of conventional 'monetary policy' would not exist. Indeed, on this view of the world, there would be no need for monetary policy. The aggregate price level would be determined solely with reference to the *numéraire* or commodity bundle unit of account, and the stability of the financial system would supposedly be preserved by competitive pressures.

The adherents of NME have put forward a vision of a system in which trade takes place without the need for monetary exchange as this is conventionally understood. They describe what are basically 'sophisticated barter systems' (Fama, 1980) or what Trautwein (1993) calls 'theories of finance without money', in which, essentially, the characteristic problems of a monetary economy are dealt with by presuming that they do not exist.

Another way of putting the point would be to say that technological advances are assumed to make the Walrasian vision of the economy a potential reality instead of a convenient theoretical fiction.

The NME scenarios are sometimes presented as extrapolations from existing trends in the financial system and sometimes as positive reform proposals. In the first case, the question arises whether such a result is a feasible outcome of actual market processes, and, in the second, whether the system would persist if somehow imposed by the governmental authorities in place of existing arrangements. In both cases, there is the overriding problem of whether it is possible to imagine the market mechanism and *a fortiori* monetary production operating without the existence of something corresponding to money and the standard problems of monetary management that this entails. It is argued below that the missing element is the credit aspect of money and the problems of 'trust and confidence' that arise whenever two or more parties enter into any contractual arrangement that goes beyond simultaneous barter. Technological changes can certainly improve the efficiency of both the trading and accounting process, and also change the external form of the various assets into which the necessary 'trust and confidence' may be reposed. It is more doubtful, however, that they will succeed in eliminating the basic features of the monetary problem.

A RETURN TO GOLD?

In contrast to the above approach, which would effectively abolish monetary theory as such, but still within the *laissez-faire* tradition, another line of argument has been that monetary theory can be reconstructed only if more explicit attention is paid to the issues raised (in that tradition) about the role of money in facilitating transactions.

Some advocates of 'free banking', which refers to the elimination of what is seen as government 'interference' in currency and banking affairs, have stressed the medium of exchange function, and have criticized the NME literature on these grounds, even though sharing with the latter group a preference for *laissez-faire* in the financial services industry. For example, White (1984, 1987, 1990) and Selgin and White (1987) cite the original 'Austrian' or Mengerian theories of money, and assert the relevance of Menger's (1892) approach even in the present day. Menger's theory attempts to explain the convergence of a market system on a common monetary *standard* purely in terms of the self-interest of traders in the system, and without the need to invoke any form of legal restrictions. An 'invisible hand' argument is used to suggest that the trader's interest in reducing transactions costs will prompt eventual convergence on a single commodity as the standard. This will be the commodity that will be the most generally acceptable or saleable to others, a property that is thought to be self-reinforcing once a particular choice begins to emerge.

Menger's account was couched in terms of a metallic commodity money such as gold, for obvious historical reasons. For the purpose of some versions of the modern free banking argument, however, it is suggested that a similar process would be equally likely to occur even in the present environment, or in some completely deregulated system of the future. In other words, the idea is that it is only the intervention of the state and state central banks in the economic process which prevents the re-emergence of some kind of 'hard money', at least as the ultimate standard. A hard money standard as such, of course, is not the same thing as the actual medium of exchange and, as in other *laissez-faire* scenarios, it is suggested that in practice there would likely be numerous competing exchange media, perhaps consisting of the brand name note and deposit liabilities of institutions resembling modern banks. In a 'mature' system (Selgin and White, 1987) it is argued that the commodity standard may not even need actually to be in circulation. It is a key point, however, that the acceptability of all the actually circulating exchange media depends on their being denominated in terms of the standard, and ultimately on a credible pledge of convertibility as the last resort.

On the issue of the separability of the monetary functions, both transactions costs arguments and the historical record are used to suggest that the unit of account function is likely to be inextricably bound up with that of the medium of exchange (White, 1984). The separation of the two functions is believed unlikely to occur spontaneously in the face of the contrary pressure to minimize calculation and negotiation costs. On this view, the separation of the unit of account and medium of exchange functions could not occur (and be maintained) except, ironically, by legislative intervention.

A number of specific criticisms can be made of the Mengerian theory, both as an exercise in evolutionary economics and as a defence for *laissez-faire* in the provision of money, as detailed in Hodgson (1992) and Dow and Smithin (1999). However, for present purposes the main point is that this approach comes to a different set of conclusions than the NME literature, in spite of a similar underlying vision of basic economic theory and a similar commitment at the policy level to *laissez-faire* and a free market in financial services. The difference centres on the idea that money must play a unique role in the transactions process in the absence of a Walrasian auctioneer, as opposed to the alternative notion that a non-monetary economy, in which a heterogeneous collection of financial assets are all more or less amenable to barter for other goods and services, is feasible. It can certainly be argued that the former represents the more realistic point of view.

However, obvious questions can be raised about the anachronistic idea that the ultimate reserve asset in a deregulated system is likely to be one of the precious metals that were historically important. Also, once it is established that functioning market economies do require some ultimate repository of purchasing power, issues of centralization, power and control over monetary policy must immediately arise, which tend to be elided in discussions of free banking. Once again, what seems to be missing from these and other discussions of the medium of exchange function, taken in isolation, is the lack of attention to the fundamental societal relationships entailed in monetary production, and the relationship between money and credit.

MONEY AS A SOCIAL RELATION

In opposition to the different variants of a commodity money theory described above, the other main line of approach to monetary issues and problems would begin with the 'social relation' of money (Ingham, 1996). This is what Schumpeter (1954) labelled the 'claims' or 'credit' approach. Money is seen as a social relationship between the economic actors, as opposed to the usual concerns of economics with relationships between those actors and commodities (as, for example, in a 'utility function'), or directly between commodities (as in a 'production function'). The power of money in the economy, and the twists and turns of the evolution of money as a social institution, are seen as ultimately as originating in the socio-political realm. But, nonetheless, the power of the socially sanctioned constructs and practices concerning money is 'real' regardless of the actually physical attributes of the 'money stuff' (Ingham, 2000), which serve as the media of exchange or medium of settlement. It is not simply nominal or symbolic, because it has a real impact on people's lives, as do other socially constituted structures and practices (Searle, 1998; Ingham, 2001).

In this line of argument, Keynes's (1930) concept of a 'money of account' would be the starting point for the basic notions of a mercantile or commercial mode of production, such as price lists, calculations of profit and wealth in monetary terms, accounting practices and so forth. This will then lead on to an elaboration of a more complete description of the social structure of monetary practice, including the development of standardized means of final payment denominated in the unit of account, and the development of secure credit relations. Such practices would be seen as the precondition for the emergence of a market-type economy, rather than its consequence.

The chartalist or neo-chartalist view (Wray, 1998) is one of the main expressions of the idea of money as a social relation, and the chartalists are quite specific as to the nature of that relation. From this perspective, money is pre-eminently state money, and the liabilities of state central banks, for example, acquire the status of *valuata* or base money because of the coercive power of the state and, in particular, because of its ability to levy taxes on its citizens payable in its own currency. Another way of putting this point is that fiscal relations are obviously one of the most important social relations. Today's 'neo-chartalism' is a modern revival of the views of Knapp (1924), the originator of the state theory of money, and also Keynes (1930), both of whom used the term 'chartal' in describing money. The approach is also described as the 'taxes drive money' view. An important implication of looking at things in this way is that control over the monetary system in this manner is seen as *enabling* a wide range of policy initiatives, which need not be constrained by essentially self-imposed financing constraints, such as the need to 'balance the budget'. This type of reasoning, in fact, was the basis of the once popular 'functional finance' version of Keynesianism (Lerner, 1943, 1947), which has now been abandoned by economic orthodoxy. Goodhart (1998) argues that, from an empirical or historical point of view, the chartalist alternative does seem to be on strong ground as compared to the alternative commodity money theory, and this calls into serious question the many complaints that continue to be made about government interference or intervention into what would otherwise be the 'natural' monetary system.

Acceptance of the empirical/historical validity of the chartalist approach does not, of course, imply that 'private money' in some sense is a logical impossibility. Historical examples have existed (Goodhart, 1998), and in present-day conditions, even if the state did abandon its monetary role, as the free-bankers advocate, presumably some powerful private institution would have to fill the void (Goodhart, 1998; Dow and Smithin, 1999). What it does do is drive home the point that the monetary order is socially constructed, rather than deriving automatically from the 'market'. Following Ingham (1996, 2000, 2001), in the most general or 'logical' sense, what seems to be required for the existence of a functioning monetary production economy is the question of establishing an 'authoritative' money of account (which obviously the state is well placed to provide). This is the essential prerequisite for a market-oriented system to exist, and it is not, *contra* the various search or tâtonnemant theories, one of the things that the market can do for itself. Such an observation is a particular application of one of the central problems in any economic theory, namely how subjective values can be supposed to produce intersubjective hierarchies of value.

The main theoretical advantage of a somewhat broad conception of what constitutes a 'monetary authority' would be simply that it does not restrict the discussion to any particular current or historical definition of what constitutes state power or a nation state. It helps, in other words, in providing a theoretically coherent basis for explanations or conjectures about 'out of sample' events and developments. For example, as mentioned, in discussing why and how 'private' monetary authorities have existed in the past, whether or not 'free banking' involving the abolition of state central banks is viable (and what would occur if this happened), whether a separation of the monetary functions is feasible or desirable, and whether or not purely technical change really does threaten the position of central banks (DeLong, 2002). Finally, in understanding what is occurring in cases where the concept of the state is itself being redefined (as it is currently with economic and monetary union – EMU – and the Euro).

Note also that certain other writers, such as Heinsohn and Steiger (2000a, 2000b) have put forward alternative formulations of what the social structure of monetary relations is believed to entail. The view of Heinsohn and Steiger (for example, 2000a) is that money can only arise in societies based on the concept of private property, and that it is created in a credit contract when property is encumbered and collateralized. This, the authors stress, is an immaterial yield which exists as a result of the legal/social relations in the society, it is not the same as a 'physical' yield resulting from the actual possession of resources. So here, then, is another version of the idea that money is a social relation, a version which might lead on to similar views on doctrinal and/or policy issues as some of the others in that vein. But this formulation raises the issue of whether the concept of money or the concept of 'property', in the above sense, comes first. Ingham (2000), *per contra*, argues that money is the logically anterior concept and quotes Weber (1924) to the effect that 'from an evolutionary standpoint money is the father of private property'.

In terms of a theory of monetary policy, which is one of our most important concerns in this volume, it can be seen that these alternative views on the logical and historical evolution of money are useful in explaining why the concept of 'monetary authority', of which the modern central bank is an example, does loom so large in the political economy of capitalist-type economic systems. Crucially, they can help to explain wherein lies the ultimate power of the monetary authority over interest rates, for example, which is (seemingly) such a deeply puzzling question to observers who prefer to think in terms of competitive money markets and similar constructs. Using the standard economic jargon it would seem that there is a distinct 'natural monopoly' element in the provision of the ultimate means of settlement in the money-using society and, moreover, that such an element is irreducible if the money-based economy is to function at all. Indeed, the natural monopoly or 'public good' argument was part of the traditional argument as to why the usual preference in favour of *laissez-faire* should be suspended or modified in the case of the payments system (Friedman, 1960; Friedman and Schwartz, 1986; Laidler, 1990). However, although this language is suggestive, and useful in some ways in locating the alternative view of money within the 'discourse' of the standard economics literature, it is misleading in others. The main problem is that it opens the door to a discussion of whether or not money satisfies the usual technical criteria for identifying a *commodity* as a public good, such as non-rivalry in consumption, non-excludability, and so on, which arguably it does not (Vaubel, 1984; White, 1988). But the thrust of the present discussion would be that these 'technical' or supply-side issues are not the main point. One the one hand, the monopoly element from the demand side for the competing promises to pay is reputational, as noted by Bagehot (1873) long ago:

> An old-established bank has a '*prestige*', which amounts to a 'privileged opportunity' though no exclusive right is given to it by law, a peculiar power is given to it by opinion[4] . . . The business of an old-established bank has the full advantage of being a simple business, and in part the advantage of being a monopoly business.

But also, as stated earlier, the point seems to be that a high degree of centralization or hierarchy in the monetary/banking system is a necessary condition if money is in fact to be money, and hence to facilitate monetary production, the taking of a long position in goods and services and the realization of monetary profits. It is in this sense that the attribute of 'money-ness' itself, rather than any particular monetary asset, exhibits public good characteristics (Dow, 1996; Dow and Smithin, 1999) and why a capitalist system needs to generate (or have generated for it) some asset with a supreme degree of 'moneyness.'

MONEY, CREDIT AND CAPITALISM

A more comprehensive approach to the basic nature and functions of money, then, suggests that the origins of money lie, not so much in the need to eliminate the inefficiency of barter in a static exchange economy, but in social practice. Its relevance to economic development is that it can provide the vehicle for the establishment of trustworthy credit relations in the real-world market economy in which both production for sale in the market and most exchange relations have a temporal dimension. Money is therefore intimately involved with issues of credit, speculation and uncertainty in decision making (Davidson, 1994). Both Wray (1990) and Trautwein (1993) identify this approach primarily with the Post Keynesians and other related heterodox schools of economists. Also relevant is the later work of Hicks (1982, 1989), which puts forward a very different view of money than in the same author's famous contributions of the 1930s, which are more usually cited.

That there is an evolutionary aspect to the relationship between the monetary and credit systems is suggested by Moore's (1988) distinction between *commodity money*, *fiat money* and *credit money* and Chick's (1986) identification of five stylized 'stages of banking' in the evolution of the modern financial system. In Chick's discussion, in a sort of compromise between the different views on the origins of money set out earlier, the evolution proceeds from an early stage in which banks are simply repositories for deposits of base money to a contemporary environment in which the banks themselves initiate lending and aggressively pursue both asset and liability management. The general idea suggested, therefore, is that monetary theory itself needs to evolve as the environment changes. One type of theory would be required under commodity money, when money consists literally of units of a physical commodity such as one of the precious metals, another under fiat money involving inconvertible paper currency issued by the state, and a third in a credit money environment when the exchange media consist primarily of the deposit liabilities of various financial institutions. In the latter case, the modern environment, the banking system itself inevitably plays a major role in the creation and destruction of money on any reasonably comprehensive definition of the money supply. An increase in bank lending will expand the asset side of bank balance sheets, causing a similar residual increase on the liabilities side, and a repayment of bank loans will have the opposite effect. The remaining question for debate in such an environment is whether there is any external constraint on this process, whether via reserve requirements in terms of some more fundamental base money or through the interest rate charged on loans of primary funds. Hicks (1967) has also argued that the relevant monetary theory must evolve with the continuing evolution of the financial system. Making a distinction between 'metallic money' and 'credit money', his view then was that 'In a world of banks and insurance companies, money markets and stock exchanges, money is quite a different thing from what it was before these institutions came into being.' However, in his last book, the posthumously published *A Market Theory of Money* (1989), Hicks substantially modifies this position in an argument that locates the foundations of money still more firmly in the relationship between money and credit similar to that outlined above. That Hicks himself placed some importance on the shift of emphasis seems to be illustrated by a passage in a communication to the author written in 1988.[5] Hicks's admonishment at the time reads as follows: '. . . you are still at the stage I was at the time of my *Critical Essays* making hard money and credit money as parallel alternatives. I now maintain that the evolution of money is better understood if one starts with *credit*! (original emphasis).' The later argument is essentially that *all* monetary economies, and not just those with developed financial institutions, have a basic credit element. In other words, that in some sense the concepts of credit and the payment of debts are fundamental to understanding the role of money in market systems at a level which goes deeper than the observation of particular institutional arrangements. Wray (1990) makes a similar point, with more emphasis on the financing of production rather than market exchange. The argument is presumably *not* that the evolutionary aspects are unimportant. Monetary theory does still need to evolve as the system evolves and, as illustrated in the works of the authors cited above, evolutionary developments obviously do radically alter how robust or fragile a particular system comes to be, whether or not accepted techniques of monetary management continue to be viable, and the practical definition of what is and is not money at any point in time. The point is rather that notions of debt and credit come in even at the basic conceptual level of the 'nature and functions of money', and not only at a particular historical juncture in the evolution of the financial system.

According to Hicks, in any but the simplest economy the representative transaction is not a simple 'spot' payment of goods for goods (under barter) or money for goods (under monetary exchange), but usually involves either deferred or advance payment (hence credit) in some way. There are three temporally separated stages: making a contract or bargain, delivery of goods or services, and delivery of means of payment. The only timing rule is that the contractual agreement comes first. In some cases, the means of payment will be delivered before the goods and services (cash in advance); in others, final payment comes after the delivery of goods and services (as in consumer or trade credit). The key point is that immediately after the initial contract is made two debts are automatically created, one in terms of 'money', the other in real goods and services. The role of money is then twofold. It plays a part in fixing the terms of the original contract, and it is also the means by which the debt is settled. In the first it is performing a role that is an amalgam of the unit of account function as listed above and the related *standard of deferred payment*, which also used to make an appearance in the old-fashioned textbooks (see Schumpeter, 1954). Hicks (as do others) calls this the *standard of value*. The standard of deferred payment is automatically included, because now the time element is taken for granted in the representative case, and for the same reason the timeless version of the unit of account would not be adequate in itself (Hicks, 1989). In its second guise, money plays a role that to some extent corresponds to what is usually meant by the medium of exchange, but which Hicks expresses, perhaps more accurately, as a *means of payment*. As in the implicit mainstream view, the *store of value* aspect of money is distinctly secondary because there will always be other stores of value, possibly with better rates of return, which do not perform the primary monetary functions. Hicks (1989) takes the view that the dual role of money, in both fixing the terms of a debt and discharging the debt, puts the textbook functions of money 'into their places in relation to one another'. However, on the issue of whether the functions can be separated, as in the NME scenarios, it is necessary to pursue Hicks's argument somewhat further and be more explicit about the precise meanings of terms such as 'means of payment' and 'money'.

The main point seems to be that, if the essence of monetary exchange and monetary production is the fixing of debt contracts in terms of 'money' and their ultimate settlement, there must obviously be some agreement on either side as to what would unambiguously constitute *final* payment. It is implicit, contrary to the NME literature, that the asset serving as the standard of value (or rather units of which serve as the standard) should itself be acceptable as final or ultimate settlement of debt. In this sense the functions are inseparable, and it may be the case that some authors might wish to reserve the term 'money' or 'cash' for the asset with this property.[6] However, as Hicks (1989) also points out, it is obviously open to the parties to any individual transaction to regard debts as settled amongst themselves via the transfer of some other asset, which is not itself the standard of value, but is nonetheless regarded as equivalent to the requisite number of units of the standard. For example, a debt owed by party A to party B might be offset by a pre-existing debt from party C to A now transferred to B for final collection. Any number of such chains of interlocking claims are possible, provided only that they are acceptable to the parties concerned: in this case provided that B has confidence that the debt from C will really be paid. Hence, as in some of the scenarios discussed above, there could be a large number of alternative assets or 'promises to pay' that do serve as actual 'media of exchange' in practice, but do not themselves possess the twin properties of defining the standard of value and representing ultimate payment. The difference between such a system and 'sophisticated barter systems', however, is the idea that the alternate exchange media, to command confidence, must all be related to the ultimate standard in some way, typically as credible promises to pay units of the standard asset. The basic problem concerning the potential instability of a monetary economy flows from this relationship. The system can be reasonably elastic and expansive when confidence in the alternative exchange media is high. These claims will then be accepted on face value and can circulate widely without actually being presented for payment for long periods. When confidence evaporates, however, for whatever reason, the system will suddenly appear to be much more unstable. The alternative exchange media will no longer seem quite so acceptable and there will be a 'scramble for liquidity', in other words for the unique asset which is regarded as representing ultimate payment.

It is the standard asset, corresponding to what is usually described in the literature as *base money*, or simply as *cash*, which will combine the twin monetary functions of a standard of value and (final) means of payment. However, it would be a mistake to assume that the ultimate asset must necessarily take the form of 'hard money', such as gold or silver, or be in exogenously fixed supply. This is not the case in current systems, for example, in which the ultimate asset consists simply of the liabilities of state-owned central banks, and which expands or contracts whenever the central bank makes advances or purchases investments. In contrast to the asset that unambiguously represents final payment, the total of other claims that are also acceptable as exchange media for the time being corresponds to what are usually described as the 'monetary aggregates' or the 'money supply'. It is easy to see why in times of rapid financial innovation this total becomes very difficult to define statistically.

It should be noted that some writers in the NME tradition also recognize that, for claims against diverse financial institutions to be acceptable, there must exist some generally accepted *medium of settlement*, (see, for example, Greenfield and Yeager, 1989). It is agreed, that is to say, that there must be something that is generally regarded as representing final or ultimate payment. In this literature, however, the settlement medium need *not* be associated with the standard of value or unit of account. The unit of account is defined by a composite commodity of some kind, but the composite itself cannot actually serve as the settlement medium, because of the inconveniences of transporting and storing the commodities involved. The actual medium of settlement is rather some more generally acceptable asset, which itself varies in unit of account value. It is then argued that price level stability can be assured by a system of 'indirect convertibility'. An exchange medium with a face value of (say) 100 units of account is supposedly always exchangeable for a quantity of the redemption medium equivalent to literally 100 units of the actual composite commodity at current market prices. Dowd (1992) presents a detailed discussion of the mechanics of this system, making an explicit distinction between the circulating medium of exchange, the 'anchor' commodity (or composite commodity) defining the unit of account, and the medium of settlement. There must be some doubt, however, as to whether the mechanism of indirect convertibility would actually be viable in a market-driven system, without (ironically) extensive 'state intervention' to enforce the rules. This would presumably be an unwelcome implication for many supporters of monetary reforms of this type, who generally tend to be supporters of *laissez-faire* in the provision of monetary services, and opponents of legal restrictions. The reason for these doubts is that the settlement medium and *not* the bundle of goods implicit in the unit of account is by definition the most acceptable asset. Hence, in the absence of more comprehensive legislation than simply fixing the unit of account, which is all that is allowed by many supporters of *laissez-faire* in financial services, there seems to be nothing to prevent the settlement medium itself from evolving into a true base money and usurping the unit of account/standard of value role (Meltzer, 1989).

THE CHOICE OF THE MONETARY STANDARD

If it is true that the system does require a basic monetary asset, which both defines the standard of value and provides the means for the unambiguous or 'final' repayment of debt, the remaining questions concern the identity of this ultimate asset, and how it comes to be chosen to perform its monetary role. As mentioned, this must in some sense be a sociopolitical process. Some modern advocates of 'free banking' would like to believe that, in the absence of government intervention, market forces would once again focus on one of the precious metals which were important in the past, and if this were the case something like the idealized hard money system would be restored. In such a system, there would presumably be scope for some elasticity in terms of innovations in the money multiplier linking the hard money base to the actual media of exchange, but ultimately the constraint represented by the relatively fixed supply of the precious metal would be binding. As (allegedly) in the old gold standard days, the possibility of monetary expansion for an individual nation would be a function of balance of payments considerations, while for the world as a whole the supply of base money would be essentially fixed, except for the activities of the mining and exploration industries. In practice, however, it is obviously more likely that, even in a contemporary innovated financial environment, the ultimate asset will continue to be the nominal liabilities of central banks backed by the coercive and legislative power of the state. This power may reside either at the national level or, as in the common currency for the EU, at a supranational level. Whatever the precise nature of the institutional arrangements, however, the most important point is that this type of regime is obviously a different matter than one in which the ultimate asset is in physically limited supply, as the liabilities of the monetary authority can be increased at will if the central institution acts as a lender in the money markets. In this case the supply of the reserve asset is (potentially) infinitely elastic, the only constraining feature being the rate of interest charged on loans of this asset.

Dow and Smithin (1999) also argue, moreover, that even if as a thought experiment state-owned central banks were abolished and somehow government was 'taken out of money', an anachronistic convergence on a new gold standard regime would be less likely than the emergence of an institution or institution(s) in the private sector which would become the monetary authority and occupy effectively the same position as a central bank. In other words, in such a deregulated modern environment the ultimate repository of purchasing power would likely come to be the liabilities of some long-established and commercially successful financial institution or institutions, which would 'socialize itself' (or themselves), as Keynes (1926) put the point. The asset which eventually comes to be widely accepted may originally have been a 'promise to pay' in terms of some pre-existing standard which occupied the central position in an earlier stage of evolution but is now in and of itself regarded as representing final payment. The basic argument is that the necessity for an ultimate means of settlement in a monetary economy probably imparts an inevitable centralizing tendency to financial systems regardless of the formal/legalistic trappings by which this is achieved. What is more relevant in the discussion of 'hard' versus 'soft' money is that, whenever the ultimate settlement medium is a *financial* asset rather than a physical asset, supplies of this asset can be readily increased simply by the central institution standing ready to make loans denominated in those terms. The interest rate charged on the loans then becomes the ultimate monetary control variable.

CONCLUSION

Following Hicks and the Post Keynesians, it seems that the best way to cut through the confusions surrounding the textbook discussions of the functions of money is to recognize that the majority of transactions in a market economy operating in real time do have the basic characteristic of an exchange of debts. Completion of the monetary side of the transaction implies a repayment of debt. The system therefore rests in an essential way on the need to establish secure credit relations, and therefore there is a requirement for a basic monetary asset that will both fix the standard of value and unambiguously represent final payment. Actual media of exchange other than the final medium of settlement can arise, but by definition they will attract less 'confidence' and must be related to the ultimate means of payment in some way, such as by redemption pledges. The notorious fragility of credit systems arises from this situation when the ultimate reliability of the substitute exchange media comes into question for some reason, and there is a flight to liquidity.

Experience with contemporary systems, in which the ultimate reserve asset consists simply of the nominal liabilities of state central banks, shows that it is not necessary for this asset to be hard money such as gold or another precious metal. All that is actually required for an asset to be accepted as final payment of debt is some kind of guarantee that others will accept it as such in some subsequent round of transactions. The obligations of the state do fulfil this requirement in the case of most governments under normal circumstances[7] (with obvious exceptions), which is why central bank liabilities are usually accepted as final payment. In fact, it may also be observed that the only reason why gold, for example, was acceptable as final payment in the past was similarly an underlying confidence that others would also accept it, either because a gold standard was actually established by government fiat (as was the case for the international gold standard of the nineteenth century) or because of the special position which the precious metals admittedly have had psychologically and socially in history. It is definitely the case, however, that monetary systems in which the ultimate reserve asset is not in relatively fixed supply will operate in a different fashion than those in which it is. In the former, supplies of the reserve asset can simply be increased when the issuing institution itself makes loans. The interest rate on those loans, rather than any quantity principle, then becomes the main instrument by which the reserve asset can be rationed.

Finally, it might be suggested that attempts to ground an explanation of the function of money solely in the need to reduce the inefficiency of barter in a static exchange economy do not go far enough. In a sense that is too easy a task, immediately opening up the possibility that 'money' could be replaced by a more or less sophisticated accounting system of exchange as soon as the technology had developed to the appropriate point. There is no technology, however, which can eliminate the uncertainty inherent in making exchange or production decisions in a market economy in real time, with the concomitant need to judge the quality of individual promises to pay on a continuous basis. This is what determines the need (if a monetary production economy is to exist at all) for some basic monetary asset embodying both the standard of value and the ultimate means of payment. Continuing changes in technology can obviously change the substantive form which this asset takes, but do not eliminate the need for it.

NOTES

1. See, for example, Binhammer and Sephton (2001).
2. Keynes's actual reference, of course, was to a 'money of account' rather than a 'unit of account'.
3. The discussion here does not attempt a detailed critique of any individual author's contribution. More details (at least for some of the earlier literature) are provided in surveys by White (1984), McCallum (1985), Meltzer (1989), Cowen and Kroszner (1994) and Selgin and White (1994).
4. Although 'chartalists' would presumably object to this particular choice of words.
5. Personal communication to the author dated 4 October, 1988.
6. This probably accounts for much of the confusion over the years on the question of whether whatever particular innovative exchange media have arisen in each era should or should not be included in the definition of money. See Moore (1988) on the debates in the early twentieth century about whether even chequing deposits in the commercial banks should be included.
7. Where 'normal circumstances' corresponds to the Knapp/Keynes requirement of being able to levy taxes effectively. See also B. Friedman (2000).

REFERENCES

Bagehot, W. (1873 [1915]), *Lombard Street: A Description of the Money Market*, London: John Murray.
Baumol, W.J. (1952), 'The transactions demand for cash: an inventory theoretic approach', *Quarterly Journal of Economics*, 66, 545–56.
Bell, S. (2001), 'The role of the state and the hierarchy of money', *Cambridge Journal of Economics*, 25, 149–63.
Binhammer, H.H. and P.S. Sephton (2001), *Money, Banking and the Canadian Financial System*, 8th edn, Toronto: Nelson Thomson Learning.
Black, F. (1970), 'Banking and interest rates in a world without money', *Journal of Bank Research*, 1, 9–20.
Blanchard, O.F. and S. Fischer (1989), *Lectures on Macroeconomics*, Cambridge, MA: MIT Press.
Chick, V. (1986), 'The evolution of the banking system and the theory of saving, investment and interest', *Economies et Sociétés*, 20, 111–26.
Clower, R. (1967), 'A reconsideration of the micro-foundations of monetary theory', *Western Economic Journal*, 6, 1–9.
Cowen, T. and R. Kroszner (1987), 'The development of the new monetary economics', *Journal of Political Economy*, 95, 576–90.
—— (1989), 'Scottish banking before 1845: a model for laissez-faire?', *Journal of Money, Credit, and Banking*, 21, 576–90.
—— (1994), *Explorations in the New Monetary Economics*, Oxford: Basil Blackwell.
Davidson, P. (1994), *Post Keynesian Macroeconomic Theory: A Foundation for Successful Economic Policies for the Twenty-First Century*, Aldershot, UK and Brookfield, US: Edward Elgar.
DeLong, J.B. (2002), *Macroeconomics*, New York: McGraw-Hill Irwin.
Dow, S.C. (1996), 'Why the financial system should be regulated', *Economic Journal*, 106, 698–707.
Dow, S.C. and J. Smithin (1999), 'The structure of financial markets and the "first

principles" of monetary economics', *Scottish Journal of Political Economy*, 46, 72–90.

Dowd, K. (1992), 'The mechanics of indirect convertibility', mimeo, University of Nottingham.

Fama, E.F. (1980), 'Banking in the theory of finance', *Journal of Monetary Economics*, 6, 39–57.

—— (1983), 'Financial intermediation and price level control', *Journal of Monetary Economics*, 12, 7–28.

Friedman, B.M. (2000), 'The role of interest rates in Federal Reserve policymaking', NBER Working Paper 8047, December.

Friedman, M. (1956), 'The quantity theory of money: a restatement', *Studies in the Quantity Theory of Money*, Chicago: University of Chicago Press.

—— (1960), *A Program for Monetary Stability*, New York: Fordham University Press.

Friedman, M. and A.J. Schwartz (1986), 'Has government any role in money?', *Journal of Monetary Economics*, 17, 37–62.

Goodhart, C.A.E. (1998), 'The two concepts of money: implications for the analysis of optimal currency areas', *European Journal of Political Economy*, 14, 407–32.

Greenfield, R.L. and L.B. Yeager (1983), 'A laissez-faire approach to monetary stability', *Journal of Money, Credit, and Banking*, 15, 302–15.

—— (1989), 'Can monetary disequilibrium be eliminated?', *Cato Journal*, 9, 405–21.

Hahn, F. (1983), *Money and Inflation*, Cambridge, MA: MIT Press.

Hall, R.E. (1982a), 'Explorations in the gold standard and related policies for stabilizing the dollar', in *Inflation, Causes and Effects*, Chicago: University of Chicago Press.

—— (1982b), '*Monetary Trends in the United States and the United Kingdom*: a review from the perspective of new developments in monetary economics', *Journal of Economic Literature*, 20, 1552–6.

Heinsohn, G. and O. Steiger (2000a), 'The property theory of interest and money', in J. Smithin (ed.), *What is Money?*, London: Routledge.

—— (2000b), 'Alternative theories of the rate of interest: a new paradigm', IKSF-Discussion Paper No. 24, University of Bremen, November.

Hicks, J.R. (1935), 'A suggestion for simplifying the theory of money', *Economica*, 2, 1–19.

—— (1937), 'Mr. Keynes and the classics', *Econometrica*, 5, 147–59.

—— (1967), 'Monetary theory and history – an attempt at perspective', *Critical Essays in Monetary Theory*, Oxford: Clarendon Press.

—— (1982), 'The credit economy', *Money, Interest and Wages: Collected Essays in Economic Theory*, vol. 2, Oxford: Basil Blackwell.

—— (1989), *A Market Theory of Money*, Oxford: Oxford University Press.

Hodgson, G.M. (1992), 'Carl Menger's theory of the evolution of money: some problems', *Review of Political Economy*, 4, 396–412.

Hoover, K.D. (1988), *The New Classical Macroeconomics: A Sceptical Inquiry*, Oxford: Basil Blackwell.

—— (1996), 'Some suggestions for complicating the theory of money', in S. Pressman (ed.), *Interactions in Political Economy: Malvern After Ten Years*, London: Routledge.

Ingham, G. (1996), 'Money is a social relation', *Review of Social Economy*, 54, 243–75.

—— (2000), 'Babylonian madness: on the historical and sociological origins of money', in J. Smithin (ed.), *What is Money?*, London: Routledge.

—— (2001), 'New monetary spaces?', paper presented at the OECD conference '*The Future of Money*', Luxemburg, July.

Innes, A.M. (1913), 'What is money?', *The Banking Law Journal*, May, 377–408.

Jones, R.A. (1976), 'The origin and development of media of exchange', *Journal of Political Economy*, 84, 757–75.

Keynes, J.M. (1926 [1972]), 'The end of laissez-faire', in *Essays in Persuasion*, vol. IX of *The Collected Writings of John Maynard Keynes*, London: Macmillan.

—— (1930), *A Treatise on Money* (2 vols), London: Macmillan.

—— (1936), *The General Theory of Employment Interest and Money*, London: Macmillan.

Kiyotaki, N. and R. Wright (1989), 'On money as a medium of exchange', *Journal of Political Economy*, 97, 927–54.

—— (1993), 'A search-theoretic approach to monetary economics', *American Economic Review*, 83, 63–77.

Knapp, G.F. (1924 [1973]), *The State Theory of Money*, New York: Augustus M. Kelley.

Laidler, D.E.W. (1990), *Taking Money Seriously and Other Essays*, London: Philip Allan.

—— (1993), *The Demand for Money: Theories, Evidence and Problems*, 4th edn, New York: Harper Collins College Publishers.

Lerner, A.P. (1943), 'Functional finance and the federal debt', *Social Research*, 10, 38–51.

—— (1947), 'Money as a creature of the state', *American Economic Review*, 37, 312–17.

McCallum, B.T. (1985), 'Bank deregulation, accounting systems of exchange and the unit of account: a critical review', *Carnegie-Rochester Conference Series on Public Policy*, 23, 13–46.

Meltzer, A.H. (1989), 'Eliminating monetary disturbances', *Cato Journal*, 9, 423–8.

Menger, C. (1892), 'On the origin of money', *Economic Journal*, 2, 239–55.

Mogidliani, F. (1944), 'Liquidity preference and the theory of interest and money', *Econometrica*, 12, 45–88.

Moore, B.J. (1988), *Horizontalists and Verticalists: The Macroeconomics of Credit Money*, Cambridge: Cambridge University Press.

Mosler, W. (1997–8), 'Full employment and price stability', *Journal of Post Keynesian Economics*, 20, 167–82.

Parguez, A. and M. Seccareccia (2000), 'The credit theory of money: the monetary circuit approach', in J. Smithin (ed.), *What is Money?*, London: Routledge.

Patinkin, D. (1965), *Money, Interest and Prices*, 2nd edn, New York: Harper & Row.

Rogers, C. (1989), *Money, Interest and Capital: A Study in the Foundations of Monetary Theory*, Cambridge: Cambridge University Press.

Samuelson, P. (1958), 'An exact consumption-loans model of interest with or without the social contrivance of money', *Journal of Political Economy*, 66, 1002–11.

Schumpeter, J.A. (1954 [1994]), *History of Economic Analysis*, London: Routledge.

Searle, J.R. (1998), *Mind, Language and Society: Philosophy in the Real World*, New York: Basic Books.

Selgin, G.A. and L.H. White (1987), 'The evolution of a free banking system', *Economic Inquiry*, 25, 439–58.

—— (1994), 'How would the invisible hand handle money?', *Journal of Economic Literature*, 32, 1718–49.

Smithin, J. (ed.) (2000), *What is Money?*, London: Routledge.

Tobin, J. (1958), 'Liquidity preference as behaviour toward risk', *Review of Economic Studies*, 25, 65–86.

Trautwein, H-M. (1993), 'A fundamental controversy about money: Post Keynesian and new monetary economics', in G. Mongiovi and C. Rühl (eds), *Macroeconomic Theory: Diversity and Convergence*, Aldershot, UK and Brookfield, US: Edward Elgar.

Turnovsky, S.J. (1999), *Methods of Macroeconomic Dynamics*, 2nd edn, Cambridge, MA: MIT Press.

Vaubel, R. (1984), 'The government's money monopoly: externalities or natural monopoly?', *Kyklos*, 37, 27–58.

Wallace, N. (1983), 'A legal restrictions theory of the demand for money and the role of monetary policy', *Federal Reserve Bank of Minneapolis Quarterly Review*, Winter, 1–7.

—— (1988), 'A suggestion for oversimplifying the theory of money', *Economic Journal*, 98, 25–36.

Walsh, C.E. (1998), *Monetary Theory and Policy*, Cambridge, MA: MIT Press.

Weber, M. (1924 [1981]), *General Economic History*, New Brunswick, NJ: Transaction Publishers.

White, L.H. (1984), 'Competitive payments systems and the unit of account', *American Economic Review*, 74, 699–712.

—— (1987), 'Accounting for non-interest-bearing currency: a critique of the legal restrictions theory of money', *Journal of Money, Credit, and Banking*, 19, 448–56.

—— (1988), 'Depoliticizing the supply of money', in T.D. Willet (ed.), *Political Business Cycles: The Political Economy of Money, Inflation and Unemployment*, Durham, NC: Duke University Press.

—— (1990), 'Competitive monetary reform: a review essay', *Journal of Monetary Economics*, 26, 191–202.

Wray, L.R. (1990), *Money and Credit in Capitalist Economies: The Endogenous Money Approach*, Aldershot, UK and Brookfield, US: Edward Elgar.

—— (1998), *Understanding Modern Money: The Key to Full Employment and Price Stability*, Cheltenham, UK and Lyme, US: Edward Elgar.

—— (2000), 'Modern money', in J. Smithin (ed.), *What is Money?*, London: Routledge.

3. Monetarism and the quantity theory of money

INTRODUCTION

By common consent, Milton Friedman was the most influential monetary economist of the twentieth century after Keynes, a view affirmed even by economists usually regarded as unsympathetic to his point of view, such as Galbraith (1987) and Heilbroner (1990). It was Friedman and his collaborators who were primarily responsible for the remarkable revival of the ancient quantity theory of money in the second half of the twentieth century, under its modern name of monetarism. Other noted economists were also influential in the development of monetarist ideas, but this chapter will concentrate primarily on the work of Friedman, whose name is undoubtedly that most firmly associated with these developments (Cagan, 1989). The discussion serves the twin purposes not only of describing a relatively recent chapter in the history of economic thought, which is important in its own right, but also, more generally, of describing the quantity theory itself through the lens of perhaps its most sophisticated version.

The quantity theory, dating back at least to the writings of Hume in the eighteenth century, and even earlier, had historically been one of the most influential methods of approaching the important questions of monetary theory and policy. However, by the time of Friedman's major contributions it was in abeyance in the aftermath of the so-called 'Keynesian revolution'. To restore it to the top of the economic agenda was therefore a notable achievement on Friedman's part. Nonetheless, as stressed by Laidler (1990), towards the end of the twentieth century the doctrine of monetarism itself seemed once again to be at a low ebb in terms of academic influence. In explaining this turn of events, some note must be taken of the social dynamics of the economics profession in academia, whose reward structure inevitably leads to some reaction against the views of the immediately preceding generation. If this were the only problem, however, the passage of time and historical distance would presumably suffice to set the record straight. It will be argued in the present chapter that there may also be some more serious difficulties, many of which relate to the debate over the basic nature and functions of money as discussed in Chapter 2 above.

Milton Friedman's essential contribution to the history of economic ideas was the revival of the view that (in some sense) 'money matters', after a period in which the conventional wisdom, following a number of popular misinterpretations of Keynes, had relegated monetary factors to a minor role in the explanation of macroeconomic phenomena. This achievement will surely continue to be recognized even by those who take a completely different view about *which* monetary variables matter, and what they matter *for*, than does Friedman. However, it may well be that the vehicle Friedman chose to make his point, the revival of the ancient quantity theory of money, has ultimately proved inadequate to the task. The application of the quantity theory in modern conditions entails the assertion that a contemporary credit economy, in which most of the exchange media consist of some subset of the deposit liabilities of financial institutions, can be made to behave 'as if' it were a simple commodity money system (Hicks, 1967; Moore, 1988; Rogers, 1989; Smithin, 1993). The monetarism of the 1960s and 1970s, against the backdrop of a relatively stable institutional structure at the time, claimed to have found the formula by which this could be achieved. However, the experience of more recent years, in which the pace of financial innovation and institutional change has picked up, has cast doubt on whether quantity-theoretic reasoning, as such, will always be reliable. In this case, and if it remains true nonetheless that money matters, some alternative and more general set of guidelines for the conduct of monetary policy will ultimately have to be found.

The next two sections describe the broad outlines of Friedman's attempted revival of the quantity theory. Then the discussion goes on to explain the relationship between the theoretical framework and the practical policy proposals that Friedman and others have made. The final three sections of the chapter then assess the challenge to Friedmanite monetarism presented by three different points of view represented in the more recent literature, and Friedman's response to them. This chapter will not discuss Friedman's technical empirical work on money in any detail, although it should be noted that there has been much debate on the technical merits of this work, as in Hendry and Ericsson (1991). Also the focus will be restricted to what Friedman himself (1953b) would describe as his 'positive' monetary theory, on the one hand, and to the practical policy proposals typically suggested by monetarists, on the other. The more esoteric issues raised by Friedman's (1969) discussion of the 'optimum quantity of money', which made a theoretical case in terms of welfare economics that there is a optimal rate of *deflation* (falling prices), are therefore excluded here, although they are taken up again in Chapter 9 below.

THE QUANTITY THEORY OF MONEY

Cagan (1989) attributes the origin of the term 'monetarism' not to Friedman but to Brunner (1968). Friedman (1983) claims to dislike the expression, but acknowledges the popular usage which identifies monetarism with his work. His own preferred description of the theory would be simply to revert to 'the quantity theory of money'. On a number of occasions (Friedman, 1974a, 1989; Friedman and Schwartz, 1982) he has dealt explicitly with the relationship between his 'restatement' of the quantity theory (Friedman, 1956) and earlier versions, including Irving Fisher's (1911) 'transactions equation', the 'income form' of the quantity theory, and the 'Cambridge cash-balances approach'. Although Friedman (1956) has complained about 'the atrophied and rigid caricature' of the quantity theory into which the work of some earlier exponents had degenerated, it will actually be convenient to begin our analysis here with just such a caricature. This will illustrate the issues that Friedman felt he had to address in his self-imposed task of developing a more up-to-date and flexible version of the theory. In the now standard notation, the *income form* of the quantity theory, which is the version surviving in the contemporary textbooks, is given by:

$$MV = PY \qquad (3.1)$$

where M stands for the nominal money supply (somehow defined), V for the 'income velocity of circulation',[1] P for the aggregate price index, and Y for real national income.

As it stands, equation (3.1) is simply a tautology. It is always possible from the published statistics to come up with a dollar figure for the average level of some measure of the money stock over a quarter or a year, and a dollar figure for the flow of national income over the same period. Their ratio, V, can then be residually determined as $V = PY/M$. The calculation of this ratio as a residual, however, would not be a very informative exercise. What turns the quantity *equation* into a more meaningful quantity *theory* is the assumptions made about the behaviour of its individual components (Humphrey, 1993).

To derive our caricature version of the quantity theory, the assumptions required are (i) that velocity, V, is essentially a constant for the purposes of the analysis; (ii) that real income, Y, is determined independently of any monetary influence; and (iii) that (in a simple closed-economy version of the model) the money supply, M, is exogenously determined by the monetary authorities. The quantity theory then becomes a very simple theory of price level determination. A change in the money supply will lead to an equiproportionate change in the price level in the same direction.

Also on these assumptions, taking logarithms of equation (3.1), differentiating with respect to time and rearranging, a dynamic version of the 'caricature' (recalling that $dV/dt = 0$) would be:

$$(1/P)(dP/dt) = (1/M)(dM/dt) - (1/Y)(dY/dt) \qquad (3.2)$$

In other words, on these assumptions the inflation rate will be equal to the rate of growth of the money supply minus the rate of growth of the real economy. This can be expressed in a more compact notation if we use the conventional symbol, π, to stand for the inflation rate $[\pi = (1/P)/(dP/dt)]$, μ to stand for the rate of growth of the money supply $[\mu = (1/M)(dM/dt]$ and g to stand for real economic growth $[g = (1/Y)(dY/dt)]$. Then equation (3.2) can be rewritten as:

$$\pi = \mu - g \qquad (3.3)$$

It is obvious that this simplistic version of the quantity theory is potentially open to attack on three separate grounds, corresponding to the three original assumptions made. First, velocity, V, may not be a constant but a variable, so that potentially some or all of the effect of any change in the money supply might be absorbed in a numerical change in velocity. Second, real income, Y, may itself be affected by monetary factors (money may not be neutral), so that some or all of a money supply change may be reflected in changes in real output rather than prices. Third, the money supply, M, may be an endogenous rather than an exogenous variable (even in the closed economy case), with causality running from nominal income to money rather than the reverse. It might be suggested that Friedman's attempt to breathe new life into the quantity theory in the post-World War II era can be understood in terms of an effort to meet each of these potential objections head on, generating a 'more relevant and subtle' version of the quantity theory (Friedman, 1956) which would be immune to these criticisms.

FRIEDMAN'S 'RESTATEMENT' AND THE MONETARY THEORY OF NOMINAL INCOME

In the early days of the monetarist controversy, attention was focused on the properties of the velocity of circulation and its reciprocal, the demand for real money balances as a fraction of real income. Friedman has made clear (Friedman, 1974a, 1989; Friedman and Schwartz, 1982) that this was because of the perception that the main point of the Keynesian revolution was precisely the assertion that velocity was highly unstable, with stress on the special case of 'absolute liquidity preference' (the liquidity trap of the textbooks) in which the demand for money would respond passively to absorb any increase in the nominal money supply.[2] This interpretation of Keynesian theory can be questioned on doctrine-historical grounds (Patinkin, 1974), but the main point here is what Friedman himself perceived the Keynesian challenge to the quantity theory to be. Kaldor (1986) does concede that there was some justification for Friedman's view in the positions taken, not by Keynes, but by some of Keynes's followers in the 1940s and 1950s, including the 'extreme-sounding statements about the variability of the velocity of circulation' in the *Radcliffe Report* (1959) in the UK. If velocity was either unstable or purely passive this would make the notion that money matters, whether for prices or output, difficult to sustain. Friedman therefore presumably originally saw his task as reformulating the quantity theory as a theory of the demand for money, in which, in the usual paraphrase, demand (and hence velocity) could be expressed as 'a stable function of a limited number of variables'. In his restatement, Friedman (1956) wrote the demand function for real money balances as:

$$M/P = f(r_b, r_e, (1/P)(dP/dt); w; Y; u) \qquad (3.4)$$

where r_b is the nominal rate of return of bonds, r_e is the nominal rate of return on equity, w is the ratio of 'human to non-human wealth', and u is a variable reflecting tastes and preferences. Given certain homogeneity assumptions, a formulation like equation (3.4) implies that the quantity equation itself can be written as:

$$MV(r_b, r_e, (1/P)(dP/dt), w, Y, u) = PY \qquad (3.5)$$

What is achieved by this transformation is that, on the one hand, the quantity theorist can escape from the restrictive assumption of constant velocity, but, on the other, velocity remains determinate and will respond in a *predictable* way to changes in the variables that affect the demand for money.

From some points of view, Friedman's approach was not really new in 1956 and could be regarded as simply a development of the Keynesian theory of money demand (Patinkin, 1974) or, even more obviously, of the approach in Hicks (1935). For the quantity theorist, however, the formulation did achieve a great deal in rescuing the theory from the first of its most obviously restrictive assumptions. This can be seen by rewriting the variable velocity form in the simplified version now common in the textbooks:

$$M/P = L(i, Y), \qquad L_i < 0, L_Y > 0 \qquad (3.6)$$

where *i* stands for the nominal rate of interest. The demand for money is therefore supposed to depend negatively on the nominal rate of interest and positively on real national income. The latter argument is what survives of the notion of transactions demand for money in the income version, and the former is the opportunity cost of holding non-interest-bearing money. Possibly, in a more contemporary analysis, of an environment in which the bulk of the money supply consists of interest-bearing liabilities of financial institutions, the opportunity cost variable should be some sort of interest rate differential rather than simply the level of nominal rates. However, in the literature under discussion it was usually assumed that money does not bear interest. The main point, in any event, is that, in a neoclassical steady-state growth equilibrium, this reformulation of the demand for money function implies only minimal modifications to the caricature version of the dynamic quantity theory.

This can be seen by using the symbol, *r*, to stand for the real, rather than the nominal, rate of interest. If π^e then stands for the *expected* rate of inflation (as of the time loans are made) then by definition we have:

$$r = i - \pi^e \qquad (3.7)$$

and, for money demand:

$$M/P = L(r + \pi^e, Y) \qquad (3.8)$$

Therefore, if there is convergence to a neoclassical steady state, output, *Y*, will be growing at its steady-state value, the real rate of interest, *r*, will be a constant (see below) and the inflation rate, π, will also converge to its long-run value, with actual and expected inflation equal. The only modification to equation (3.2) which would then be required for it to be consistent with equation (3.8) is for the coefficient on output growth now to be different from unity, to take account of the different effect of real income changes on the demand for money implied by the general functional form.[3]

In terms of the traverse from one steady-state rate of money growth to another, there must be one further modification to the traditional quantity theory story to take account of the 'overshooting' (or 'undershooting') of the inflation rate that must now occur. In the case of an increase in the rate of monetary growth, for example, the steady-state inflation rate will also eventually increase according to the modified version of equation (3.2). However, with real rates roughly constant, this increase in inflation will also cause an increase in the nominal rate of interest. Therefore, according to the demand for money function in equations (3.6) or (3.8), the steady-state demand for real balances must be reduced. Given that the starting point of the exercise is an increase in the rate of nominal monetary growth, the necessary deflation of real balances can only occur if at some point in the transition the rate of inflation is actually *greater* than both the rate of monetary growth and its own ultimate long-run value. Hence the overshooting phenomenon.[4] This type of modification, however, does not damage the basic quantity theory logic for the long run or steady state. Also, as price behaviour corresponding to the overshooting phenomenon has actually been observed, in hyperinflationary situations for example (Cagan, 1956), the changes can again be represented as a move in the direction of making the theory more flexible and realistic. Allowing for these modifications, Friedman's reformulation of the theory of money demand, together with the historical correlations between growth rates of broad money and nominal income found in the empirical work of Friedman and Schwartz (1963, 1982), was sufficient to convince many economists at the time that the quantity theory was not after all vulnerable to attack on the grounds of instability in velocity.

Even if the velocity issue is decided, however, and given the ultimate objective of explaining the relationship between monetary changes and prices, another potential line of attack for opponents is to assert that changes in the rate of monetary growth will primarily be reflected in changes in real income rather than just nominal income and prices. Another element of the perceived Keynesian challenge was therefore precisely along those lines (Friedman, 1974a; Friedman and Schwartz, 1982). According to Friedman (1989), a key assumption made by both Keynes and his followers[5] was that either nominal prices or wages could be treated as an 'institutional datum' for short-run analysis. Again, such an interpretation can be challenged on doctrine-historical grounds (Tobin, 1974; Davidson, 1974; Patinkin, 1974), but, from Friedman's point of view, allowing institutional or sociological elements to play any significant part in the determination of wages or prices would represent another clear threat to the quantity theory. Money supply changes would then primarily affect real output and employment, for as long as these elements remained a determining factor. It may seem that Friedman's view of the Keynesian challenge involves an element of 'overkill' by including *both* unstable velocity *and* rigid prices, but presumably it seemed necessary also to provide an answer to those 'Keynesians' who had accepted the velocity argument and gone on to emphasize nominal rigidities.

Friedman's solution to the problem of the effect of money on real income was actually similar to that of the earliest writers on the quantity theory, such as Hume, centuries before (Humphrey, 1993). Essentially, the impact of money on output was conceded for the short run, but *not* for the long run. Monetary changes would be 'non-neutral' in the short run, but neutral (or superneutral) in the long run. In this way, Friedmanite monetarism was able to retain the basic proposition about the long-run relationship between the rate of growth of the money supply and the inflation rate, while at the same time providing a coherent explanation for major business cycle fluctuations, which could in turn be presented as a viable alternative to the orthodoxy of the day. The blame for both types of economic problem could be laid firmly at the door of central banks.

For the long run, Friedman (1974a) believes that the economy converges to an equilibrium or permanent growth rate that is independent of any monetary influence, and reflects only the real forces of productivity and thrift. The real rate of interest, identified with the marginal product of capital, also depends only on real factors, and for the purposes of monetary analysis can be treated as a constant. These assumptions are in the spirit of the neoclassical growth model (Tobin, 1974; Blanchard and Fischer, 1989), but in Friedman's case they reflect more directly the influence of the 'Chicago special case' in Knightian capital theory (Burstein, 1963; Friedman, 1974a; Leijonhufvud, 1981). The vision is one in which a capitalist economy is capable of a more or less indefinite expansion at a steady rate. Either there are ultimately no fixed factors or technological advance may be presumed to offset whatever physical limitations do exist, and therefore the marginal product of capital can reasonably be treated as a constant. These assumptions are of fundamental importance for monetary theory, implying that there is a unique natural rate of interest, a real rate, which can never be permanently altered by monetary policy. This is a view that goes back (at least) to Ricardo and Thornton (Smithin, 1989) and essentially predisposes the resulting theory to come to long-run monetarist conclusions (Keynes, 1936). It is also closely connected with the other 'natural rate' popularized by Friedman, the natural rate of unemployment (Friedman, 1968).

The short-run non-neutrality of monetary changes, on the other hand, arises because at least some economic actors (labour, for example) will be slow to realize the implications of an unanticipated change in the rate of monetary growth and will fail to fully incorporate this change in their inflationary expectations (Friedman, 1968, 1989). This will impart some (temporary) elements of nominal rigidity or money illusion into the system, enough to account for short-run non-neutrality and explain why increases (decreases) in the rate of monetary growth will tend to increase (decrease) output growth in the short run (Friedman and Friedman, 1980). Ironically, the main difference between this and what is called the 'Keynesian' model in textbooks can only be how pervasive and long-lasting the non-neutralities are expected to be. For Friedman they are explicitly temporary. Eventually, expectations will catch up and any real effects from monetary changes will dissipate (Friedman, 1968). Appeal is made to an 'adaptive expectations' process (for example, Friedman, 1974a) to generate this conclusion.

The fact that Friedman's version of the quantity theory could allow for short-run non-neutrality, while retaining the traditional long-run relationship between money and prices, was an extremely important factor in enhancing the plausibility and acceptability of the theory. It meant that the quantity theory could no longer be accused of bankruptcy in the face of historical episodes like the Great Depression (Friedman, 1974b). Friedman and Schwartz's (1963) explanation of the slump in the United States in the 1930s was precisely that the money stock fell by one-third between 1929 and 1933. Yet this could still be consistent with the view that in the long run changes in the money supply would only affect prices, and that given enough time the real economy would always bounce back from a downturn even as severe as that of the 1930s.

It should be noted that Friedman was always reluctant to specify the precise details of the transition from a short-run disturbance to the assumed long-run situation. This is why his version of the quantity theory is described as a 'monetary theory of nominal income' (Friedman, 1974a; Friedman and Schwartz, 1982). The implication is that all that can be definitely said is that an increase in the money supply, M, will cause an increase in nominal income, PY, but that exactly how much of this will be in real output, Y, as opposed to prices, P, and with how much of a lag, is more difficult to state precisely. Empirically, for advanced industrial nations such as the USA, the UK or Japan, it is suggested that an unanticipated increase (decrease) in the rate of growth of nominal money shows up as an increase (decrease) in nominal income with a six to nine month lag and, at first, affects mostly real income rather than prices. The impact on prices is then supposed to come about 18 months to two years later (Friedman, 1983).

The final requirement for Friedman's version of the quantity theory to hold is that the money supply, M, should be capable of a reasonably precise definition, and that it should be amenable to control by some central authority. For the small open economy with fixed exchange rates it is recognized that the domestic money supply will actually be determined endogenously in response to balance of payments developments (Humphrey, 1993). This in itself, however, would not be inconsistent with monetarism. Historically, the 'price-specie-flow' mechanism was an integral part of the original quantity theory (Friedman and Schwartz, 1982; Humphrey, 1993). The same logic (that is, of the price-specie-flow mechanism under a gold standard) can easily be adapted to a fiat money fixed exchange rate world. These balance of payments considerations, however, do explain why

Friedman (1953c) has been an advocate of flexible exchange rates. Only in the latter case would an individual national monetary authority be able unilaterally to control its own inflation rate. Otherwise, it would be necessary to apply one version or another of 'global monetarism' (Humphrey, 1993) to explain developments in the world money supply and world inflation rates.

A more serious challenge to the exogeneity of the money supply would come from the recognition that in a modern credit economy the bulk of the exchange media are the liabilities of various financial institutions rather than physical commodities or fiat note issues. This gives rise to two problems. The first is that of defining the money supply in these circumstances. In other words, which liabilities of which institutions should be included? The second is the observation that the liabilities side of the balance sheets of these financial institutions will change endogenously whenever changes are made on the asset side, when loans are extended or retired.

In their empirical work, Friedman and Schwartz (1963, 1982) apparently did not consider the definitional issue to be a major problem, at least for the economies and time periods they studied (the USA for 1867–1960, and the USA and the UK for 1867–1975). A 'broad' definition of the money supply, referring to currency plus adjusted demand and time deposits in commercial banks, seemed to suffice (Friedman and Schwartz, 1982).

As for the problem of money creation, the answer given by the monetarists has been that in a fractional reserve banking system the process of credit creation is nonetheless constrained by the need for banks to hold reserves of the base money of the system to satisfy the intermittent demands of their depositors for 'cash' payment. Outside of a commodity money system, the monetary base consists essentially of the nominal liabilities of the central bank, and the required reserves to deposit ratio may be determined either by legislation or prudent banking practice. Hence, following Friedman (1960), if C stands for currency in the hands of the public, D stands for those bank deposits included in the relevant definition of the money supply, R for bank reserves, and H for the monetary base ('high-powered money'), we have:

$$M = [(1 + C/D)/(C/D + R/D)]H \tag{3.9}$$

which is known as the 'money multiplier' relationship. Thus, if both the reserves to deposits ratio, R/D, and the cash to deposits ratio determined by the public, C/D, are fairly stable, and also if the central bank can control the size of its own balance sheet (and hence control H), the argument is that the money supply, M, will also be under control, and will change in some determinate ratio to H.

MONETARIST POLICY PROPOSALS

The typical policy proposals which Friedman and other monetarists have
derived from the theory outlined above are well known. The suggestion is
that the rate of growth of the money supply should be low on average,
steady and predictable (Friedman, 1983). A low average growth rate will
supposedly deliver a low inflation rate, and steady and predictable growth
will eliminate a major cause of the business cycle. The particular policy proposal with which Friedman's name has been associated is that the rate of
growth of the money supply (somehow defined) should simply be a constant, set to deliver roughly stable prices (Friedman, 1960, 1968, 1983).
Friedman is aware that more sophisticated or 'optimal' rules might be
devised,[6] but has opted for constancy on the political grounds that it would
be easier to gain public support and understanding for a simple rule
(Friedman, 1983).

Friedman's views on appropriate monetary policy, however, have evolved
over time. In a set of proposals put forward in the late 1940s (Friedman,
1948) he was, at first, explicitly concerned with the interaction between
monetary and fiscal policy. It was suggested that tax and expenditure
parameters be set to balance the federal government budget at a high level
of employment, implying surpluses in boom years and deficits in a depression. Further, deficits should be money-financed rather than bond-financed
and (symmetrically) the money supply should be reduced when there is a
surplus. The combined fiscal and monetary response therefore would
provide 'defense in depth' against the business cycle (ibid.). However, there
should be no other changes in the money supply, and the money stock and
price level should be stable on average. In order for monetary responses to
be 'entirely automatic', Friedman further proposed that the banking
system be subject to 100 per cent reserves requirements. These early proposals therefore seem to reflect two sets of influences. One was the concern
with 'automatic stabilizers' and 'functional finance', which were much in
vogue at Friedman's time of writing. The second was the 100 per cent
reserves tradition at the University of Chicago associated with Friedman's
precursor, Henry Simons (Friedman, 1948). This can be seen as one way of
dealing with the perennial problem (for the quantity theorist) of making a
credit money system behave 'as if' it is a commodity money system.

Twelve years later, in Friedman's *Program for Monetary Stability* (1960),
the policy proposals put forward are somewhat different. The concern with
automatic stabilizers is dropped, and the recommendation for a constant
rate of monetary growth makes its first appearance. To facilitate this at the
level of national monetary policy, Friedman explicitly calls for an end to
the Bretton Woods system of fixed exchange rates and a move to flexible

rates. There is still a recommendation for 100 per cent reserves, but it is no longer such an essential part of the overall scheme (ibid.), and the constant growth rule is presented as desirable in itself even if the other reforms are not made.

The idea of constancy is thereafter retained in one form or another in most of Friedman's subsequent proposals. The 100 per cent reserves idea, however, does not reappear in later works such as Friedman (1968, 1983, 1985) or Friedman and Friedman (1980). Explicitly or implicitly, reliance is placed on the stability of the money multiplier relationship.

Perhaps the most interesting evolution in Friedman's thinking over the years is about the appropriate definition of the money supply to which the monetary rule should apply. It is precisely this issue that, intuitively, is likely to cause difficulties for the practical application of monetarist ideas in a credit money world in which any line drawn between money and 'near money' is ever-shifting. At first this was not treated as a particularly important problem. In 1960, for example, it was suggested that it did not much matter which definition of money was adopted 'as long as . . . it is at least as broad as currency plus adjusted demand deposits' (the M1 of the day). Friedman (1960) would himself at that time have opted for M2. By 1980, however, in *Free to Choose*, in the context of a draft constitutional amendment for the USA, the proposed rule applies only to the narrow monetary *base* (Friedman and Friedman, 1980). Apparently, the need for legal precision in the case of a constitutional proposal forced a recognition that the institutional structure (and hence the definition of M) is constantly changing. For the policy to work, there must still be an implicit assumption that some real-world counterpart to the theoretical 'M' continues to exist, and that it is linked to the base by a version of equation (3.9), but now it is no longer assumed that this magnitude will be easy to identify in practice.[7]

By the mid-1980s, Friedman was making even more concessions to the problems caused by financial innovation. At this point the preferred monetary policy was a *zero* rate of growth of the monetary base, and it was now suggested that, if the pace of financial innovation were to continue in the range of historical experience (thereby raising the money multiplier), this would be consistent with stable or mildly declining prices (Friedman, 1985). These changes in the proposed definition of the monetary aggregate to be controlled obviously do reflect the serious difficulties that have arisen in attempts to implement monetarist policies in practice, in an environment in which financial innovation implies continual change in the spectrum of assets acceptable as money.

MONETARISM AND THE NEW CLASSICAL SCHOOL

As stated by Laidler (1990), monetarism was at the height of its purely academic influence more than a quarter of a century ago, and although its subsequent decline in prestige surely owes something to the difficulties mentioned above, probably equally important in terms of mainstream economics was the rise of what was originally called the 'rational expectations' school, later the 'new classical' school, in the 1970s and 1980s. This is ironic as, to begin with, new classical ideas were seen as strengthening the monetarist model (ibid.). Indeed, at one point Tobin (1981) could refer to the new classicals as 'Monetarists Mark II' (Hoover, 1984). Eventually, however, the logic of new classical theory ended up by tending to undermine the monetarist position in the eyes of many academic economists.

Monetarists do believe that in some sense 'money matters', but in two distinct ways. In the long run, money matters for the average inflation rate, whereas in the short run it matters for the ups and downs of the business cycle, particularly for the most severe episodes. New classical theory did retain monetarist notions about the long-run determinants of the inflation rate, but when taken literally and pushed to its logical conclusion, it threatened the monetary theory of the business cycle.

As is well known, the rational expectations component of new classical theory caused great stress to be laid on the different effects of 'anticipated' and 'unanticipated' changes in monetary policy. Anticipated changes should, supposedly, quickly be reflected in the nominal contracts which 'rational agents' are prepared to undertake, and therefore should have no real effects. Only genuinely unanticipated changes, which must by definition be random or unsystematic, could therefore be non-neutral. Friedman (1974a) had also used the vocabulary of 'actual' and 'anticipated' changes, but these terms were employed in a less precise way than by members of the new classical school and the expectations formation process in monetarism was modelled by what was essentially an adaptive expectations mechanism. This allowed for considerable short-run non-neutrality, but was unacceptable on theoretical grounds in the rational expectations view. The monetarist constancy rule itself was given only weak support by the new approach. Under market-clearing rational expectations, no *systematic* monetary policy, simple or complicated, would have any real effects.

In the early days, nonetheless, new classical theory did allow for a 'monetary misperceptions' theory of the business cycle, which was not dramatically inconsistent with monetarism (Lucas, 1981). However, it was soon pointed out that official money supply data are widely publicized with a short lag, and that therefore the empirical counterpart of unanticipated money in the rational expectations sense is a trivial magnitude, which could hardly be held responsible for business cycle fluctuations of the magnitude observed in practice (Laidler, 1990). By the mid-1980s, the monetary mis-perceptions theory of the business cycle had therefore fallen out of favour (McCallum, 1986). The new classical economists, beginning with the con-tribution by Kydland and Prescott (1982), then responded by developing a new completely non-monetary explanation of the business cycle, the so-called 'real business cycle' theory (Ryan and Mullineux, 1997). This, if suc-cessful, would rule out monetarist concerns entirely.

From some points of view, it is curious that such a position should become popular in the 1980s and 1990s (Smithin, 1990a, 1990b), as the evi-dence from that period, whether in terms of casual observation of current events or from more sophisticated statistical methods (Laidler, 1990), obvi-ously provides little support for the view that the activities of central banks have no real effects. Among academic economists the so-called 'new Keynesian' school[8] were prepared to respond to this evidence by reinstat-ing some role for nominal rigidities (with certain other theoretical innova-tions) in their theoretical models. However, this sort of explanation was anathema to the new classicals, and in many influential circles *all* monetary explanations of the cycle languished, along with the monetary mispercep-tions theory.

Laidler (1990), interestingly, locates the reason for these difficulties in a lack of attention by monetarists and others to the type of issues concern-ing the nature of money and its role in the socioeconomic system, that were discussed in the previous chapter. Specifically, it is suggested that the expli-citly Walrasian framework of most contemporary economic theory, includ-ing new classical theory, provides little scope for adequately developing the foundations of monetary theory from first principles. Evidently, a theory in which money plays no essential role will have difficulty in providing a mon-etary theory of the business cycle, or of any other macroeconomic phenom-enon.

It might have been thought that monetarism would be immune from these theoretical difficulties. After all, the point has been made that Friedman's method is actually Marshallian (partial equilibrium) rather than Walrasian (Hoover, 1984; Rogers, 1989). This is a view which Friedman himself appar-ently accepts (Friedman, 1974a). Nonetheless, as Laidler (1990) suggests, the fact is that Friedman's version of monetarism paid no more attention to the specifics of the role played by money in the capitalist or 'market' economy than did the new classicals. Hence monetarism was vulnerable at a theoretical level as soon as macroeconomists began to take the Walrasian-type system seriously as a vehicle for explaining aggregate economic phe-nomena.

In fact, Friedman himself has occasionally cited the Walrasian scheme with approval, in spite of his Marshallian pedigree, notably in the discussion of the natural rate of unemployment in the famous AEA Presidential Address (Friedman, 1968). Even more significantly, Friedman's (1956) original theory of the demand for money *explicitly* made no attempt to inquire into the nature of the services provided by money, on the argument that the demand for money was just a special case of demand theory in general. This explicit rejection of any deeper inquiry into the role played by money in the economy, which must have seemed a fruitful simplification at the time, had serious consequences later on. In the end, the theoretical foundations of monetarism could be undermined just as easily as those of new classical monetary theory. This is somewhat ironic for an approach whose *raison d'être* was to re-establish the view that money matters.

MONETARISM AND FREE BANKING

The recent upsurge of advocacy for *laissez-faire* in the banking industry, as described, for example, by Dowd (1996, 2000) represents another challenge to Friedmanite monetarism from what might otherwise have seemed a friendly quarter. The free banking argument is a potential problem for Friedman because he has been an outspoken advocate of *laissez-faire* in other spheres (Friedman and Friedman, 1962, 1980), and it is natural for critics to inquire why should this not also apply in the realm of banking and finance.

Although the monetarist rule would restrict the purely *discretionary* activities of government central banks, it certainly does not promote anything like *laissez-faire* in banking. There is no suggestion that central banks should be abolished, that government monopoly in the provision of currency should be withdrawn, or that there should be no role for government in the provision of monetary services. In addition, at times monetarists have suggested reforms which would actually increase government control of the banking system, as in the proposal for 100 per cent reserve requirements.

Friedman's original attitude to this question was that a stable monetary framework is simply a necessary condition for the market system to function (and hence to gain the benefits of free markets in other areas), but that it is unlikely that the market itself would generate such a framework. The monetary system was therefore seen as a legitimate arena for government 'intervention', on a par with the provision of a legal system or national defence (Friedman, 1960).

The later literature surveyed by Cowen and Kroszner (1994), Selgin and White (1994) and McCallum (1985), however, represented a new challenge to which Friedman and Schwartz (1986) at one point explicitly responded. They referred back to Friedman's earlier discussion of government involvement in money and banking in which he put forward four defences for government intervention (Friedman, 1960). These were, first, the tendency of commodity-based systems to evolve into fiduciary systems because of the resource costs involved; second, the scope for fraud and deception, and the difficulty of enforcing promises to pay once fiduciary elements are present; third, 'technical monopoly' features in the production of a fiduciary currency; and, finally, the third party externalities which arise when there are serious monetary disorders (Friedman and Schwartz, 1986). After examining the arguments put forward more recently, the authors claim to find little reason for altering Friedman's original views. They are somewhat dismissive of the case for a unit of account divorced from the medium of exchange, referring with approval to the counter-arguments of White (1984) and McCallum (1985). The modern free banking school as such, however, is treated more sympathetically, and the authors go so far as to agree that in some hypothetical counterfactual history market-based money and banking arrangements might have performed more satisfactorily than existing systems involving government intervention (Friedman and Schwartz, 1986). However, they also assert that the political realities make it unlikely that any free banking system could actually emerge from the currently existing situation, so that the question is not practical politics. In this, as they acknowledge, they come to essentially the same position reached much earlier by writers such as Bagehot (1873) and Smith (1936).

ENDOGENOUS MONEY

Yet another theoretical and empirical challenge to basic monetarist propositions relates to the issue of causality in the quantity equation, and this has also re-emerged with particular force in recent years.

As discussed above, if the monetarist proposition of a relatively stable velocity of circulation is granted, the monetary theory of nominal income then asserts that causality flows from left to right in the quantity equation, from money, M, to nominal income, PY. However, the arguments of many Keynesian and Post Keynesian economists, including Kaldor (1986), Moore (1988), Dow and Saville (1990) and Lavoie (1992), and also those of the European circuit school (see Graziani, 1990; Nell and Deleplace, 1996; Parguez and Seccareccia, 2000), suggest that this is not a realistic proposition in modern credit economies. The argument is that, when the money supply, on any reasonable definition, consists mostly of the deposit liabilities of various kinds of financial institutions, money is created essentially as a by-product of the lending activities of those institutions. It may therefore make more sense to think in terms of an increase in nominal income, PY, being financed by an increase in bank lending, which then leads residually to an increase in money, M, on the other side of bank balance sheets. In other words, the causality in the quantity equation goes from right to left, from PY to M.

This view is often called the 'endogenous money' approach, as discussed in more detail in Chapter 5 below, but this expression should be used with care. It would be agreed, for example, that the money supply is endogenous technically speaking, under either an international gold standard or a pure fiat money regime with fixed exchange rates. This, however, would not damage the quantity theory itself as long as causality goes from left to right in equation (3.1). The key point in the Post Keynesian view is the idea that changes in nominal income in some sense *cause* changes in money. For many writers this is bound up with the fact that the Post Keynesians typically take a different view of the causes of inflation than the monetarists, specifically that inflation is essentially a 'cost-push', and particularly a 'wage-push', phenomenon (Moore, 1988; Kaldor, 1986; Laidler, 1989). Hence, in a standard sequence, a spontaneous rise in the nominal wage bill would give rise to an increase in the demand for bank credit and be accommodated by an increase in the money supply (Moore, 1988).

Monetarists must recognize that bank deposits *per se* are indeed an endogenous variable created when bank loans are extended, but they have argued that this real-world complication is adequately dealt with by an appeal to the money multiplier mechanism. The expansion of bank balance sheets is constrained by the availability of base money, and the base in turn is supposed to be amenable to control by the central bank (Laidler, 1989). The Post Keynesians counter that the base itself is also endogenous in real-world central banking systems. The argument is that in practice central banks cannot refuse to accommodate demands for borrowed reserves at the 'discount window', as this would mean abandoning their responsibility for the liquidity of the system and the 'lender of last resort' function (Moore, 1988; Kaldor, 1986; Dow and Saville, 1990). All they can do is change the terms on which they are prepared to make accommodations, the discount rate or bank rate, and this rate or (more likely in current practice) a closely related inter-bank rate on central bank liabilities then becomes the ultimate monetary policy instrument.[9]

The challenge to Friedman posed by this argument is that it provides an alternative, internally coherent, interpretation of the statistical correlations between the growth rates of money and nominal income on which the monetarists have based their case. These can no longer be regarded as proving monetarist propositions simply by themselves, the basic point being the obvious one that correlation is not causality. Friedman's response to this has been that the evidence that he and Schwartz have marshalled, particularly the evidence about the timing of lags and leads, does point to the main causal connection running from money to income, albeit with allowance for some feedback effects in the opposite direction (Friedman, 1970; Friedman and Schwartz, 1982). Tobin (1970), however, has provided a theoretical model which casts doubt on the timing argument, and Moore (1988) has reported evidence that so-called 'Granger–Sims causality' runs from the monetary aggregates to the monetary base in the USA, and not vice versa. Laidler (1989) concedes that the empirical evidence about the causality between money and nominal income is inconclusive, and that reasonable people may disagree about it. However, to accept this position would seem to be to substantially undercut the impact of Friedman and Schwartz's empirical correlations.

CONCLUDING REMARKS

In addition to the considerations outlined above, the loss of influence suffered by monetarism must also owe something to the empirical problems thrown up by the so-called 'monetarist experiments' in policy making of the 1980s (Smithin, 1990b). Around 1979–82, in several jurisdictions, and in particular in the two nations which Friedman and Schwartz had studied in *Monetary Trends in the United States and the United Kingdom*, the authorities announced themselves as essentially converted to monetarist ideas. They accepted monetarist views on the link between money growth and inflation, on the need to target the growth rates of whatever statistical monetary aggregates were thought to be the empirical counterparts of the theoretical '*M*' of the quantity equation (M1 in the USA, M3 in the UK) and on the need to lower the targets to reduce inflation.

In both these jurisdictions (and elsewhere) it is fair to say the authorities tried very hard to carry the policies out, but the results of the experiments were very confusing from the point of view of monetarist theory. Money certainly seemed to matter in the 1979–82 period, as real interest rates were forced up to high levels, real exchange rates appreciated, severe recessions ensued and eventually inflation rates came down. However, the course of events seemed to bear little relationship to previous monetarist predictions about the process (Smithin, 1990a, 1990b; B. Friedman, 1988; Goodhart, 1989). In particular, the behaviour of the monetary aggregates, which were supposed to be crucial to the exercise, was not that predicted beforehand. Rates of growth of the broader monetary aggregates, for example, were actually seen to *increase* for some time as the recessions set in and inflation began to fall. Similarly, in the recovery years later in the decade of the 1980s, rapid growth rates of the published monetary aggregates should have led to very high inflation rates on monetarist principles (B. Friedman, 1988), but in practice inflation did not really begin to increase for five or six years, and then not in commensurate magnitude. Eventually, monetary targeting was abandoned by most central banks and monetary policy essentially reverted to a traditional interest rate and/or exchange rate focus (B. Friedman, 1988; Goodhart, 1989).

The conclusion that might reasonably be drawn from all this is that money did indeed 'matter' during the period of the monetarist experiments, but not necessarily in the way in which Friedman and other monetarists had suggested. Evidently, the proximate reason for the breakdown was that the 1980s were also an era of rapid deregulation and financial innovation, in which inevitably the traditional interpretations of monetary aggregates become blurred.

It might be suggested that the difficulties involved with interpreting the monetary experience of the 1980s mirror the difficulties that we have with evaluating Friedman's ultimate contribution to the discipline. Friedman has passionately insisted that money matters, and first did so at a time when the majority opinion in the economics profession was all but ignoring monetary issues. This must be counted as a real contribution that will outlast the contemporary partial reversion to the opposite point of view. However, it cannot be said that he has succeeded in providing an unambiguously convincing account of exactly which monetary variables are important and precisely how they affect the economy, certainly not one which would be adequate to satisfy all the critics cited above. The difficulties experienced with the definition and meaning of the monetary aggregates during a period of financial innovation are indicative of the basic problem. The point may ultimately be that the attempt to refurbish the traditional quantity theory such that it could be applied equally to credit money economies as well as simple commodity money economies was heroic but quixotic. It appears that modern financial systems are too complex, or change too rapidly, to be fully explicable in those terms.

NOTES

1. In the income version of the quantity theory, the term 'velocity of circulation' is clearly something of a misnomer, with connotations originally deriving from the transactions version, as in Fisher (1911). However, this terminology seems to have been generally retained, albeit misleadingly, and is the conventional usage.
2. This slides over the distinction made by Friedman (1974a) between 'short-run' and 'long-run' absolute liquidity preference. Such a distinction may have a bearing on the question

of whether or not a permanent 'underemployment equilibrium' may be presumed to exist, but it is not really relevant in terms of the motivation for Friedman's interest in the stability of the demand for money function. On this point, see Leijonhufvud (1981).

3. It has been an issue in the empirical literature whether the income elasticity of money demand is greater than, or less than, unity. Some of Friedman's empirical work seemed to indicate the former (Friedman, 1974a), implying that real money balances are a superior or 'luxury' good. Goldfeld (1989), however, reports that other researchers have found lower elasticities.

4. See the relevant passages in Parkin (1982) for a clear textbook description of this process.

5. Monetarist writers tend not to draw the distinctions implied by the title of Leijonhufvud's well-known book *On Keynesian Economics and the Economics of Keynes* (1968), or to distinguish between different schools of Keynesians in the manner of Coddington (1983).

6. As mentioned, Friedman's own 'optimum quantity of money' rule (Friedman, 1969) would require a deflation to reduce nominal interest rates to zero. (See also Friedman, 1968).

7. See also the discussion in Smithin (1984).

8. See Mankiw and Romer (1991). As with monetarist interpretations of 'Keynesian economics', it is a highly debatable point whether the new Keynesian theory has any close relationship to anything actually written by Keynes.

9. Post Keynesians differ, however, on the question of how effective interest rate changes might be in terms of their impact on other macroeconomic variables, as compared with (say) the traditional tools of fiscal policy.

REFERENCES

Bagehot, W. (1873 [1915]), *Lombard Street*, London: John Murray.

Blanchard, O.J. and S. Fischer (1989), *Lectures on Macroeconomics*, Cambridge, MA: MIT Press.

Brunner, K. (1968), 'The role of money and monetary policy', *Federal Reserve Bank of St. Louis Review*, 50, 8–24.

Burstein, M.L. (1963), *Money*, Cambridge, MA: Schenkman Publishing Co.

Cagan, P. (1956), 'The monetary dynamics of hyperinflation', in M. Friedman (ed.), *Studies in the Quantity Theory of Money*, Chicago: University of Chicago Press.

——— (1989), 'Monetarism', in J. Eatwell, M. Milgate and P. Newman (eds), *The New Palgrave: Money*, London: Macmillan.

Coddington, A. (1983), *Keynesian Economics: The Search for First Principles*, London: George Allen & Unwin.

Cowen T. and R. Kroszner (1994), *Explorations in the New Monetary Economics*, Oxford: Basil Blackwell.

Davidson, P. (1974), 'A Keynesian view of Friedman's theoretical framework for monetary analysis', in R.J. Gordon (ed.), *Milton Friedman's Monetary Framework: A Debate with his Critics*, Chicago: University of Chicago Press.

Dow, J.C.R. and I.D. Saville (1990), *A Critique of Monetary Policy: Theory and British Experience*, Oxford: Clarendon Press.

Dowd, K. (1996), 'The case for financial laissez-faire', *Economic Journal*, 106, 679–87.

——— (2000), 'The invisible hand and the evolution of the monetary system', in J. Smithin (ed.), *What is Money?*, London: Routledge.

Fisher, I. (1911), *The Purchasing Power of Money*, New York: Macmillan.

Friedman, B.M. (1988), 'Lessons on monetary policy from the 1980s', *Journal of Economic Perspectives*, 2, 51–72.

Friedman, M. (1948 [1953a]), 'A monetary and fiscal framework for economic stability', in *Essays in Positive Economics*, Chicago: University of Chicago Press.
—— (1953b), 'The methodology of positive economics', *Essays in Positive Economics*, Chicago: University of Chicago Press.
—— (1953c), 'The case for flexible exchange rates', *Essays in Positive Economics*, Chicago: University of Chicago Press.
—— (1956), 'The quantity theory of money – a restatement', in M. Friedman (ed.), *Studies in the Quantity Theory of Money*, Chicago: University of Chicago Press.
—— (1960), *A Program for Monetary Stability*, New York: Fordham University Press.
—— (1968), 'The role of monetary policy', *American Economic Review*, 58, 1–17.
—— (1969), *The Optimum Quantity of Money and Other Essays*, Chicago: Aldine Publishing Co.
—— (1970), 'The new monetarism: comment', *Lloyds Bank Review*, October, 52–5.
—— (1974a), 'A theoretical framework for monetary analysis', in R.J. Gordon (ed.), *Milton Friedman's Monetary Framework: A Debate with his Critics*, Chicago: University of Chicago Press.
—— (1974b), 'Comments on the critics', in R.J. Gordon (ed.), *Milton Friedman's Monetary Framework: A Debate with his Critics*, Chicago: University of Chicago Press.
—— (1983), 'Monetarism in rhetoric and in practice', *Bank of Japan Monetary and Economic Studies*, 1, 1–14.
—— (1985), 'The case for overhauling the Federal Reserve', *Challenge*, July–August, 4–12.
—— (1989), 'Quantity theory of money', in J. Eatwell, M. Milgate and P. Newman (eds), *The New Palgrave: Money*, London: Macmillan.
Friedman, M. and R. Friedman (1962), *Capitalism and Freedom*, Chicago: University of Chicago Press.
—— (1980), *Free to Choose*, New York: Harcourt Brace Jovanovich.
Friedman, M. and A.J. Schwartz (1963), *A Monetary History of the United States, 1867–1960*, Princeton: Princeton University Press.
—— (1982), *Monetary Trends in the United States and the United Kingdom: Their Relation to Income, Prices and Interest Rates, 1867–1975*, Chicago: University of Chicago Press.
—— (1986), 'Has government any role in money?', *Journal of Monetary Economics*, 17, 37–62.
Galbraith, J.K. (1987), *Economics in Perspective: A Critical History*, Boston: Houghton Mifflin.
Goldfeld, S.M. (1989), 'Demand for money: empirical studies', in J. Eatwell, M. Milgate and P. Newman (eds), *The New Palgrave: Money*, London: Macmillan.
Goodhart, C.A.E. (1989), 'The conduct of monetary policy', *Economic Journal*, 99, 293–346.
Graziani, A. (1990), 'The theory of the monetary circuit', *Economies et Sociétés*, 24, 7–36.
Heilbroner, R. (1990), 'Analysis and vision in the history of modern economic thought', *Journal of Economic Literature*, 28, 1097–114.
Hendry, D.F. and N.R. Ericsson (1991), 'An econometric analysis of UK money demand in *Monetary Trends in the United States and the United Kingdom* by Milton Friedman and Anna Schwartz', *American Economic Review*, 81, 8–38.
Hicks, J.R. (1935), 'A suggestion for simplifying the theory of money', *Economica*, 2, 1–19.

—— (1967), *Critical Essays in Monetary Theory*, Oxford: Clarendon Press.

Hoover, K.D. (1984), 'Two types of monetarism', *Journal of Economic Literature*, 22, 58–76.

Humphrey, T.M. (1993), *Money, Banking and Inflation: Essays in the History of Monetary Thought*, Aldershot, UK and Brookfield, US: Edward Elgar.

Kaldor, N. (1986), *The Scourge of Monetarism*, 2nd edn, Oxford: Oxford University Press.

Keynes, J.M. (1936), *The General Theory of Employment Interest and Money*, London: Macmillan.

Kydland, F.E. and E.C. Prescott (1982), 'Time to build and aggregate fluctuations', *Econometrica*, 50, 1345–70.

Laidler, D.E.W. (1989), 'Dow and Saville's *Critique of Monetary Policy* – a review essay', *Journal of Economic Literature*, 27, 1147–59.

—— (1990), *Taking Money Seriously and Other Essays*, London: Philip Allan.

Lavoie, M. (1992), *Foundations of Post-Keynesian Economic Analysis*, Aldershot, UK and Brookfield, US: Edward Elgar.

Leijonhufvud, A. (1968), *On Keynesian Economics and the Economics of Keynes*, New York: Oxford University Press.

—— (1981), *Information and Coordination: Essays in Macroeconomic Theory*, New York: Oxford University Press.

Lucas, R.E. Jr. (1981), *Studies in Business-Cycle Theory*, Cambridge, MA: MIT Press.

Mankiw N.G. and D. Romer (eds) (1991), *New Keynesian Economics*, Cambridge, MA: MIT Press.

McCallum, B.T. (1985), 'Bank deregulation, accounting systems of exchange, and the unit of account: a critical review', *Carnegie-Rochester Conference Series on Public Policy*, 23, 13–45.

—— (1986), 'On "real" and "sticky-price" theories of the business cycle', *Journal of Money, Credit, and Banking*, 18, 379–414.

Moore, B.J. (1988), *Horizontalists and Verticalists: The Macroeconomics of Credit Money*, Cambridge: Cambridge University Press.

Nell, E.J. and G. Deleplace (eds) (1996), *Money in Motion: The Post Keynesian and the Circulation Approaches*, London: Macmillan.

Parguez, A. and M. Seccareccia (2000), 'The credit theory of money: the monetary circuit approach', in J. Smithin (ed.), *What is Money?*, London: Routledge.

Parkin, M. (1982), *Modern Macroeconomics*, Scarborough, Ontario: Prentice-Hall Canada.

Patinkin, D. (1974), 'Friedman on the quantity theory and Keynesian economics', in R.J. Gordon (ed.), *Milton Friedman's Monetary Framework: A Debate with his Critics*, Chicago: University of Chicago Press.

Radcliffe, Rt. Hon. the Lord (1959), *Report of the Committee on the Working of the Monetary System*, London: HMSO, Cmnd 827.

Rogers, C. (1989), *Money, Interest and Capital: A Study in the Foundations of Monetary Theory*, Cambridge: Cambridge University Press.

Ryan, C. and A.W. Mullineux (1997), 'The ups and downs of modern business cycle theory', in B. Snowdon and H.R. Vane (eds), *Reflections on the Development of Modern Macroeconomics*, Cheltenham, UK and Lyme, US: Edward Elgar.

Selgin, G. and L.H. White (1994), 'How would the invisible hand handle money?', *Journal of Economic Literature*, 32, 1718–49.

Smith, V. (1936 [1990]), *The Rationale of Central Banking and the Free Banking Alternative*, Indianapolis: Liberty Press.

Smithin, J. (1984), 'Financial innovation and monetary theory', *Three Banks Review*, December, 26–38.

—— (1989), 'Hicksian monetary economics and contemporary financial innovation', *Review of Political Economy*, 1, 192–207.

—— (1990a), 'Empirical and conceptual problems in contemporary macroeconomics', *British Review of Economic Issues*, 12, 73–95.

—— (1990b), *Macroeconomics after Thatcher and Reagan: The Conservative Policy Revolution in Retrospect*, Aldershot, UK and Brookfield, US: Edward Elgar.

—— (1993), 'La pensée monétaire de Milton Friedman face aux théories contemporaines', in M. Lavoie and M. Seccareccia (eds), *Milton Friedman et son œuvre*, Paris: Dunod.

Tobin, J. (1970), 'Money and income: post hoc ergo propter hoc?', *Quarterly Journal of Economics*, 84, 301–17.

—— (1974), 'Friedman's theoretical framework', in R.J. Gordon (ed.), *Milton Friedman's Monetary Framework: A Debate with his Critics*, Chicago: University of Chicago Press.

—— (1981), 'The monetarist counter-revolution today: an appraisal', *Economic Journal*, 91, 29–42.

White, L.H. (1984), 'Competitive payments systems and the unit of account', *American Economic Review*, 74, 699–712.

4. Short-run non-neutralities, nominal rigidities, misperceptions and the concept of the Phillips curve

INTRODUCTION

When asking the question how the activities of the 'monetary authorities' such as central banks affect the actual economy, the most popular answer has usually been that they can only have a transitory effect, at most, on the so-called 'real' economic variables. The conviction is that ultimately monetary changes can only affect inflation rates. This was certainly the position of the monetarist school, for example, as discussed in the previous chapter. There have obviously been challenges to this point of view over the centuries, but the present era seems to be characterized, once again, by a particularly firm belief on the part of most economists in the doctrine of the 'long-run neutrality of money'. This may be why, for example, professional opinion is apparently so sanguine about the consequences of such things as deliberately deflationary policies at the national level, and such concentrations of international financial power as the 'single currency' in Europe or 'dollarization' in the Americas. Whenever it seems that in practice there *have* been definite consequences of monetary changes on economic activity (in either direction) it is explained that these can only be of a short-run or temporary nature, caused by such things as 'nominal rigidities', ' wage/price stickiness' or 'misperceptions', and are therefore bound to disappear eventually. The purpose of the present chapter is to pursue this type of argument in more detail.

Another way of looking at this material is as a (partial) exposition of what Krugman (2002) calls 'old-fashioned macro', which (in his opinion) is more useful for policy analysis for economists in government circles and in the financial markets than the more esoteric products of contemporary academic economic theorists. This present exposition does not necessarily endorse the 'usefulness' of this approach, primarily because of the continued underlying commitment within it to 'natural rate' ideas and concepts. Nonetheless, it is true that a straightforward aggregate demand and supply focus does make clear the essential points in a way that the more obscure/

abstract discussions do not, and Krugman explicitly identifies 'sticky prices' as one of the key elements of the debate. In what follows, the focus is on the 'AD–AS approach to long-run versus short-run analysis' (ibid.), rather than the Hicksian IS/LM model, which Krugman also endorses.[1] Another feature of the discussion which follows is that it is mostly cast in dynamic terms, wherever possible, involving growth rates and inflation rates, rather than in static terms involving only output and price levels. This allows for a more direct comparison with the 'alternative' monetary model of inflation and growth, to be developed in Chapter 7 below.

HISTORICAL CONSIDERATIONS

In fact, for more than 250 years, since the early days of capitalism even before the industrial revolution, it has usually been the dominant or mainstream opinion that the activities of central banks matter for real economic variables *only* to the extent that the economic system is characterized by temporary frictions of the types mentioned above. Without too much damage to the underlying barter–exchange model, it can be agreed that there will be some degree of inertia in levels or rates of change of money wages or prices, and that this may prevent them from immediately adjusting to monetary policy changes. This is enough to account for some measure of non-neutrality in the short run. However, as the economic 'agents' or actors are ultimately supposed to care only about real wages and relative prices, the argument continues that, in the nature of things, any stickiness in money wages and prices can only be a transitory phenomenon. In the final analysis, wages and prices must eventually adjust to the requirements of a real economic equilibrium impervious to merely monetary changes. From this point of view, it would not much matter whether monetary policy is conceived of as arbitrary changes in the quantity of base money or as changes in interest rates which provide the incentive or disincentive for the other players to take credit denominated in term of central bank liabilities. In either case, while it would be conceded that monetary policy changes may have a temporary effect on real variables while the nominal rigidities persist, they would still be neutral in the long run and could not permanently change the real economic equilibrium.

One of the most pervasive features of the current economics literature, at both the textbook level and in more advanced circles, is the extent to which an appeal to nominal rigidities to explain short-run monetary non-neutrality continues to be associated particularly with 'Keynesian economics'. However, as pointed out by Leijonhufvud (1968), in a famous book, by Smithin (1988) and by Laidler (1996), this is a serious misinterpretation of the historical record. In fact nominal wage rigidity, in particular, was always part of the *traditional* explanation of temporary 'lapses from full employment'. If anything, the intent of Keynes's work was to draw attention away from this feature. The persistence of the idea that rigid or sticky wages is a peculiarly Keynesian concept can only be attributed to a widespread lack of knowledge of the history of the discipline on the part of today's mostly technically trained economists.

An explicit statement of the implications of short-run nominal rigidities can be found as far back as the mid-eighteenth century in Hume's presentation of the quantity theory. Hume (1752) qualified a statement of the long-run quantity theory relationship between money and prices in the following terms:

> notwithstanding this conclusion, which must be allowed just, it is certain, that, since the discovery of mines in America, industry has increased in all the nations of Europe . . . and this may justly be ascribed . . . to the increase of gold and silver . . . in every kingdom, into which money begins to flow in greater abundance than formerly, every thing takes a new face: labour and industry gain life; the merchant becomes more enterprising, the manufacturer more diligent and skilful . . . To account . . . for this phenomenon, we must consider that though the high price of commodities be a necessary consequence of the increase of gold and silver, yet it follows not immediately upon that increase . . . some time is required before the money circulates through the whole state . . . At first, no alteration is perceived; by degrees the price rises, first of one commodity, then of another; till the whole at last reaches a just proportion with the new quantity of specie . . . In my opinion, it is only in this interval or intermediate situation, between the acquisition of money and the rise of prices, that the increasing quantity of gold and silver is favourable to industry. When any quantity of money is imported into a nation, it is not at first dispersed into many hands; but is confined to the coffers of a few persons, who immediately seek to employ it to advantage . . . we shall find, that it must first quicken the diligence of every individual, before it increases the price of labour . . . There is always an interval before matters be adjusted to their new situation; and this interval is as pernicious to industry, when gold and silver are diminishing, as it is advantageous when these metals are increasing.

The point of quoting Hume at such length is to illustrate that, in spite of the vast quantity of economic writing and research which has taken place since his time, and (as stressed earlier) the change in the monetary system away from a commodity money base, the economist's basic understanding of the reasons for short-term monetary non-neutrality has not changed all that much in the past two and a half centuries. It is thought that a monetary expansion may cause a temporary increase in output and employment, and a monetary contraction a decrease, but only in a transitional period during which nominal prices are gradually adjusting to the new situation. In the long run, the quantity theory is assumed to hold. Essentially

this same point has been rehashed in the economic literature of each suc-
ceeding generation, albeit using different terminology and different analytical techniques, up to and including at least some of the variants of the
so-called 'new Keynesian' school of today. Therefore, although there does
seem to be recurring controversy in each era over the precise quantitative
implications of short-run monetary neutrality, it can be strongly argued
that this issue is *not* actually the main area of dispute over the extent of the
powers of monetary policy. Apart from some periods in which very extreme
views have been in the ascendancy, as with the early versions of 'new classical' economics a couple of decades ago, it has usually been agreed that
central bank activities can indeed have a short-run impact on real economic
variables such as output and employment. However, in contrast to the
effective consensus on short-run issues, the question of whether monetary
changes can have a *permanent* effect on real variables has been much more
controversial. This has usually been strongly denied by mainstream economic opinion.

To continue with the historical story, 50 years after Hume's explanation
of the role of short-run nominal rigidities we find Henry Thornton making
a similar point, in a discussion of whether or not downward pressure on the
exchange rate should always be met with a 'tight money' policy on the part
of the Bank of England. Thornton (1802) writes as follows:

> It is true, that if we could suppose the diminution of bank paper to produce per-
> manently a diminution in the value of all articles whatsoever, and a diminution
> . . . in the rate of wages also, the encouragement to future manufactures would
> be the same . . . The tendency, however, of a very great and sudden reduction of
> the accustomed number of bank notes, is to create an *unusual* and *temporary* dis-
> tress, and a fall in price arising from that distress. But a fall arising from a tem-
> porary distress, will be attended with probably no correspondent fall in the rate
> of wages; for the fall of price, and the distress, will be understood to be tem-
> porary, and the rate of wages, we know, is not so variable as the price of goods.
> There is reason, therefore, to fear that the unnatural and extraordinary low price
> of which we now speak, would occasion much discouragement of the fabrica-
> tion of manufactures. (Original emphasis)

Into the twentieth century, nominal wage rigidity was also a popular
explanation of the mass unemployment of the 1930s, and discussion of this
point was certainly not confined to Keynes (Smithin, 1988). For example,
Pigou (1933) whose work was criticized by Keynes (1936) as a prime
example of the 'classical' school, quite explicitly wrote as follows:

> With . . . free competition . . . and labour perfectly mobile . . . [there] will always
> be at work a strong tendency for wage-rates to be so related to demand that
> everybody . . . is employed . . . such unemployment as exists at any time is due

wholly to the fact that changes in demand conditions . . . tak[e] place and . . . frictional resistances prevent the appropriate wage adjustments from being made instantaneously.

Evidently it is the latter part of this quotation that is particularly relevant for present purposes. Similar remarks were also made by Viner (1936), actually in the course of a review of the *General Theory*.

It seems that it was only in the post-World War II era that short-run nominal wage rigidity came to be mistakenly identified as an exclusively 'Keynesian' proposition. This interpretation was particularly prominent in textbooks in the United States whose version of Keynesian economics was that based on the 'neoclassical synthesis'. Within this framework there was simply no other feasible explanation for unemployment caused by monetary or other demand shocks. It is noteworthy also that the monetarist model, supposedly the antithesis of the Keynesian project according to the same textbooks, required a very similar postulate to explain the influence of money on the business cycle in addition to its long-run impact on inflation. Yeager (1997), drawing on the work of Warburton (1981), describes a tradition of 'monetary disequilibrium theory' in the first half of the twentieth century, which implicitly should be extended forward to include Friedmanite monetarism. According to Yeager, this tradition should be sharply distinguished from Keynesianism, but nonetheless did rely on nominal rigidities of one sort or another to explain the short-run non-neutrality of money.

As it happened, both textbook monetarism and textbook Keynesianism came unstuck in the 1970s with the rise of the new classical school and rational expectations theory, as exemplified by Lucas (1972, 1981) and Sargent and Wallace (1975). By the 1970s, both of the former groups had tended to rely on straightforward adaptive expectations mechanisms, as embodied in the expectations-augmented Phillips curve, to explain non-neutrality in the transitional phase after a change in monetary policy. Hence they were both vulnerable to the charge that 'rational economic agents' would not form expectations in this way. The adaptive expectations schemes could be seen as suggesting that the economic actors would continuously make systematic errors in expectations formation, a possibility ruled out by the supposedly more theoretically appealing 'rational expectations' assumption. If the only source of non-neutrality is expectational error, however, the early new classical models also thereby ruled out the non-neutrality of systematic monetary policy, even in the short run. In effect, the short run, as this was conventionally understood, was abolished. As Laidler (1996) points out, almost all macroeconomic theories up to that time, and most afterwards, had indeed relied on temporary disequilibrium or non-market-clearing explanations of the business cycle. What was 'new' about the new classical economics that began with Lucas (1972) was the proposed abandonment of this tradition, dating back at least to the passage from Hume quoted above.

A notable feature of the economics scene in the twentieth century, however, was the relatively short shelf-life of new academic fashions, and it was quickly realized that the most distinctive features of the early new classical models revolved around the assumption of continuous market clearing rather than rational expectations *per se*. Hence the notion of nominal wage rigidity was soon revived in the guise of the overlapping contracts models of Fischer (1977) and Taylor (1980). These constructs were, in fact, the first generation of 'new Keynesian' models and provided a framework the properties of which were, once again, not dissimilar to those suggested by Hume. The plausibility of some such explanation for the impact of money on real variables was enhanced for many by the experience of the monetary policy-induced recessions in several jurisdictions in the 1980s (Smithin, 1990a, 1990b), which seemed to belie the extreme policy irrelevance results of the new classical models of the 1970s.

From the point of view of 'highbrow opinion' (Robertson, 1963) in the contemporary economics mainstream, however, a main objection to models of overlapping contracts, and indeed to any realist approach which simply postulates some degree of nominal wage and price rigidity as an empirical fact of life, from which implications can be drawn, is the methodological *obiter dicta* that some sufficiently complex microtheoretical rationale should be provided as to why the ubiquitous 'rational economic agents' would choose to set wages and/or prices in that way. Therefore, as described by Mankiw and Romer (1991), Dixon (1997) and Snowdon and Vane (1997), one objective of some later contributions to the misleadingly named 'new Keynesian' economics was precisely to provide just such a rationale. To the extent that this succeeds, however, it seems clear that it does little more than put a contemporary mathematical gloss on an argument which, as has been shown, was already well-established.

In fairness, it is true the rubric 'new Keynesian' eventually came to include a wide variety of fairly disparate approaches, some of which, if pushed to their logical conclusion, ultimately might even come to threaten the underlying 'natural rate' assumption (Mankiw, 1992; Dixon, 1997; Snowdon and Vane, 1997). Examples would be the concept of 'hysteresis' (discussed below), or perhaps a generalization of notions of 'imperfect competition' to the macroeconomic level. Nonetheless, there still seems to be a shying away from the drawing of such conclusions at the policy-making and broad doctrinal levels, and in those contexts it seems fair to say that the basic explanation of monetary non-neutrality has actually changed very little from the explanations of Hume or the monetary disequilibrium theorists. The main macroeconomic theme is still that the power of central banks and other authorities to affect real economic variables is limited to a relatively short time horizon.

An opposite approach, of course, is provided by those economists (usually out of the academic mainstream) who would argue that the nominal rigidities themselves are a fairly permanent feature of the economic scene. For example, some of the published views of the later Hicks (1955, 1982c, 1989), in which the rate of change of money wages is taken to be essentially an exogenous variable determined by the sociological and political factors influencing the collective bargaining process, can be interpreted in this way. Similar remarks might apply to the theories of inflation put forward by some of the Post Keynesian authors (Coddington, 1983; Laidler, 1996).

THE LUCAS SUPPLY CURVE

The version of the generic nominal stickiness/misperceptions argument that was most popular in the latter half of the twentieth century revolved around the so-called 'Lucas supply curve' named after Lucas (1972), which, in a deterministic version, would be:

$$y(t) = y^N + \beta[p(t) - p(t)^e], \qquad \beta > 0 \qquad (4.1)$$

where $y(t)$ is the (log of) real GDP, y^N is the supposed 'natural rate' of output, $p(t)$ is the (log of) the aggregate price level in time (t), and $p(t)^e$ is the (log of) the price level which was expected to prevail in t, at the time the relevant decisions about output, labour supply and so on were being made (that is, in the previous period). What equation (4.1) purports to say is that, if the actual price level in period (t) turns out to be greater than expected when contracts were being made and nominal wages were being set, this will tend to increase the level of output above the so-called 'natural rate'. This is the 'misperceptions' theory of output fluctuations.

THE PHILLIPS CURVE

The Lucas supply curve discussed above is clearly very closely related to the concept of the Phillips curve named after the work of Phillips (1958), or at least to its later 'expectations-augmented' version (Laidler, 1990, 1996; Leeson, 2002).

Actually, the original Phillips curve was something of an anomaly in terms of the historical developments sketched above, because initially Phillips's findings did, for a time, seem to persuade a large number of economists that demand-oriented policies, including monetary policies, could have permanent real effects. The original Phillips curve was an empirical relationship, documented by Phillips (1958), between the rate of change of money wages and unemployment in Britain from 1861 to 1957. Given the close association between wage inflation and price inflation, the idea of a price inflation/unemployment trade-off seemed to follow. The concept was then taken up and propagated in such contributions as Lipsey (1960) and Samuelson and Solow (1960). So, during the 1960s, contrary to the historic *tendenz* of classical ideas it was apparently widely believed that there existed a permanent and stable negative trade-off between inflation and unemployment, which could be exploited for policy purposes. It would therefore be possible for either monetary or fiscal policy to reduce unemployment permanently, but only at the 'cost' of a permanently higher inflation, or vice versa. On this view, each society would have to assess the relative costs of inflation and unemployment and choose some 'optimal' mix of the two. A linear version of the price-inflation Phillips curve would be:

$$\pi(t) = \alpha[U^N - U(t)], \qquad \alpha > 0 \tag{4.2}$$

where U^N has the connotation of Friedman's 'natural rate' of unemployment. But note the implication that unemployment can be permanently held down below this level, as long as the inflation rate is high enough. The Phillips curve in this sense, however, was soon in trouble in academia and among policy makers. There were two main problems. The first was simply that this does conflict with what were described above as the basic presumptions of classical and neoclassical economics, namely that economic decisions should be based on real (inflation-adjusted) magnitudes rather than nominal magnitudes. This point was made in two highly influential articles by Phelps (1967) and Friedman (1968).[2] Second, during the 1970s, the Phillips curve trade-off seemed to be actively misleading owing to the occurrence of 'stagflation' in the real-world data during that decade. There were episodes in which *both* inflation *and* unemployment increased in various jurisdictions. It is worth pointing out, however, that the apparent empirical failures came well *after* the basic theoretical challenge. They were only decisive in the sense that they gave credence to the latter. But, in any event, belief in a permanent trade-off between inflation and unemployment very quickly declined. It was argued that the short-run or 'expectations-augmented' Phillips curve could shift bodily whenever there was a change in inflationary expectations. In the mainstream macroeconomic models of the late twentieth century any postulated trade-off between inflation and unemployment was explicitly short term. In the long run, any rate of inflation at all was thought compatible with the *natural rate* of unemployment, which later came to be called (more neutrally) the NAIRU.[3] The long-run Phillips curve was assumed to be vertical. It can be seen that this mode of thought fully restores the status quo ante, and provides a macroeconomic framework that would have been fully comprehensible to Hume or Thornton. To illustrate, the 'expectations-augmented' version of the Phillips curve would be:

$$\pi(t) = \alpha[U^N - U(t)] + \pi^e(t) \tag{4.3}$$

Now the key point is that when actual and expected inflation are equal, unemployment will be at its 'natural' rate, as then we have $U^N = U(t)$. There is therefore no long-run trade-off between actual inflation and unemployment, only a temporary, or short-run, trade-off. This is a conclusion that is right in line with the ethos of classical orthodoxy.

To see the connection between the Phillips curve type of formulation and the Lucas supply curve, note that we can lag the supply equation (4.1) by one period and subtract. Also assume that the trend level of GDP itself is evolving over time via some growth process. This gives:

$$y(t) - y(t-1) = y^N(t) - y^N(t-1) + \beta[p(t) - p(t)^e] - \beta[p(t-1) - p(t-1)^e] \tag{4.4}$$

And, defining the growth rate as $g(t)$ and the inflation rate as $\pi(t)$, as before, this becomes:

$$g(t) = g^N + \beta[\pi(t) - \pi(t)^e] \tag{4.5}$$

where g^N is the 'natural rate' of growth. This is a 'dynamic' version of the original supply relationship outlined above. Finally, as suggested for example in the first edition of the best-selling textbook by Dornbusch and Fischer (1978), note that there must be some relationship between growth relative to trend and the unemployment gap, along the lines of 'Okun's Law',[4] such as:

$$g(t) - g^N = \gamma[U^N - U(t)] \qquad \gamma > 0. \tag{4.6}$$

So letting $\alpha = \gamma/\beta$ by definition, it can be seen that equation (4.5) boils down to the same thing as the 'expectations-augmented' Phillips curve in equation (4.3).

THE STICKY-WAGE MODEL AGAIN

Mankiw (1992), in another of the best-selling textbooks of the late twentieth century, showed that there are actually a number of other ways to
derive the Lucas supply curve, which are all consistent with contemporary
orthodox economic thinking. Four alternative models were developed,
including the 'sticky-wage' model, the 'worker-misperception model', the
'imperfect-information model' and the 'sticky-price model'. Each of these,
when all is said and done, can yield expressions similar to (4.1) or (4.3)
above. It would be repetitive to go through each of these derivations, but
perhaps in the light of the historical discussion above, the 'sticky-wage'
version is of particular interest.

In this model it is assumed that firms/entrepreneurs will hire more labour
on average if the real wage falls, and that if more labour is hired there will
be more output. The stickiness of wages comes about because the nominal
wage for a certain period, t, is assumed to be set before that period on the
basis of expectations formed earlier. For example:

$$W(t) = [W/P]^N/P(t)^e \qquad (4.7)$$

where $[W/P]^N$ is the equilibrium real wage, supposedly aimed at by the
parties to the wage bargain, and has the connotation of a 'natural' or
market-determined rate as above. Equation (4.7) then says that the nominal
wage is fixed beforehand on the basis that it would realize the natural real
wage if expectations are realized. Of course, they will not turn out to be
correct in each period, so that the actual real wage will be:

$$W(t)/P(t) = [W/P]^N[P(t)^e/P(t)] \qquad (4.8)$$

Then, taking logs, this will give:

$$w(t) - p(t) = \omega^N + p(t)^e - p(t) \qquad (4.9)$$

where ω^N is a shorthand notation for the (log of) the target or 'natural' rate
of real wages. Now suppose that the relationship between a change in
actual real wages and the actual level of output can be written.

$$y(t) = y_0 - \beta[w(t) - p(t)] \qquad (4.10)$$

where, by construction, β is the same positive coefficient introduced earlier:
Hence:

$$y(t) = y_0 - \beta\omega^N - \beta[p(t)^e - p(t)] \qquad (4.11)$$

From (4.10) there must also be a 'natural rate of output':

$$y^N = y_0 - \beta\omega^N \qquad (4.12)$$

implying that:

$$\omega^N = 1/\beta[y_0 - y^N] \qquad (4.13)$$

Finally, using (4.13) in (4.11):

$$y(t) = y^N + \beta[p(t) - p(t)^e] \qquad (4.14)$$

which is the same as equation (4.1) above. This will also yield the dynamic or growth equation (4.5) if the natural rate of output itself (and by implication the equilibrium real wage also) evolves over time.

ADAPTIVE EXPECTATIONS AND 'RATIONAL' EXPECTATIONS

We can now use a complete macroeconomic model derived from the above to give a standard textbook-style expression of the old idea that money is neutral in the long run but non-neutral in the short run, as this had evolved by the end of the twentieth century. Actually, the reference in this particular case should be to so-called 'superneutrality', as the assumed monetary instrument will be a change in the rate of growth of the money supply, rather than a change in its level. The relevant equations of the model are:

$$\pi(t) = \mu(t) - g(t) \qquad (4.15)$$

$$g(t) = g^N + \beta[\pi(t) - \pi(t)^e] \qquad (4.16)$$

$$\mu(t) = x(t) + \varepsilon(t) \qquad (4.17)$$

$$\pi(t)^e - \pi(t-1)^e = \lambda[\pi(t-1) - \pi(t-1)^e], \qquad 0 < \lambda \leq 1 \qquad (4.18a)$$

$$\pi(t)^e = E[\pi(t)] \qquad (4.18b)$$

In the above, equation (4.15) is simply a dynamic version of the quantity theory, derived from $M(t)V(t) = P(t)Y(t)$, assuming that velocity, V, is roughly constant. The inflation rate, $\pi(t)$, is then equal to the rate of monetary growth, $\mu(t)$, minus the rate of growth of the real economy, $g(t)$, as in

Chapter 3 above. This serves as the simplest possible version of aggregate demand for this framework. Equation (4.17) is a dynamic version of the Lucas supply curve, which says that the actual growth rate will deviate from the 'natural' growth rate to the extent that the actual inflation rate turns out to be greater or less than the expected inflation rate. Equation (4.17) is then the most straightforward version possible of a 'monetary policy rule' (Taylor, 1999), to determine the rate of growth of the money supply. This expression contains a deterministic element, $x(t)$, relating to deliberate policy, but it also introduces a component based on the statistical theory favoured by contemporary economic theorists. This is brought in via the device of an 'error term', assumed to be 'normally distributed' with mean zero. In effect, the rule says that the authorities are trying to achieve some particular rate of money growth, $x(t)$, in period t, but that also, as a practical matter, they will make random errors. The errors are the $\varepsilon(t)$, the expected values of which, however, are zero on average. Obviously, more sophisticated rules than this simple expression could be suggested, for example by allowing feedback on the realized economic growth rate itself, the unemployment rate or the inflation rate, in some way which is thought 'optimal'. It should also be recalled, as stressed throughout, that in reality the monetary policy instrument is more likely to be a short-term interest rate of some kind rather than the rate of money growth directly. But neither of these caveats affects the main point about monetary neutrality or non-neutrality in the short run, and we simply follow the standard literature in taking changes in money growth as the point of departure. So the policy rule here is that the monetary authorities usually attempt to keep the rate of growth of the money at a constant level, with the error term allowing for the fact that they will make random mistakes. A *systematic* monetary policy change would be a decision to either increase or decrease $x(t)$ permanently. An increase would be what is usually described as an expansionary policy, and a decrease a contractionary policy.

Equations (4.18a) and (4.18b) are rival methods of suggesting how inflationary expectations are formed, and in effect represent the rival sides of the main macroeconomic 'debate' of the 1970s and 1980s, between adherents of 'adaptive expectations' and 'rational expectations'.[5] Equation (4.18b) suggests that expectations are formed adaptively as originally suggested by Cagan (1956). This assumes that current period expectations of inflation are adjusted from what was expected last period only by some fraction, λ, of the mistake (as it turned out) between actual inflation last period and what was originally expected. From a commonsense point of view this might be regarded as a reasonable rule of thumb, and implies that current expected inflation is a weighted average of all the inflation rates actually experienced in the past. Moreover, again seemingly reasonably, the weights decline geometrically so that the greatest emphasis is placed on the most recent experience. This can be seen by rearranging (4.18b) such that:

$$\pi(t)^e = \lambda\pi(t-1) + \lambda(1-\lambda)\pi(t-2) + \lambda(1-\lambda)^2\pi(t-3) + \ldots\ldots\ldots \quad (4.19)$$

The simplest version of this would let $\lambda = 1$, so that expected inflation just depends on the inflation rate that was actually experienced last period. In that case, (4.18a) and (4.19) can be simplified to:

$$\pi(t)^e = \pi(t-1) \quad (4.20)$$

The other version of expectations formation, however, equation (14.18b), represents *soi-disant* rational expectations, where $E[\ldots]$ is the 'expectations operator'. What is supposedly rational, from this point of view, is that expectations of the inflation rate should be given by the statistical expected value of the inflation rate, generated by the equations of the model itself.

The reason for the tension or discrepancy between these different methods of modelling expectations has its roots in the implicit philosophical underpinnings of neoclassical microeconomics, combined with the insistence that the *same* methodology be applied to macroeconomic and monetary issues (Smithin, forthcoming). These underpinnings are (a) the insistence on methodological individualism, (b) the idea that all economic actors are members of the species *homo economicus*, and (c) also that the only decision-making procedure available to such atomistic agents is optimization subject to constraints. So, if the players do form expectations adaptively by some rule of thumb, they are not optimizing, not using all available information, and so on. They are not keeping to the rules of the game (Fletcher, 2000; Smithin, 2002, forthcoming), and 'rational agents' supposedly would not do that. What is 'rational', then, is for these agents or actors to actually figure out the workings of the economic regime under which they are living, and form expectations on that basis. It implies working out some approximation to the statistical expected value of the relevant variable (in this case, inflation) as generated by the model at hand. It should be noted that this not only introduces a particular philosophical approach to economic methodology, but also makes the tacit assumptions that the models employed are *a priori* correct, for example that the concept of 'natural rates' of unemployment, growth or interest rates is reasonable, and, moreover that, if that is so, the economic actors concerned are cognitively competent to realize as much. All of these assumptions are clearly of questionable legitimacy, but the main question to be asked at present is how these competing views of expectations are supposed to affect economic behaviour. In the context of our simple model, what will be the effect of a change in monetary policy, interpreted as a permanent change in the rate of growth of the money supply?

SOLVING THE MODELS

For the Marshallian short run, the competing views on how 'inflationary expectations' are supposed to be formed will make a good deal of difference to the analysis. Suppose, for example, as in equations (4.18a) and (4.20), that they are formed by the simple version of adaptive expectations, whereby the inflation rate expected this period is simply that which occurred in the recent past. Using equations (4.20), (4.17) and (4.15) in (4.16) we obtain:

$$g(t) = g^N + \beta[x(t) + \varepsilon(t) - g(t) - \pi(t-1)] \tag{4.21}$$

or:

$$g(t) = g^N + \beta[x(t) + \varepsilon(t) - g(t) - x(t-1) - \varepsilon(t-1) + g(t-1)] \tag{4.22}$$

Then, using the notation Δx to stand for $[x(t) - x(t-1)]$, corresponding to a deliberate change in the rate of monetary growth, we have:

$$g(t) = [\beta/(1+\beta)]g(t-1) + [1/(1+\beta)]g^N + [\beta/(1+\beta)][\Delta x + \varepsilon(t) - \varepsilon(t-1)] \tag{4.23}$$

Under adaptive expectations, then, in the short-run growth will depend not only on 'policy shocks', but also on deliberate changes to the monetary growth rate (the systematic part of monetary policy). An increase in the rate of growth of the money supply, for example, will cause an increase in the GDP growth rate and a reduction in money supply growth a fall in the GDP growth rate, or even a recession. So monetary policy does 'matter', at least temporarily. If the systematic component of monetary policy undergoes no further changes, however ($\Delta x = 0$), the system will eventually converge to a long-run equilibrium level:

$$g = g^N + \beta[\varepsilon(t) - \varepsilon(t-1)] \tag{4.24}$$

The eventual steady state is therefore defined by the natural rate of growth, disturbed only by the random 'policy shocks'. The overall formulation, then, yields a neat pseudo-mathematical demonstration of what had actually long been the basic model, combining short-run non-neutrality (or non-superneutrality) with long-run neutrality (or superneutrality), the history of whose more 'verbal' expositions was sketched above.

But what happens when expectations are formed (supposedly) rationally according to equation (4.19a)? In fact, part of the reason for the initial furore raised by the concept of rational expectations when first introduced to macroeconomics 25 to 30 years ago was that it seemed to disturb this tidy solution to the distinction between the long run and short run, while at the same time claiming to be more consistent than the adaptive version with respect to approved economic theory and methodology. To see this, note that 'rationally' the expected value of the inflation rate can be worked out directly from equation (4.16):

$$\pi(t)^e = E[\pi(t)] = E[\mu(t)] - E[g(t)] \tag{4.25}$$

or, simply:

$$\pi(t)^e = x(t) - g^N \tag{4.26}$$

where $x(t)$, it should be recalled, is the systematic (or announced) part of monetary policy and should be known to everyone. If we then use (4.26), (4.15) and (4.17) in (4.16), the result is:

$$g(t) = g^N + [\beta/(1 + \beta)]\varepsilon(t) \tag{4.27}$$

So, in this case, under rational expectations, real GDP growth is *always* at its natural rate except for the random policy disturbances. This result, when first articulated, was certainly appealing for economists who believe in *laissez-faire* and hence are suspicious of government involvement in the economy. The systematic or deliberate use of monetary policy apparently has no effect whatsoever (except on the inflation rate). It does not affect the growth rate or unemployment at all, even in the short run. Ironically, is it only the random policy errors which have any impact. Therefore, from the perspective of political economy, this so-called *policy irrelevance* result had a powerful ideological charge: government can only make things worse, it cannot make things any better. But unfortunately, for the traditionalist, it also seemed to wreck the argument that allows for some short-run real impact of monetary changes for the sake of realism, while nonetheless insisting on the quantity theory for the long run. From a traditionally 'classical' point of view, complete policy irrelevance could seem to be too much of a good thing.

This defect could be repaired in a number of obvious ways. For example, by allowing nominal wages to be set in advance for more than one period (as in theories of overlapping contracts and staggered wage setting), or perhaps by recognizing that information itself is costly to acquire, and therefore that to use some simple rule of thumb in forming expectations might be 'rational' after all. However, debates of this kind are open-ended and can go on forever. Looking at the matter from first principles, it seems clear that *if* the basic premise is an economy that always eventually reverts to some 'natural' state (including natural rates of growth, unemployment and real interest), then the 'monetary disequilibrium theorists' (Yeager, 1997) must have common sense on their side in trying to explain the actual deviations from, or fluctuations around, these natural levels. Rigidities, misperceptions, imperfections of various kinds can be the only explanation. It can also be argued, however, that a far more significant debate would be whether or not this particular way of looking at the economy, as if it behaves rather like a pendulum which always swings back to some pre-determined position, is in itself either an accurate or a useful way of thinking about socioeconomic issues. This more far-reaching debate is taken up briefly in the next section of the present chapter, and then in more detail in the two chapters to follow.

HYSTERESIS AND PERSISTENCE

One concept that did seem to put something of a dent into traditional natural rate models is the concept of hysteresis (a term originally borrowed from physics), which was introduced in the mid-1980s (Blanchard and Summers, 1986; Wyplosz, 1987) and has since been discussed in both the heterodox and the orthodox literature (Setterfield, 1993; Ball, 1999). The original debate followed on from the observation that mass unemployment (specifically in Europe) in the late twentieth century seemed to be a far more deep-rooted problem than could be explained by conventional models. The suggested explanation was that the time path of an economic variable, such as the unemployment rate, or the level of real GDP, may depend crucially on its own past history. For example, workers who are unemployed during a recession lose job skills, and the experience itself will adversely affect them, both socially and emotionally. They may therefore become less 'employable', and the overall employment picture will get worse. Similarly, if an industrial plant closes down during a recession it is unlikely to be as efficient when it reopens as it was originally. Hence it may not be reasonable to assume that a policy-induced recession, for example, will leave no permanent scars. To recognize these issues of hysteresis and path-dependency would presumably not restore any precise quantitative notion of a trade-off between inflation and unemployment, as in the original Phillips curve. However, it might tend to dispel the notion that the real effects of monetary policy are temporary and/or can safely be ignored, even given a fairly conventional understanding of the relationship between money and the economy.

We can illustrate the concept of hysteresis, in a Phillips curve format, as follows. The expectations-augmented Phillips curve is:

$$\pi(t) = \alpha[U^N - U(t)] + \pi^e(t) \tag{4.28}$$

Therefore, when $\pi(t) = \pi^e(t)$:

$$U(t) = U^N \tag{4.29}$$

This natural rate, in turn, supposedly depends on a vector of relevant variables, $\mathbf{Z}$, all of which (according to conventional thought) relate mainly to the supply side. Therefore, we can write:

$$U^N = b\mathbf{Z} \tag{4.30}$$

The steady-state or equilibrium value of the actual unemployment rate is also:

$$U = b\mathbf{Z} \tag{4.31}$$

But the point about the hysteresis argument is that U^N may also depend on the past actual realized values of U. The natural rate itself may be indexed with respect to time. For example, we may have:

$$U^N(t) = aU(t-1) + b\mathbf{Z}, \qquad 0 \le a \le 1 \tag{4.32}$$

There are three possible cases. The first is the standard textbook formulation, where $a = 0$, and the natural rate does *not* evolve over time. In this case, the steady-state value of the natural rate remains as given in equation (4.31) and never changes unless there is an exogenous change in $\mathbf{Z}$. It is an unvarying centre of gravity for the system.

The second case would have $0 < a < 1$. This is usually referred to as the case of *persistence*. There is, in fact, an ultimate steady-state value for the natural rate (and hence also for the actual unemployment rate), which is:

$$U = b\mathbf{Z}/(1-a) \tag{4.33}$$

There is a steady state, and this preserves something of the traditional notion of an economic pendulum. But, as the natural rate in each period is evolving according to equation (4.32), it takes a long time to reach the ultimate equilibrium, hence the idea of persistence (for example, of mass unemployment.) Ironically also, however, note that, if this scenario holds it would actually justify traditional conservative scepticism about the possibility of monetary policy, or any other demand-side policy, relieving this unemployment. It is the 'natural rate' itself which is sticky here, so it would be plausible to make the argument that any attempt to relieve unemployment will quickly dissipate in inflation, even *if* unemployment is abnormally high at the present time. Some support is thereby given for one of the most popular economic arguments, do nothing.

The situation, though, is much different if genuine *hysteresis* applies, which in this context would require $a = 1$. Now there is no steady-state solution for the unemployment rate, and hence the concept of the natural rate ceases to apply. The actual unemployment rate simply follows a 'random walk with drift', according to:

$$U(t) = U(t-1) + b\mathbf{Z} \tag{4.34}$$

If this is the case, then the idea of a unique long-run equilibrium, impervious to monetary policy change, would indeed suffer a blow, and this would represent a move away from the traditional economic thinking as described above.

CONCLUDING REMARKS

Summing up the issue of monetary non-neutrality as a result of nominal rigidities, Smithin (1990a) argues that although, if these exist, the issue cannot be ignored as a matter of practical policy, nonetheless, at a deeper theoretical level, there is a much more fundamental underlying debate about the power of central banks and other policy makers to affect those economic variables of significance for economic welfare. In the case of central banks, this specifically concerns whether or not their acknowledged influence over short-term nominal interest rates can translate into a *permanent* impact on both the level and term structure of real rates of interest prevailing in the economy, and hence also have a permanent impact on other real economic variables, including the growth rate of GDP and unemployment. This latter debate is discussed in more detail in Chapter 6.

NOTES

1. In the present volume the issues arising in that context are taken up in Chapter 6.
2. Recall the discussion in Chapter 3 above.
3. NAIRU stands for 'non-accelerating inflation rate of unemployment'.
4. Although note that the participants in this debate did not actually disagree on any fundamental issue in monetary economics. They were all mainstream neoclassical economists.
5. At that time, the US data suggested that for unemployment to fall by one percentage point GDP would have to be growing at 2.5 per cent to 3 per cent above trend (Dornbusch and Fischer, 1978). Whether these precise numbers hold for other times and places is beside the present point, which is simply that some such relationship must exist.

REFERENCES

Ball. L. (1999), 'Aggregate demand and long-term unemployment', *Brookings Papers on Economic Activity*, 2, 189–236.

Blanchard, O.J. and L. Summers (1986), 'Hystereris and the European unemployment problem', in S. Fischer (ed.), *NBER Macroeconomics Annual*, Cambridge, MA: MIT Press.

Cagan, P. (1956), 'The monetary dynamics of hyperinflation', in M. Friedman (ed.), *Studies in the Quantity Theory of Money*, Chicago: University of Chicago Press.

Coddington, A. (1983), *Keynesian Economics: The Search for First Principles*, London: George Allen & Unwin.

Dixon, H.D. (1997), 'The role of imperfect competition in new Keynesian economics', in B. Snowdon and H.R. Vane (eds), *Reflections on the Development of Modern Macroeconomics*, Cheltenham, UK and Lyme, US: Edward Elgar.

Dornbusch, R. and S. Fischer (1978), *Macroeconomics*, New York: McGraw-Hill.

Fischer, S. (1977), 'Long term contracts, rational expectations and the optimal money supply rule', *Journal of Political Economy*, 85, 191–206.

Fletcher, G. (2000), *Understanding Dennis Robertson: The Man and his Work*, Cheltenham, UK and Northampton, MA, USA: Edward Elgar.

Friedman, M. (1968), 'The role of monetary policy', *American Economic Review*, 58, 1–17.

Hicks, J.R. (1955 [1982b]), 'Inflation and the wage structure', reprinted in *Money, Interest and Wages: Collected Essays on Economic Theory*, vol. 2., Oxford: Basil Blackwell.

—— (1982c), 'The credit economy', reprinted in *Money, Interest and Wages: Collected Essays on Economic Theory*, vol. 2., Oxford: Basil Blackwell.

—— (1989), *A Market Theory of Money*, Oxford: Oxford University Press.

Hume, D. (1752 [1987]), 'Of money', in *Essays Moral, Political and Literary*, ed. E.F. Miller, Indianapolis: Liberty Classics.

Keynes, J.M. (1936), *The General Theory of Employment Interest and Money*, London: Macmillan.

Krugman, P. (2002), 'There's something about macro', (*http://web.mit.edu/krugman/www/islm.html*).

Laidler, D.E.W. (1990), *Taking Money Seriously and Other Essays*, London: Philip Allan.

—— (1996), 'Wage and price stickiness in macroeconomics: a historical perspective', in F. Capie and G.E. Wood (eds), *Monetary Economics in the 1990s*, London: Macmillan.

Leeson, R. (2002), 'Expectations-augmented Phillips curve', in B. Snowdon and H.R. Vane (eds), *An Encyclopedia of Macroeconomics*, Cheltenham, UK and Northampton, MA, USA: Edward Elgar.

Leijonhufvud, A. (1968), *On Keynesian Economics and the Economics of Keynes*, New York: Oxford University Press.

Lipsey, R.G. (1960), 'The relation between unemployment and the rate of change of money wages in the UK, 1862–1957: a further analysis', *Economica*, 27, 1–32.

Lucas, R.E Jr. (1972), 'Expectations and the neutrality of money', *Journal of Economic Theory*, 4, 103–23.

—— (1981), *Studies in Business-Cycle Theory*, Cambridge, MA: MIT Press.

Mankiw, N.G. (1992), *Macroeconomics*, New York: Worth Publishers.

—— and D. Romer (eds) (1991), *New Keynesian Economics*, Cambridge, MA: MIT Press.

Phelps, E.J. (1967), 'Phillips curves, expectations of inflation and optimal inflation over time', *Economica*, 34, 254–81.

Phillips, A.W. (1958), 'The relation between unemployment and the rate of change of money wages in the United Kingdom, 1861–1957', *Economica*, 25, 283–300.

Pigou, A.C. (1933), *The Theory of Unemployment*, New York: Augustus M. Kelley.

Robertson, D. (1963), *Lectures on Economic Principles*, London: Fontana Press.

Samuelson, P.A. and R. Solow (1960), 'Analytical aspects of anti-inflation policy', *American Economic Review*, 50, 177–94.

Sargent, T.J. and N. Wallace (1975), 'Rational expectations, the optimal monetary policy instrument and the optimal money supply rule', *Journal of Political Economy*, 83, 241–54.

Setterfield, M. (1993), 'Towards a long-run theory of effective demand: modelling macroeconomic systems with hysteresis', *Journal of Post Keynesian Economics*, 15, 347–64.

Smithin, J. (1988), 'On flexible wage policy', *Economies et Sociétés*, 12, 277–85.

—— (1990a), *Macroeconomics after Thatcher and Reagan: The Conservative Policy Revolution in Retrospect*, Aldershot, UK and Brookfield, US: Edward Elgar.

—— (1990b), 'Empirical and conceptual problems in contemporary macroeconomics', *British Review of Economic Issues*, 12, 73–9.

—— (2002), 'Review of Fletcher, *Understanding Dennis Robertson: The Man and his Work* (2000)', *Eastern Economic Journal*, 28, 440–42.

—— (forthcoming), 'Macroeconomic theory, (critical) realism, and capitalism', in P.A. Lewis (ed.), *Transforming Economics: Perspectives on the Critical Realist Project*, London: Routledge.

Snowdon, B. and H.R. Vane (1997), 'To stabilize or not to stabilize: is that the question?', in B. Snowdon and H.R. Vane (eds), *Reflections on the Development of Modern Macroeconomics*, Cheltenham, UK and Lyme, US: Edward Elgar.

Taylor, J.B. (1980), 'Aggregate dynamics and staggered contracts', *Journal of Political Economy*, 88, 1–23.

—— (ed.) (1999), *Monetary Policy Rules*, Chicago: University of Chicago Press.

Thornton, H. (1802 [1962]), *An Inquiry into the Nature and Effects of the Paper Credit of Great Britain*, ed. F.A. von Hayek, New York: Augustus M. Kelley.

Viner, J. (1936), 'Mr Keynes on the causes of unemployment', *Quarterly Journal of Economics*, 51, 147–67.

Warburton, C. (1981), 'Monetary disequilibrium theory in the first half of the twentieth century', *History of Political Economy*, 13, 286–99.

Wyplosz, C. (1987), 'Comment', in R. Layard and L. Calmfors (eds), *The Fight Against Unemployment*, Cambridge, MA: MIT Press.

Yeager, L.B. (1997), *The Fluttering Veil: Essays in Monetary Disequilibrium*, ed. G. Selgin, Indianapolis: Liberty Fund.

5. The real bills doctrine, interest rate pegging and endogenous money

INTRODUCTION

The purpose of this chapter is to discuss some of the alternatives to the quantity theory of money that have been put forward over the years. By this is meant not only views that are in direct opposition to the quantity theory, but also those that can be seen as complementary to, or developments of, quantity-theoretic reasoning, as, for example, in the case of Wicksell, discussed below.

Turning first, however, to the outright opposition, it is true that in the long history of economic thought there have been several recurring episodes when views based on the quantity theory of money, and hence bearing a close family resemblance to twentieth-century monetarism, have been urged on policy makers. Naturally, on each occasion opposing views have also been advanced. In the English-language literature, numerous episodes from British monetary history, in particular, are frequently cited to illustrate these clashes. These would include the 'bullionist controversy' of the 1797–1821 period (Laidler, 1989a; Humphrey, 1993),[1] the 'currency school/banking school' debates of the mid-nineteenth century leading up to the passage of Peel's Bank Charter Act of 1844 (Schwartz, 1989; Humphrey, 1993) and the controversy over the return to the gold standard (at the prewar parity) in the aftermath of World War I (Kaldor, 1986).[2] The emphasis placed by many writers on the British historical experience and debates obviously reflects the relative importance of Britain and the Bank of England in the world economy of the nineteenth and early twentieth centuries. In the mid-twentieth century, after British power had waned, the focus shifted very decisively to the American debate, as illustrated by the discussion of Friedman's work above, and a plethora of later developments in the US literature. In the future, presumably, the focus may well pass on elsewhere.

In the historical context, the version of the quantity theory held in common by bullionists, the currency school, and others, was that inflationary over-issue of central bank notes, the effective monetary base of the system, could be prevented by insisting on gold convertibility. The 1844

Act, which separated the 'banking' and 'issue' departments of the Bank of England, and required that any note issue above a fixed 'fiduciary' amount should be backed 100 per cent by gold reserves, represented a historical highpoint in the acceptance of these ideas. However, as pointed out by Bagehot (1873), in practice the provisions of the Act were judiciously suspended during each subsequent crisis (in 1847, 1857 and 1866), whenever they threatened to become binding.

Twentieth-century monetarism differed from these nineteenth-century principles in not having the convertibility feature, relying instead on strict rules governing the issue of fiat money. The basic ethos, however, was similar in that the rate of growth of the monetary base is to be strictly determined by impersonal forces, with the overall objective of limiting inflationary pressures. Although, under a gold standard, it was true that the domestic monetary base could change as a result of inflows and outflows of specie caused by balance of payments developments, those same forces ensure that domestic price levels cannot deviate very much from those prevailing in the rest of the world. World prices, in turn, were held to be free from excessive inflationary pressure owing to the relatively fixed global supplies of the precious metal.

Just as there have been enthusiastic supporters of the quantity principle over the centuries, there has also been no shortage of economists and commentators who have opposed it. These would include the 'anti-bullionists' of the Napoleonic era who defended the Bank of England against the charge of over-issue (Laidler, 1989a), and the 'banking school' in the debates over Peel's Act in the mid-nineteenth century. The latter, to employ modern terminology, were believers in discretionary monetary management, as opposed to the rigid 'rules' of the type incorporated in the 1844 Act (Schwartz, 1989).

The vision shared by the various opponents of the quantity principle was essentially one in which an ideal monetary system should respond endogenously to the 'needs of trade'. From this point of view the role, and even the duty, of the banking system was to accommodate the demands of merchants and manufacturers for finance. Quantity-theoretic prescriptions, arbitrarily restricting the quantity of bank lending, would be seen as stifling trade and real economic activity. Appeal was made to such concepts as the 'real bills doctrine' (Humphrey, 1993; Green, 1989; Mints, 1945) and the 'law of reflux' (Schwartz, 1989; Seccareccia, 1996) to argue that inflationary over-issue would not occur if the banks restricted themselves to a certain type of short-term commercial lending or, in general, to the financing of real productive activity.

It would be tempting to include the US 'monetarist versus Keynesian' debates of the mid-twentieth century as a more recent example of the debate between supporters of the quantity theory of money and its critics, but this would be misleading. The problem in this case would be that, by the end of this particular debate, before both groups were eclipsed by the shifts of academic fashion in the 1980s and 1990s, the US Keynesians (meaning by this proponents of the type of model described as 'Keynesian' in the textbooks) had developed a theory which hardly differed from monetarism in any important respect. The so-called 'Keynesian' model, by this time, would have included exogenous money, a stable demand for money function, and a 'natural rate' of output towards which the economy is always tending. For an economist who accepted this perspective, the only possible source of disagreement with the monetarists would be over such issues as the length of the transition period from one long-run equilibrium position to another, the precise degree of wage rigidity, and whether or not the automatic adjustment mechanisms might benefit from the assistance of activist government policy in the short run. As Leijonhufvud (1981) has put this point, 'someone whose macrobeliefs consist of neoclassical growth, variable velocity . . . and lags in wage adjustment should not fight Milton Friedman but join him'. More substantive opposition to the quantity principle in the modern era has been provided by such groups as the Post Keynesians in the United States, the United Kingdom and elsewhere, and the 'circuit school' in continental Europe, who have insisted on the endogeneity of the money supply in the credit economy. These issues were touched on in Chapter 3 above, and are discussed in more detail below. However, they are rarely emphasized in textbook discussions of monetarists and Keynesians.

At the other end of the ideological/theoretical spectrum, it should also be noted that some economists might feel that a simple dichotomy between supporters of the quantity principle and its opponents is probably *too* simple. From a certain point of view, the opposition between (say) the currency school and the banking school and their modern descendants is simply an intramural dispute about what appropriate central bank policy should be. The adherents of 'free banking' and other *laissez-faire* scenarios would urge on the contrary that the key question should be whether or not a central bank should even exist. Therefore White (1984) and Schwartz (1989) identify a third school in the nineteenth-century debates, the 'free banking school', who, like the currency school and the banking school, also have their intellectual descendants today. Smith (1936) and Yeager (1990)[3] go even further and suggest a four-way classification of authors from the history of thought, along the lines of their positions both on the currency principle versus the banking principle, and also on free banking versus central banking. They are able to find at least some candidates to fit into each box.[4] The details of the latter debate, however, have been discussed elsewhere in this volume, and this chapter will concentrate primarily on the former set of issues.

CREDIT MONEY AND COMMODITY MONEY

It might be argued that the most basic common element in the views of supporters of the quantity principle over the years, from Hume and Ricardo down to the present, is that a commodity money system, in which money consists only of units of some physical commodity such as one of the precious metals, is in some sense the 'ideal'. It is not suggested, of course, that contemporary quantity theorists regard this as literally a realistic proposition for an actual modern economy. There was no advocacy of commodity money in monetarism, for example, and the evolution of fiat money and credit-based systems is not denied. The point is rather that the proposals put forward for regulating the currency are designed to make the actual credit system behave 'as if' it were a commodity-based system. The objective is to design a practical system that will mimic the properties of a theoretical commodity money economy as closely as possible (Hicks, 1967a; Rogers, 1989; Smithin, 1984). It can be argued, for example, that this was as true of Friedman's proposals of the mid-twentieth century as it was of the Bank Charter Act more than a hundred years before.

Similarly, if there is a common thread in the writings of quantity theory opponents it is that this type of restriction is impractical, and may be actively damaging to economic prosperity by placing the financial system in a straitjacket. The fragility as well as the benefits of the credit system are emphasized, and various alternative principles of monetary policy are put forward, usually reflecting the view that monetary management is more of an 'art' than a science. The basic argument is that skilful discretionary actions are required to steer a safe course between inflation and deflation and to avoid financial crisis.

Hicks (1967a) clearly identifies both points of view in the course of a critique of Ricardo's version of the quantity theory. Hicks claims that Ricardo's views were predicated on a pure commodity money regime and hence were already obsolete by the time of Ricardo's writings on money in the period 1808–23. According to Hicks, Ricardo's monetary economics was inferior to that of Thornton in *The Paper Credit of Great Britain* (1802), which, as the title of the work suggests, already takes a developed credit system as its starting point. As Hicks portrays it, much of the history of monetary economics can be understood in terms of positions taken on either side of this issue. The followers of Ricardo maintain 'that all would be well if by some device credit money could be made to behave like metallic money' (Hicks, 1967a) whereas the descendants of Thornton take seriously the evolution of the credit system and hence the necessity of monetary management.

Thornton, as Hicks (1967b) is aware, is actually something of a special case because he could also be considered 'a moderate bullionist' (Laidler, 1989a, quoting Viner, 1937), and is cited with approval in that role by such authors as Capie and Wood (1989), Humphrey (1993), Laidler (1989a) and Mints (1945). Both monetarists and anti-monetarists can find things to applaud in Thornton. Hicks (1967b) attempts to resolve this paradox by suggesting that the hard money aspect of Thornton's views relates to the provision of a long-run sheet anchor for the monetary system, but that Thornton was indeed ahead of his time in recognizing some of the short-run difficulties of the management of a credit system.[5]

THE REAL BILLS DOCTRINE

One of the main alternatives to quantity-theoretic principles which has re-emerged at various times is the so-called 'real bills doctrine'. This, however, is often treated simply with derision in the modern literature, and Laidler (1989a) refers to it unambiguously as 'the real bills fallacy'. Nonetheless, as related by Green (1989), Humphrey (1993), Laidler (1989a), Schwartz (1989) and Mints (1945), it has had a long history. The name derives from a famous passage in Adam Smith's *Wealth of Nations* (1776) suggesting that prudent banking practice requires limiting discounts (lending) to 'a real bill of exchange drawn by a real creditor upon a real debtor, and which, as soon as it becomes due is really paid by that debtor'. Similar ideas (with land rather than real bills as security) can be traced as far back as the infamous financier John Law, in France, writing 70 years earlier (Mints, 1945). The real bills doctrine was also advanced by some anti-bullionists during the bullionist controversy and, in the form of the law of reflux, by Tooke and Fullarton of the banking school later in the nineteenth century. Into the twentieth century, a form of the real bills doctrine was actually enshrined in the US legislation setting up the Federal Reserve System in 1913 (Sargent, 1979).

In the literature on the history of economic thought, there is some dispute as to whether Adam Smith ever did actually advocate the version of the real bills doctrine that most writers find fallacious. Rather, he can be interpreted as having simply suggested a prudent rule of thumb for an individual bank in a system that is already on a metallic standard (Glasner, 1992; Laidler, 1989a; Perlman, 1989). Similarly, questions have been raised about the relationship between the real bills doctrine *per se*, and the later 'law of reflux' of Tooke and Fullarton of the banking school. The law of reflux asserts the impossibility of over-issue by competitive banks, because of repayments of bank loans or redemption demands by the public. This proposition is often treated as equivalent to the real bills doctrine, but, according to Skaggs (1991) and Glasner (1992), the two are conceptually distinct. On this interpretation, the operation of the law of reflux explains rather why it is *necessary* to suggest some prudent rules of thumb or guidelines for lending at the level of the individual bank.

In the present chapter, however, we are not primarily concerned with the above issues, but explicitly with the 'aggregative' version of the real bills doctrine, in its guise as a rival to the quantity principle for the purposes of control of the price level. From the latter point of view, the real bills doctrine is a proposed criterion for regulating overall bank lending in a system in which the bulk of the exchange media are the nominal liabilities of financial institutions, issued as a by-product of their credit-creating activities, and without any necessary reference to an underlying metallic standard. It is suggested that, if banks restricted themselves to short-term commercial lending to finance the production and distribution of goods in process (in other words precisely 'real bills'), this would provide a system in which the money supply would change endogenously, would be optimally responsive to the needs of trade and yet also deliver price stability.

The real bills doctrine in this sense is regarded as fallacious because in reality any number of promises to pay can be issued in connection with the forward delivery of a given quantity of goods (that is, the same goods can be sold any number of times), and also, importantly, because the money value of any quantity of goods that supposedly backs these bills must itself also contain a price component. In the aggregate the real bills criterion provides no check on inflation, because any arbitrary money price increases of the goods concerned will be automatically validated by the forthcoming increases in the nominal money supply. The following simple model, derived from Humphrey (1993), will illustrate the latter point. In an economy with real output fixed at the full employment level, Y_f, suppose that the money supply in existence in the current period, $M(t)$, is related to the value of last period's production via the real bills criterion:

$$M(t) = eP(t-1)Y_f \tag{5.1}$$

In this expression, the coefficient, e, represents the proportion of the value of last period's production financed by bank loans. Also let the money supply created by last period's production be spent on current period output at current prices according to a quantity-type equation:

$$M(t)V = P(t)Y_f \tag{5.2}$$

Combining equations (5.1) and (5.2) then yields the following difference equation in the price level:

$$P(t) = eV[P(t-1)] \tag{5.3}$$

The point is that if the coefficient in equation (5.3), eV, is greater than unity (which seems to be the case that most critics of the real bills doctrine have in mind), this difference equation is not stable and the price level will be continuously increasing. Moreover, although there is a stable case, involving $0 < eV < 1$, this cannot be economically relevant as the only possible equilibrium value of the price level would then be zero. Only in the case where the coefficient, eV, was fortuitously equal to unity would prices be stable (at a level determined by some arbitrary initial condition). Although this simple construct is evidently not a watertight model of a credit economy, it suffices to illustrate the basic point that the real bills doctrine is not adequate to prevent inflationary over-issue.

As mentioned, Laidler (1981) defends Adam Smith's version of the real bills doctrine on the grounds that Smith's original proposal was made against a background of gold convertibility. In other words, it was the convertibility feature, rather than the real bills criterion itself, which was supposed to be the true safeguard against general over-issue. In this regime, in a small open economy the domestic price level is tied down by the world price level, which in turn is determined by the cost of gold production. Under such circumstances, appeal to the real bills criterion might therefore justifiably be interpreted as a reasonable rule of thumb for the individual bank. However, an attempt to apply the same logic for a central bank in the circumstances of an inconvertible currency (as was the case in the bullionist debate) would fall apart on the grounds outlined above.

As illustrated by Laidler's (1984) critique of Sargent and Wallace (1982), there seems to have been some confusion in the later twentieth-century literature about the precise content of the historical real bills doctrine and its relationship to other proposed criteria for the conduct of monetary policy. Some writers, including Sargent (1979) and Humphrey (1993), have seemed to suggest that the real bills criterion is substantively the same as cheap money policies, or, more generally, the suggestion that central banks should conduct monetary policy with reference to a nominal interest rate target. Although it is true that some of the same issues and arguments do arise in the latter context, this characterization is not quite accurate. At an earlier stage Mints (1945), for example, in an authoritative volume, cited the view that interest rates are the controlling factor in monetary policy as a 'significant competitor' to the real bills view. As Laidler (1984) has stressed, it seems that the main point about the real bills doctrine was the view that bank lending should be restricted to a limited subset of assets, and that this restriction by itself would be enough to provide stability. The criterion expressed in this way pays little or no attention to the incentives or disincentives faced by bank customers themselves in their decisions whether or not to take credit. Monetary policy conducted with reference to interest rates, however, obviously explicitly does just that, and is therefore conceptually distinct from the real bills doctrine as this was conventionally understood.

The alternative idea mentioned by Mints is that the inflation rate will depend on the difference between the interest rate charged by the banking system and the rate of return that can be earned by the use of borrowed funds. This has a history dating at least from the time of Thornton's work, mentioned above (Mints, 1945), continuing through Wicksell's *Interest and Prices* (1898) almost a century later (Laidler, 1996), down to the Austrian and Swedish schools of the inter-war period (Seccareccia, 1990). It is also, arguably, once again reflected in the close attention central banks seem now to pay to interest rate policy (Taylor, 1993; B. Friedman, 2000; Lewis and Mizen, 2000). The following section takes up the issue in more detail.

INTEREST RATES AND INFLATION

In an environment in which the money supply consists primarily of claims on the liabilities side of bank balance sheets, it is obviously not surprising that many authors have identified interest rates charged by the banking system as being an important factor in determining the demand for bank credit, and hence how rapidly both sides of bank balance sheets will expand. In a system with an inconvertible currency and a central bank, the liabilities of the central bank itself will represent the primary reserves for the other financial institutions in the system (B. Friedman, 2000). Hence, in principle, the interest rate charged by the central bank, historically usually known as the bank rate or the discount rate, can be seen as the linchpin of the entire system (Keynes, 1930). There have been different institutional mechanisms in existence at different times and places for making the bank rate 'effective' (Keynes, 1930). For example, in current US practice the inter-bank 'federal funds rate' is regarded as the main monetary policy instrument, rather than the discount rate *per se*. Nonetheless, it is clear that it is central bank monopoly supply of the ultimate monetary base which gives it power over the former interest rate as well as the latter (B. Friedman, 2000). These observations lead on to the argument that it is the level of interest rates effectively set by the central bank in the particular institutional context, or the 'policy-related' rate (IMF, 2001), *relative* to the rate of return which can be earned by using borrowed funds, that will determine the nominal rate of expansion of the system as a whole, and hence the inflation rate. The money supply itself adjusts endogenously to the incentives provided by interest rate changes.

Specifically, the traditional argument has been that, if the interest rate charged by the banking system is less than the return to be had on projects employing the borrowed funds, this will provide an incentive for borrowing as long as the differential persists, and hence a continuing expansion of the money supply and inflation. Similarly, if the central bank rate is higher than the rate of return elsewhere there will be deflation. Thornton, credited by Humphrey (1993), Laidler (1989a) and Mints (1945) with being the originator of this doctrine, stated that everything depends 'principally on a comparison of the rate of interest taken at the bank with the current rate of mercantile profit' (Thornton, 1802). Wicksell (1898), in his discussion of the 'cumulative process' nearly a century later, made the same analysis hinge on the difference between the 'money rate' and the 'natural rate' of interest, or, using a slightly different terminology, between the 'market rate' (meaning, confusingly, that set by the bank) and the 'natural rate' (Laidler, 1989a).

A key point that has recurred in most discussions of this issue is that whatever corresponds to the natural rate is assumed to be determined *outside the monetary system*, as if in some hypothetical capital market in which borrowing and lending can take place without the intermediation of money. It is regarded as a real phenomenon determined by the ubiquitous forces of 'productivity and thrift', and cannot be altered by purely monetary forces. Therefore, from the point of view of monetary analysis, it is argued that this magnitude can be treated essentially as a constant. The implication is that, if the monetary interest rate (the policy-related rate set by the central bank) does not conform to the rate determined on the capital market, there will be an irreconcilable disequilibrium situation, resulting in continuous inflation or deflation.

This idea of a natural rate of interest determined outside the monetary process and impervious to monetary manipulation has been a persistent theme in monetary economics for the past two centuries and more. Thornton (1802) denied that 'an increase in bank loans, by furnishing capital, may reduce the profit on the use of it' (see also Mints, 1945), and this was also the view of Ricardo (1817) in a famous passage, which begins, 'the rate of interest on money . . . is *not* regulated by the rate at which the banks will lend' (emphasis added), and was later explicitly criticized by Keynes in the *General Theory* (1936). According to Wicksell (1898), the natural rate of interest is the 'the rate which would be determined by supply and demand if real capital were lent in kind without the intervention of money'. Although this rate can change as a result of a change in the under-lying real equilibrium, in principle it is the money rate that eventually has to come into line and not vice versa. A rate of interest somehow determined in a 'real' capital market and immutable to monetary changes was also a major plank of Chicago monetary theory in the twentieth century (Burstein, 1963; Leijonhufvud, 1981; Smithin, 1989). Furthermore, pos-sibly because of the success of monetarism in the 1960s and 1970s, it remains an implicit assumption in the mainstream analysis of monetary policy today. In Chapter 6 below, it will be argued that in a credit economy the assumption is highly questionable, as the availability of money loans to entrepreneurs must stimulate investment projects which otherwise could not be carried out. In the present chapter, however, we simply note the prevalence of this view and its influence on theories of inflation in the Thornton/Wicksell mode.

Let $i(t)$ stand for the 'money rate' or policy rate set by the banking system in time (t), and r^N for the natural rate (assumed constant for present pur-poses). Then a simple version of these interest rate-based theories, corre-sponding to the caricature version of the basic quantity theory in Chapter 3, might have the rate of increase of nominal loans (and hence the rate of increase of the nominal money supply) responding to the gap between $i(t)$ and r^N.[6] For example:

$$(1/M)(dM/dt) = a[r^N - i(t)], \qquad a > 0 \qquad (5.4)$$

If, for the sake of simplicity, it is again assumed that the rate of output is fixed at the full employment level, and we then apply quantity-theoretic rea-soning to the effect that the inflation rate will be roughly equal to the rate of growth of the money supply, a simple theory of inflation emerges. Using the previous notation that $(1/P)(dP/dt) = \pi$, this will be:

$$\pi = a[r^N - i(t)] \qquad (5.5)$$

In short, if the rate of interest set by the banking system is below the natural rate, the result will be inflation, whereas if this 'policy rate' is above the natural rate there will be deflation. It should be noted from this argument that supporters of this type of theory, such as Wicksell, do not need to rep-resent themselves as having overturned the quantity theory by this argu-ment, but simply as having provided a more realistic version of the quantity theory appropriate for an economy with a developed credit system (Laidler, 1993). From this point of view, a setting of the 'bank rate' different from the natural rate can explain the mechanics of how additional credit money gets into circulation in a system with a sophisticated banking sector, but in other respects much of the familiar quantity theory 'world view' can remain intact.

Although equations (5.4) and (5.5) are adequate to give the flavour of theories in which 'the rate of interest charged by the banks, in relation to the rate of return on funds borrowed, is the controlling factor' (Mints, 1945), there are still a number of problems, which reflect the fact that the historical discussions of the approach rarely made an explicit distinction between so-called 'real' and 'nominal' rates of interest in the manner that is widely accepted today. In modern terminology, a nominal rate of interest is simply the percentage rate actually quoted in loan transactions, whereas the real rate is this nominal rate adjusted for expected inflation. It is presumed that the former, rather than the latter, is important for economic decision making. It is usual to attribute the first recognition of the distinction between real and nominal interest rates to Irving Fisher (1896), but its full acceptance by the economics profession did not really occur until the inflationary period of the 1970s. When economists such as Wicksell used terms such as 'real' or 'money' interest rates, therefore, this was not necessarily in their present-day meanings.

A lack of attention to Fisher's distinction, however, does make formulations like equations (5.4) and (5.5) difficult to interpret. Presumably the natural rate, r^N, must be a real rate in the modern sense, and therefore to be consistent the argument really should run that potential borrowers would have an incentive to increase or decrease their indebtedness when the *real* bank rate differs from the standard set by the natural rate. Most of the historical discussions, however, have seemed to involve the *nominal* bank rate or 'market rate', or were simply confused about these distinctions. One problem which arises from this confusion is that, if we interpret the natural rate to be a real rate and the bank rate to be a nominal rate, the traditional idea that the bank rate must adjust itself to the natural rate (Wicksell, 1898) seems to require a *deflation* when nominal interest rates are set too low rather than an inflation (McCallum, 1986). Suppose the nominal bank rate is permanently set at the level, i, and the natural rate, r^N, is interpreted as a real rate. In this case, abstracting from population growth and depreciation, and so on, a neoclassical equilibrium at the margin will require the real rate charged by banks, r, to be equal to the natural rate, or:

$$r = r^N \qquad (5.6)$$

The definition of r, however, is:

$$r = i - \pi^e \qquad (5.7)$$

And, in the steady state (when $\pi^e = \pi$):

$$r = i - \pi \qquad (5.8)$$

This then implies:

$$\pi = i - r^N \qquad (5.9)$$

So, in other words, it would seem that a setting of the nominal bank rate below the natural rate must imply *deflation* rather than inflation if the marginal equality of the corresponding real interest rate concepts is ever to be achieved. A negative association of nominal interest rates and inflation would, of course, be perfectly acceptable in the monetarist model with an exogenously determined rate of monetary growth and constant real interest rates. However, it is the opposite of the relationship predicted in the Wicksellian tradition with nominal rates as the instrument. If we are to come to an understanding of the problem consistent with modern economic ideas, therefore, and if the Wicksell/Thornton-type arguments regarding a cumulative process are to relate to a nominal interest rate peg, they must be interpreted as purely disequilibrium phenomena in which the marginal equality in (5.7) is never achieved.

In the light of this discussion, it might also be helpful to consider whether the idea of the real bank rate (more generally a real 'policy-related' rate) is itself a useful concept. By this is simply meant the nominal monetary policy instrument less expected inflation, as in the usual definition of a 'real' rate. In general:

$$i(t) = r(t) + \pi(t)^e \qquad (5.10)$$

or:

$$r(t) = i(t) - \pi(t)^e \qquad (5.11)$$

Now use this in equation (5.5):

$$\pi(t) = a\{r^N - [r(t) + \pi(t)^e]\} \qquad (5.12)$$

and, in the case when expectations are accurate:

$$\pi(t) = a\{r^N - [r(t) + \pi(t)]\} \qquad (5.13)$$

Finally, solving for the inflation rate:

$$\pi(t) = [a/(1+a)][r^N - r(t)]. \qquad (5.14)$$

This recasts the basic neo-Wicksellian theory in terms of discrepancies in real interest rates. If monetary policy is such that the *real* rates set by the central bank are less than the natural rate, the result is inflation, and vice versa if the real bank rate is set higher than the natural rate. Wisdom in monetary policy could be seen as achieving a 'policy-related' real rate which exactly mirrors the supposedly market-determined natural rate. By luck or judgment, the goal is to achieve, not by any supposedly automatic equilibrating mechanism inherent in the market but by 'policy', the desired state of:

$$r(t) = r^N \qquad\qquad (5.15)$$

in which case, according to (5.14), there will be no inflation.

For some time in the mid-twentieth century, particularly in the period between the publication of Keynes's *General Theory* and the later rise of monetarism and the new classical school, the objective of monetary policy was, in fact, often seen as specifically to provide cheap money in the sense of low *nominal* rates of interest (B. Friedman, 1988; Howson, 1989; Humphrey, 1993; Kaldor, 1986). Before the advent of monetarism, the famous *Radcliffe Report* in Britain in 1959 (Kaldor, 1986) was one of the most influential statements of the point of view that control over interest rates should be the main monetary policy instrument (as opposed to the quantity of base money), while also stressing some perceived limitations as to what an activist monetary policy could be expected to achieve. However, to the extent that these early arguments for interest rate control placed the emphasis on nominal rates rather than real rates, they obviously did lend themselves to criticisms that were a combination of Thornton/Wicksell considerations and the traditional critique of the real bills doctrine. Later, during the period in which monetarism was in the ascendant, the concept of an interest rate target for monetary policy was dismissed as an anachronism, and interest rate settings by the central bank were only discussed, if at all, from the perspective that very short-run changes were seen as one of the alternative techniques for achieving given monetary base targets (Courchene, 1976). But this was only one of the 'three strands of thought' on bank rate policy identified earlier by Keynes (1930).

In his famous Presidential Address to the American Economic Association, Friedman (1968) explicitly addressed the possibility of pegging interest rates, only to dismiss it, arguing that attempts to peg the interest rate 'too low' would result in a disequilibrium situation and ever-accelerating inflation. This was presented as an updated version of Wicksell's analysis, with the caveat, as suggested above, that Wicksell failed to distinguish between real and nominal interest rates. In the early 'new classical' literature (Sargent and Wallace, 1975; Sargent, 1979), the even stronger claim was made that interest rate pegging would lead to *indeterminacy* of the aggregate price level, as opposed to mere inflationary instability, and therefore was not, in some sense, a coherent policy.[7] The latter result, however, seems to be an artefact of the simple models which were employed rather than a genuine economic problem. Inflationary instability has certainly been observed in many real world economies, but it is difficult to imagine what the empirical counterpart to an 'indeterminate' price level would be. More formally, as shown by MacKinnon and Smithin (1993), it is always possible to develop consistent models that involve lagged nominal variables as well as pegged interest rates, and hence can readily determine inflation rates. From this starting point, price level determinacy (but not necessarily stability) will follow, given only an initial condition on at least one of the nominal variables at some point in the past. McCallum (1986) and Edey (1989) have also illustrated monetary rules which can simultaneously employ an interest rate instrument and provide determinate price levels by paying attention to realized nominal magnitudes, and Cottrell (1989) points out that even a minimal degree of nominal price rigidity automatically solves the determinacy problem.

The Friedman (1968) Wicksellian result was later rehabilitated at a more rigorous level by Cottrell (1989) and Howitt (1992), using models in which expectations are formed via adaptive learning mechanisms. These procedures avoid the counter-intuitive results obtained by McCallum (1986), illustrated above, whereby under perfect foresight low settings of the nominal interest rate should lead to deflation rather than inflation. The Wicksell/Thornton mechanism is thereby reinterpreted as a suggestion that a nominal interest rate peg that is too low or too high will lead to inflationary or deflationary instability. All these discussions, however, continue to rest on the assumption that there is a unique natural rate of interest, which remains unaffected by monetary manipulation, and therefore a unique natural level of output and employment. The possibility that the rate of interest in the capital markets is itself not immutable, and may interact with the level of interest rates established in the financial sector, is not addressed in any detail (Smithin, 1989).

In the area of practical policy making, the relative lack of attention paid to the interest rate instrument by academic theorists turned out to be something of an embarrassment after the collapse of the monetary targeting experiments of the early 1980s, which forced central banks around the world to revert to a pragmatic interest rate and/or exchange rate focus (Goodhart, 1989; B. Friedman, 1988). By the beginning of the twenty-first century, this was a *fait accompli*. According to B. Friedman (2000): '[in the late 1960s] . . . the Federal Reserve, like most central banks at that time, made monetary policy by setting interest rates. The same is once again true today. In retrospect, much of the intervening experience proved to be a historical detour.'

This evolution is more or less explicit in contemporary discussions of monetary policy. For example, the often-cited 'Taylor rule' for the federal funds rate, after Taylor (1993), for example, in the version discussed by Lewis and Mizen (2000), suggests that the following simple reaction function was a reasonable characterization of the way in which the US central bank was actually setting interest rates around the turn of the twentieth and twenty-first centuries:

$$i(t) = \theta_0 + \theta_1[\pi(t-1) - \pi^*] + \theta_2[y(t-1) - y^N(t-1)] + \pi(t-1) \quad (5.16)$$

This suggests that the rule that the Fed was following *is* actually couched in 'real' terms with the lagged inflation term explicitly serving as a proxy for expected inflation (Taylor, 1993). According to the rule the central bank will tend to raise short real interest rates whenever lagged inflation, $\pi(t-1)$, is seen to exceed some arbitrary target π^*, and also when the economy is supposedly 'growing too fast', that is, if lagged output, $y(t-1)$, was above the presumed natural or 'capacity' rate at that time, $y^N(t-1)$. The Wicksellian pedigree of the above is obvious if the coefficient, θ_0, is also interpreted as the natural rate or the 'equilibrium real interest rate' (Lewis and Mizen, 2000).

THE POST KEYNESIAN THEORY OF ENDOGENOUS MONEY

As mentioned in the earlier discussion of Friedman's work, perhaps the most consistent challenge to quantity theory reasoning has come from Post Keynesian economists, and those such as the circuitists who hold similar views on the endogeneity of money (Lavoie, 1992). As related by Kaldor (1970, 1986) the basic idea here has been not to deny the correlation between monetary growth and inflation, but to argue rather that causality in the quantity equation, $MV = PY$, runs from right to left, not from left to right, from PY to MV. This comes about in a credit economy simply because increases in aggregate nominal income, from whatever cause, give rise to a demand for finance from the banking system which, in turn, for the most part is accommodated at the prevailing rate of interest. There may be some caveats to this for individual borrowers, due to the principle of increasing risk, but not to any serious extent for the system as a whole 'expanding in step' (Lavoie, 1992, 1996). With the increase on the asset side of bank portfolios, the liabilities side (the volume of bank deposits) increases also and, as bank deposits are the bulk of the money supply, the original rise in nominal income is validated.

The Post Keynesians have a basically different theory of inflation from that of the monetarists and other quantity theory advocates. Inflation is essentially a 'cost-push' phenomenon and, in the case where wage costs are a large proportion of total costs, this implies that a major cause of inflation is 'wage-push' generated by the demands of labour unions in the struggle over income distribution (Robinson, 1979; Moore, 1988; Kaldor, 1986; Laidler, 1989b). Increases in the nominal wage bill are then accommodated by increases in bank loans to finance these costs, and hence by increases in the money supply.

To illustrate, we follow the exposition by Seccareccia (1996) of the theory of Weintraub (1978), combining the quantity equation set out in Chapter 3 with an alternative simple mark-up explanation of price formation. This gives the following two equations:

$$MV = PY \qquad (5.17)$$

and:

$$P = kWN/Y \qquad (5.18)$$

where k is the mark-up factor, and WN is the nominal wage bill. Assume also that both the velocity of circulation and the mark-up factor are constants, such that $dV/dt = dk/dt = 0$. Then, taking logs of both expressions and differentiating with respect to time, we obtain:

$$(1/P)(dP/dt) = (1/M)(dM/dt) - (1/Y)(dY/dt) \qquad (5.19)$$

and:

$$(1/P)(dP/dt) = (1/W)(dW/dt) + (1/N)(dN/dt) - (1/Y)(dY/dt) \qquad (5.20)$$

Combining equations (5.18) and (5.19) then gives:

$$(1/M)(dM/dt) = (1/W)(dW/dt) + (1/N)(dN/dt) \qquad (5.21)$$

This states that the rate of growth of the money supply (which in turn will determine the inflation rate) will be determined by the rate of growth of the nominal wage bill. Post Keynesians would argue that this is a causal relationship. In other words, the increase in the nominal wage bill causes the

increase in the money supply, and hence inflation, via bank financing of the
wage bill. Note that this mechanism is not subject to the charge of price
level indeterminacy as prices and their rate of change are already 'tied
down' by the level and exogenous rate of change of nominal wages. As suggested by Hicks (1955), this type of economy is therefore on a 'labour standard'. Note also that, if the production function in this economy is given
by $Y = AN$, where A is labour productivity, we can use equations (5.21) and
(5.19) to yield:

$$(1/P)(dP/dt) = (1/W)(dP/dW) - (1/A)(dA/dt) \qquad (5.22)$$

which makes the statement that there will be inflation if the rate of growth
of money wages is faster than that of productivity (Robinson, 1979).

Seccareccia (1996) has discussed some of the logical difficulties that need
to be addressed in this type of 'fundist' model. One of these is that, in a self-
contained circuit in which the money supply increases when loans are
extended, and is reduced once again via the law of reflux when loans are
repaid, the 'wage fund' by itself will not be arithmetically large enough to
enable firms to realize monetary profits. If only the wage bill is borrowed
and the money supply only expands by this amount, it is arithmetically
impossible for firms to generate enough monetary receipts to pay principal
plus interest, let alone to realize a monetary profit. As Seccareccia points
out, this deficiency is usually remedied in theoretical models by introducing an autonomous deficit spending sector such as the government, or alternatively, in a two-sector model, by arranging the purchases from one sector
by another such that effectively the total value of production is loan-
financed. Other alternatives along these lines are illustrated in the model
presented in Chapter 7 below.

Another perhaps more obvious point is that, as with the monetarist
model, it is difficult to distinguish between correlation and causality in the
empirical counterpart to equation (5.21). In fact, both monetarists and
Post Keynesians would concede that there is an empirical correlation
between the rate of growth of the nominal wage bill and the rate of growth
of some measures of the money supply. The question of causality, however,
of whether an increase in the money wage bill causes an increase in the
nominal money supply or vice versa, is more difficult to solve, as the very
persistence of these debates would testify.

As in the Thornton/Wicksell scenarios, the Post Keynesians take the ultimate monetary control variable available to the authorities to be the discount rate or bank rate, or its equivalent, in other words the 'terms on which'
the central bank stands ready to accommodate the demand for loans by
other financial institutions. The argument is that, in practice, central banks

cannot close the 'discount window' as implied in the base control approach, as this would mean abandoning their responsibility for the liquidity of the system and abdicating the 'lender of last resort' role (Moore, 1988; Kaldor, 1986; Dow and Saville, 1990). They can only discourage applications to the discount window by setting higher discount rates. For the Post Keynesians, however, unlike the case in the Thornton/Wicksell scenarios, the view tends to be that changes in the bank rate have little *direct* effect on the inflation rate, which is already predetermined by the rate of change of the nominal wage bill. A given increase (decrease) in the nominal interest rate therefore automatically implies a similar increase (decrease) in the real rate. This in turn will only affect the economy by its impact on aggregate demand. Some Post Keynesians, moreover, are sceptical that interest rate changes have much effect even in this area (Earl, 1990).

The Post Keynesian model reverses the causal sequences of orthodox theory in which output is determined on the supply side and the inflation rate is determined by aggregate demand. In Post Keynesian theory, the inflation rate is determined on the supply side, via cost-push, and the volume of output is determined by effective demand (Robinson, 1979; Coddington, 1983; Dutt and Amadeo, 1990). Hence the rate of interest plays a different role than in models descended from Thornton and Wicksell. If it is also believed that interest rates do not have much impact on aggregate demand, because (say) the rate of investment is interest-inelastic (Moore, 1988), monetary policy may also be seen as rather ineffective. The most common viewpoint is that 'tight money' is likely more effective in causing a recession than is cheap money in promoting recovery, in the latter case because of depressed expectations. This is a position that can perhaps be traced back to Keynes's own views as expressed in the *General Theory*,[8] although in other statements both before and after 1936 Keynes showed much greater confidence in the efficacy of monetary (interest rate) policy (Hirai, 1997).

THE DEMAND SIDE OF A SIMPLE POST KEYNESIAN MODEL

For the sake of completeness, given that the price level is determined on the supply side in the basic Post Keynesian model, this section will also briefly review the complementary demand side of that model. Output and employment are thought to be determined by aggregate demand, and influenced by income distribution, rather than being essentially predetermined by the natural rate of growth. As mentioned, this is precisely the opposite to the monetarist and similar constructs, where the supply side determines output in principle, and demand changes only affect prices (Coddington, 1983; Dutt and Amadeo, 1990).

In the closed economy, the starting point is the usual expenditure breakdown of GDP:

$$Y = C + I + G \qquad (5.23)$$

where C is consumption, I is investment and G is government expenditure. Also it is a truism that all income, including aggregate income, can either be taxed away by the government, spent or saved. So:

$$Y = C + S + T \qquad (5.24)$$

where S is savings and T is taxation. From (5.23) and (5.24) we derive the familiar equilibrium condition for the 'circular flow' (Schumpeter, 1934) namely, 'injections = withdrawals':

$$I + G = S + T \qquad (5.25)$$

Now assume that the savings function depends on income distribution, and for simplicity on the gross (before-tax) profit share and wage share:[9]

$$S = s_\Pi \Pi + s_W WN, \qquad s_\Pi > s_W \qquad (5.26)$$

where s_Π *and* s_W are the propensities to save out of gross profits and wages, respectively. Now divide through by Y, and define the wage share as $\psi = WN/Y$. We obtain:

$$S/Y = s_\Pi + (s_W - s_\Pi)\,\psi \qquad (5.27)$$

Finally, use (5.25) in (5.27) and solve for Y:

$$Y = \{1/[s_\Pi + (s_W - s_\Pi)\,\psi]\}[I + (G - T)] \qquad (5.28)$$

The expression $\{1/[s_\Pi + (s_W - s_\Pi)\psi]\}$ is clearly the so-called 'multiplier', and this result has the fundamentally 'Keynesian' character that an increase in investment, an increase in the national accounts budget deficit and also a redistribution in favour of the wage share (the group with the highest propensity to consume), will all tend to increase output and employment.

Finally, it can also be seen that, if the propensities to save on the part of the income receiving groups are equal such that $s_\Pi = s_W = s$, the multiplier will reduce to, for example:

$$dY/dI = 1/s \qquad (5.29)$$

or, as $s = 1 - c$, where c is the 'propensity to consume':

$$dY/dI = 1/(1 - c) \qquad (5.30)$$

This last expression is the simple expenditure multiplier, as derived in the many generations of introductory macroeconomics textbooks following that of Samuelson (1948). Essentially, all of these expositions have assumed a common propensity to consume in their versions of the Keynesian model.

CONCLUDING REMARKS

In this chapter several of the alternatives to simple quantity-theoretic reasoning have been discussed, including the much-criticized real bills doctrine, the neo-Wicksellian view that the interest rate charged by the central bank, more generally the 'policy-related' rate, is the controlling factor, and the Post Keynesian theory of endogenous money which allows for cost-push inflation.

Taking the contents of this chapter and the previous two together, it therefore appears that there are three main alternative theories of inflation, each of which, however, has many variants and offshoots in the literature. The three main views are (1) the monetarist/quantity theory/mainstream approach, in which inflation is ultimately determined by the autonomous rate of growth of base money, (2) the Wicksell/Thornton approach, in which inflation depends on the discrepancy between the 'market rate' (rather policy rate) and the 'natural rate' of interest, and (3) cost-push/wage-push approaches which attribute inflation to increases in nominal production costs such as wage costs.

In terms of the treatment of the complexities of the credit money environment and the evolution of financial systems, the monetarist-type approach differs from other approaches, even those which are in sympathy ideologically, in the attempt to sidestep the issue of money endogeneity and reduce the analysis of the credit economy to terms similar to those applicable to a commodity money system.

At the next level of theoretical principle, however, the important dividing line seems to be between theories which assume the existence of a natural rate of interest (impervious to monetary manipulation) and those which do not. Essentially, all theories which assume the existence of a natural rate have a common theoretical core and will eventually come to essentially similar conclusions about the role of money in a market economy. This is why Wicksell, for example, who explicitly used the term 'credit economy', and who had a sophisticated understanding of the properties of alternative monetary systems, could nonetheless regard his work primarily as an embellishment of the quantity theory. In hypothetical economies with a natural rate of interest, the equilibrium output is also fixed by that assumption and, whether we are considering autonomous changes in the money supply or administered changes in a 'money' rate of interest, these can only ultimately affect the demand side of the economy and inflation rates. Of the different approaches discussed above, actually only the Post Keynesian theories seem to work in a fundamentally different manner, with output determined by the demand side, and inflation determined mainly on the supply side through cost-push. However, it should also be noted that the non-neutrality of money in these models seems to be attributable mainly to the assumption of 'horizontal aggregate supply curves' (Moore, 1988; Coddington, 1983; Dutt and Amadeo, 1990), rather than directly to any of the alternative theories of the rate of interest which have been developed.

If there is a common criticism of all the approaches discussed so far, it is that they all, in their different ways, rely too heavily on the analytical procedure of a 'dichotomy' (Coddington, 1983) between aggregate demand and aggregate supply, and hence make too little progress in 'pushing monetary theory back to becoming a theory of output as a whole' (Keynes, 1936). A further alternative approach to these issues is offered in Chapter 7 below.

NOTES

1. This was the period of the 'Bank Restriction' during the wars against France in the Revolutionary and Napoleonic eras, when the Bank of England suspended the gold convertibility of its notes. The controversy was about the effects of the suspension, and when and how to restore convertibility.
2. This drastic step was advocated by the Cunliffe Committee in 1919 and finally carried out by Winston Churchill as Chancellor of the Exchequer in 1925. The policy was heavily criticized by Keynes (1925) in his pamphlet *The Economic Consequences of Mr. Churchill.* The restored gold standard was finally abandoned during the financial crisis of 1931.
3. The latter in the context of a new introduction to a reprint of Smith's book.
4. According to Yeager (1990), most of the historical supporters of free banking were also opponents of the currency principle. A prominent exception would be the Austrian economist Ludwig von Mises, whose work inspires a number of the proponents of free banking today.
5. See Smithin (1996) for further discussion.
6. As illustrated by the work of Humphrey (1993) a more historically accurate representation of Wicksell's argument would have the price level, rather than its rate of change, responding to the interest differential. In the 'neo-Wicksellian' formulation here debtors are assumed to be willing to take on obligations at a faster rate the greater is the differential.

7. This in spite of the historical record as later discussed in B. Friedman (2000), and cited above.
8. The model presented in Chapter 7 below suggests a different channel whereby changes in (real) interest rates can have an effect on output, namely via the supply side.
9. In other words, the assumption is that any increases in taxes will be taken up entirely out of savings rather than reduced consumption.

REFERENCES

Bagehot, W. (1873 [1915]), *Lombard Street*, London: John Murray.

Burstein, M.L. (1963), *Money*, Cambridge, MA: Schenckman Publishing Co.

Capie, F. and G.E. Wood (1989), 'Introduction: the Henry Thornton lectures', *Monetary Economics in the 1980s*, London: Macmillan.

Coddington, A. (1983), *Keynesian Economics: The Search for First Principles*, London: George Allen & Unwin.

Cottrell, A. (1989), 'Price expectations and equilibrium when the interest rate is pegged', *Scottish Journal of Political Economy*, 36, 125–40.

Courchene, T.J. (1976), *Money Inflation and the Bank of Canada*, Montreal: C.D. Howe Institute.

Dow, J.C.R. and I.D. Saville (1990), *A Critique of Monetary Policy: Theory and British Experience*, Oxford: Clarendon Press.

Dutt, A.K. and E.J. Amadeo (1990), *Keynes's Third Alternative: The Neo-Ricardian Keynesians and the Post Keynesians*, Aldershot, UK and Brookfield, US: Edward Elgar.

Earl, P.E. (1990), *Monetary Scenarios: A Modern Approach to Financial Systems*, Aldershot, UK and Brookfield, US: Edward Elgar.

Edey, M. (1989), 'Monetary policy instruments: a theoretical analysis', in I. Macfarlane and G. Stevens (eds), *Studies in Money and Credit*, Research Department, Reserve Bank of Australia.

Fisher, I. (1896), *Appreciation and Interest*, New York: American Economic Association.

Friedman, B.M. (1988), 'Lessons on monetary policy from the 1980s', *Journal of Economic Perspectives*, 2, 51–72.

—— (2000), 'The role of interest rates in Federal Reserve policymaking', NBER Working Paper 8047, December.

Friedman, M. (1968), 'The role of monetary policy', *American Economic Review*, 58, 1–17.

Glasner, D. (1992), 'The real bills doctrine in the light of the law of reflux', *History of Political Economy*, 24, 867–94.

Goodhart, C.A.E. (1989), 'The conduct of monetary policy', *Economic Journal*, 99, 293–346.

Green, R. (1989), 'Real bills doctrine', in J. Eatwell, M. Milgate and P. Newman (eds), *The New Palgrave: Money*, London: Macmillan.

Hicks, J.R. (1955 [1982]), 'Inflation and the wage structure', reprinted in *Money, Interest and Wages: Collected Essays on Economic Theory*, vol. 2, Oxford: Basil Blackwell.

—— (1967a), 'Monetary theory and history – an attempt at perspective', *Critical Essays in Monetary Theory*, Oxford: Clarendon Press.

—— (1967b), 'Thornton's *Paper Credit* (1802)', *Critical Essays in Monetary Theory*, Oxford: Clarendon Press.

Hirai, T. (1997), 'A study of Keynes's economics (I) – from *A Treatise on Money* to *The General Theory*', *Sophia Economic Review*, 43, 67–136.

Howitt, P. (1992), 'Interest rate control and non-convergence to rational expectations', *Journal of Political Economy*, 100, 776–800.

Howson, S. (1989), 'Cheap money', in J. Eatwell, M. Milgate and P. Newman (eds), *The New Palgrave: Money*, London: Macmillan.

Humphrey, T.M. (1993), *Money Banking and Inflation: Essays in the History of Monetary Thought*, Aldershot, UK and Brookfield, US: Edward Elgar.

IMF (2001), *World Economic Outlook*, International Monetary Fund, Washington, DC, May.

Kaldor, N. (1970), 'The new monetarism', *Lloyds Bank Review*, July, 1–18.

—— (1986), *The Scourge of Monetarism*, 2nd edn, Oxford: Oxford University Press.

Keynes, J.M. (1925), *The Economic Consequences of Mr. Churchill*, London: Hogarth Press.

—— (1930), *A Treatise on Money* (2 vols), London: Macmillan.

—— (1936), *The General Theory of Employment Interest and Money*, London: Macmillan.

Laidler, D.E.W. (1981), 'Adam Smith as a monetary economist', *Canadian Journal of Economics*, 14, 185–200.

—— (1984), 'Misconceptions about the real bills doctrine and the quantity theory: a comment on Sargent and Wallace', *Journal of Political Economy*, 92, 149–55.

—— (1989a), 'The bullionist controversy', in J. Eatwell, M. Milgate and P. Newman (eds), *The New Palgrave: Money*, London: Macmillan.

—— (1989b), 'Dow and Saville's *Critique of Monetary Policy*: a review essay', *Journal of Economic Literature*, 27, 1147–59.

—— (1993), 'Was Wicksell a quantity theorist?', in H. Barkai, S. Fischer and N. Liviatian (eds), *Monetary Theory and Thought: Essays in Honour of Don Patinkin*, London: Macmillan.

Lavoie, M. (1992), 'Jacques Le Bourva's theory of endogenous credit-money', *Review of Political Economy*, 4, 36–46.

—— (1996), 'Horizontalism, structuralism, liquidity preference, and the principle of increasing risk', *Scottish Journal of Political Economy*, 43, 275–300.

Leijonhufvud, A. (1981), 'The Wicksell connection: variations on a theme', *Information and Coordination: Essays in Macroeconomic Theory*, New York: Oxford University Press.

Lewis, M.K. and P.D. Mizen (2000), *Monetary Economics*, Oxford: Oxford University Press.

MacKinnon K.T. and J. Smithin (1993), 'An interest rate peg, inflation and output', *Journal of Macroeconomics*, 15, 769–85.

McCallum, B.T. (1986), 'Some issues concerning interest rate pegging, price level determinacy, and the real bills doctrine', *Journal of Monetary Economics*, 17, 135–60.

Mints, L.W. (1945), *A History of Banking Theory in Great Britain and the United States*, Chicago: University of Chicago Press.

Moore, B.J. (1988), *Horizontalists and Verticalists: The Macroeconomics of Credit Money*, Cambridge: Cambridge University Press.

Perlman, M. (1989), 'Adam Smith and the paternity of the real bills doctrine', *History of Political Economy*, 21, 77–90.

Ricardo, D. (1817 [1973]), *The Principles of Political Economy and Taxation*, London: J.M. Dent & Sons.

Robinson, J. (1979), 'Foreword', in A.S. Eichner (ed.), *A Guide to Post Keynesian Economics*, White Plains, New York: M.E. Sharpe.

Rogers, C. (1989), *Money, Interest and Capital: A Study in the Foundations of Monetary Theory*, Cambridge: Cambridge University Press.

Samuelson, P.A. (1948), *Economics: An Introductory Analysis*, New York: McGraw-Hill.

Sargent, T.J. (1979), *Macroeconomic Theory*, New York: Academic Press.

—— and N. Wallace (1975), 'Rational expectations, the optimal monetary policy instrument and the optimal money supply rule', *Journal of Political Economy*, 83, 241–54.

—— (1982), 'The real bills doctrine versus the quantity theory: a reconsideration', *Journal of Political Economy*, 90, 1212–36.

Schumpeter, J.A. (1934 [1983]), *The Theory of Economic Development: An Inquiry into Profits, Capital, Credit Interest and the Business Cycle*, New Brunswick, NJ: Transaction Publishers.

Schwartz, A.J. (1989), 'Banking school, currency school, free banking school', in J. Eatwell, M. Milgate and P. Newman (eds), *The New Palgrave: Money*, London: Macmillan.

Seccareccia, M. (1990), 'The two faces of neo-Wicksellianism in the 1930s: the Austrians and the Swedes', in D. Moggridge (ed.), *Perspectives on the History of Economic Thought*, vol. 4, Aldershot, UK and Brookfield, US: Edward Elgar.

—— (1996), 'Post Keynesian fundism and monetary circulation', in E.J. Nell and G. Deleplace (eds), *Money in Motion: The Post Keynesian and Circulation Approaches*, London: Macmillan.

Skaggs, N.T. (1991), 'John Fullarton's law of reflux and central bank policy', *History of Political Economy*, 23, 457–80.

Smith, A. (1776 [1981]), *An Inquiry into the Nature and Causes of the Wealth of Nations*, Indianapolis: Liberty Fund.

Smith, V.C. (1936 [1990]), *The Rationale of Central Banking and the Free Banking Alternative*, Indianapolis: Liberty Press.

Smithin, J. (1984), 'Financial innovation and monetary theory', *Three Banks Review*, 144, 26–38.

—— (1989), 'Hicksian monetary economics and contemporary financial innovation', *Review of Political Economy*, 1, 192–207.

Taylor, J.B. (1993), 'Discretion versus policy rules in practice', *Carnegie-Rochester Conference Series on Public Policy*, 39, 195–214.

Thornton, H. (1802 [1962]), *An Inquiry into the Nature and Effects of the Paper Credit of Great Britain*, New York: Augustus M. Kelley.

Viner, J. (1937), *Studies in the Theory of International Trade*, New York: Harper Bros.

Weintraub, S. (1978), *Capitalism's Inflation and Unemployment Crisis*, Reading, MA: Addison-Wesley.

White, L.H. (1984), *Free Banking in Britain: Theory, Experience, and Debate, 1800–45*, Cambridge: Cambridge University Press.

Wicksell, K. (1898 [1965]), *Interest and Prices*, New York: Augustus M. Kelley.

Yeager, L.B. (1990), 'Introduction', in V.C. Smith, *The Rationale of Central Banking and the Free Banking Alternative*, Indianapolis: Liberty Press.

6. Money, interest rates and output

THE NATURAL RATE OF INTEREST

As illustrated in Chapters 4 and 5 above, although economists of a wide range of opinion can accept (to a greater or lesser degree) that monetary policy will be non-neutral in the short-run due to nominal rigidities, this need not compromise the still more deeply held belief that purely monetary factors will not affect the ultimate long-run equilibrium, or growth path, of the economy.

The basis of the latter position is the idea that the rate of interest, at its most fundamental level, is a 'real' rather than a monetary phenomenon. Hence, almost by definition, it cannot be permanently affected by the activities of central banks. We are asked to imagine that in principle a rate of interest exists which represents the outcome of the 'true' motives of borrowers and lenders as these would be revealed *if* they could somehow interact in a capital market operating without the intervention of money, banks or other financial institutions. This is what Wicksell (1898a, 1898b) called the 'natural rate of interest', although the basic idea long antedates Wicksell's contribution. The next step in the argument is to assert that the real-world complications caused by the actual existence of money and banks do not, in fact, have any lasting impact on the motives of those engaged in the supposedly more fundamental barter capital transactions. The natural rate as established by the imaginary barter transactions is then taken to be the most basic determinant of the complex of interest rates actually observed in reality. Interest rates expressed in money terms must ultimately conform to the natural rate, and not vice versa. Given these premises, it follows that central bank influence over the level and term structure of interest rates can only be temporary at best, and that in the long run money must be neutral.

This set of ideas, in one version or another, has a history as long as the quantity theory, and is really the ultimate basis of that theory, even though this is not always acknowledged. Both Leijonhufvud (1981) and Rogers (1989) point out that disagreements over the mechanism of interest rate determination lie at the heart of much confusion and disagreement in monetary economics, although this fact is not obvious to many present-day, mainly technically-trained, economists who seem to have lost sight of the basic issues in a welter of controversy over other less central matters.

An obvious response to the natural rate doctrine would be that the idea of interest rates being somehow determined on barter-oriented capital markets is as much a theoretical fiction as commodity exchange taking place in Walrasian barter markets with the aid of an 'auctioneer'. Such a concept takes no account of the actual historical evolution of capitalism and the market system, or of the internal logic of that system. In reality, the rise of banking and financial systems, and their continued evolution, has in itself been a main determinant of the type and volume of borrowing and lending that can be carried on at any point in time, and hence also of the type and volume of real economic activity that can be undertaken. Moreover, as pointed out above, in real-world systems the activities of financial intermediation and the monetary payments systems are inextricably interconnected to the point where artificial discussions between 'monetary' and 'financial' issues are untenable. In this type of environment, fictional natural rates determined in barter markets would seem to have little practical relevance, and it is more likely that causality would actually run from the complex of interest rates determined on the financial markets *to* real economic activity and not vice versa.

In the history of economic thought, however, this type of response to the natural rate doctrine has rarely been made. The dominating conception has been the idea of a generic rate of interest determined on barter capital markets and impervious to monetary manipulation in the long run, and this persists up to and including the present day. Some authors, such as Moore (1988a, 1988b) and Smithin (1989), have suggested that Keynes (1936) was an exception to the usual consensus, as he did insist on reversing the direction of causality in the determination of interest rates. Again, however, if this was one of Keynes's main intended contributions, the message has evidently not survived in modern so-called 'Keynesian' or 'new Keynesian' economics.

Referring again to some of the historically important works in monetary economics, cited earlier, we can see how concepts similar to that of a natural rate of interest have been a more or less permanent feature of the literature. Recall, for example, Thornton's (1802) idea that the inflation rate depended on the difference between the rate of interest charged by the central bank and the 'rate of mercantile profit'. It was a key point for Thornton that this so-called 'rate of profit' could not itself be affected by changes in purely monetary variables. As he put it:

> The reader, possibly, may think that an extension of bank loans, by furnishing additional capital, may reduce the profit on the use of it, and may thus lessen the temptation to borrow . . . It has already been remarked that capital by which the term *bona fide* property was intended, cannot be suddenly and materially increased by any emission of paper. That the rate of mercantile profit depends

on the quantity of this *bona fide* capital and not on the amount of the nominal value which an encreased emission of paper may give to it, is a circumstance . . . easy to point out. (Original emphasis)

Ricardo (1817) held a similar point of view, as illustrated by the following often-cited passage:

> with respect to the interest for money; it is not regulated by the rate at which the banks will lend, whether it be 5, 4 or 3 per cent., but by the rate of profits which can be made by the employment of capital, and which is totally independent of the quantity or value of money. Whether a bank lent one million, ten million, or a hundred millions, they would not permanently alter the market rate of interest; they would only alter the value of the money which they thus issued . . . The applications to the bank for money . . . depend on the comparison between the rate of profits that may be made by the employment of it and the rate at which they are willing to lend it. If they charge less than the market rate of interest, there is no amount of money which they might not lend; if they charge more than that rate none but spendthrifts and prodigals would be found to borrow of them.[1]

Wicksell (1898b) in the preface to *Interest and Prices* is explicit about what is meant by the natural rate of interest:

> This natural rate is roughly the same thing as the real interest of actual business. A more accurate, though rather abstract, criterion is obtained by thinking of it as the rate which would be determined by supply and demand if real capital were lent in kind without the intervention of money.

On the issue of whether the natural rate can be affected by monetary policy, Wicksell (1898a) describes the then forthcoming *Interest and Prices* as providing:

> the only completely satisfactory explanation of . . . [what] . . . is usually regarded almost as an axiom in economics, namely, that the level of interest on money is not in the last instance determined by a shortage or surplus of money, but by a shortage or surplus of real capital . . . the relation of cause and effect immediately becomes clear, as soon as it can be assumed that a lasting difference between the natural rate of interest and the rate of interest on money would at once . . . lead to a rise or fall in commodity prices.

The assumption of a natural rate of interest that cannot be permanently affected by monetary policy was also very much a part of mid-twentieth century monetarism. In Friedman's classic statement in his AEA Presidential Address (1968), he refers directly to Wicksell:

> Thanks to Wicksell we are acquainted with the concept of a 'natural' rate of interest and the possibility of a discrepancy between the 'natural' rate and the

'market' rate. *The preceding analysis can be translated fairly directly into Wicksellian terms.* The monetary authority can make the market rate less than the natural rate only by inflation. (Emphasis added)

Similarly, somewhat later in the same paper, Friedman states a general conclusion about the limitations of monetary policy in the following terms: 'the monetary authority . . . cannot use its control over nominal quantities to peg a real quantity – *the real rate of interest*, the rate of unemployment, the level of real national income' (emphasis added).

The concept of a non-monetary natural rate of interest also continues as an important plank of mainstream monetary economics today. Statements about this property are usually more careful than in the historical examples quoted above because, as pointed out by McCallum (1991), 'superneutrality' in this sense is not a robust theoretical property of any of the formal monetary models in use in mainstream economics today. Rather the property must be imposed in these models as one of the initial conditions.[2] Nonetheless, the view still seems to be that as a practical matter this is a reasonable assumption to make. The following passages from Barro (1988) might be taken as representative. Describing a specific monetary model, a version of which was later published in the *Journal of Monetary Economics* (Barro, 1989), the author writes: 'The main restriction in this specification is that movements in the expected real rate are independent of monetary disturbances . . . it is . . . important that monetary policy cannot affect the expected real interest rate in this model.' Barro then lists a number of the sources of monetary non-neutrality in contemporary models and discusses their theoretical and empirical limitations. He goes on to summarize:

> Overall, I treat the expected real interest and output as exogenous with respect to money because I lack an alternative specification that I regard as theoretically or empirically superior. However, even if this assumption is wrong, it may still be satisfactory in the present context if money matters mostly for nominal variables – such as the price level and the nominal interest rate – and only secondarily for real variables.

Similarly, surveying contemporary models of inflation, McCallum (1991) argues that in general, in these models, 'superneutrality is not strictly implied but departures should be minor'. What all of these quotations establish is that variations on the theme of a natural rate of interest invariant to monetary policy measures has been influential in monetary economics for two hundred years and more, and continues to be so to this day, in spite of what Keynes had to say on the matter earlier in the twentieth century. On this issue certainly, the so-called 'Keynesian revolution' was evidently a failure.

However, it can also be argued that, once we move away from the pure commodity money framework of the quantity theory and recognize the actual role of 'money' as an indispensable part of the credit system, the natural rate doctrine is not particularly convincing. If, as argued above, the credit-based system cannot function without the existence of a basic monetary asset, in the sense of an unambiguous standard of value and ultimate means of payment, it would seem that the rate of interest charged on loans of that asset should play a key part in determining, not only the nominal, but also the real variables of the system. The business of borrowing and lending and therefore the formation of physical capital, and real economic activity in general, could hardly get off the ground without the assistance of the monetary system in this sense. It would seem to be a reasonable argument to make, therefore, that the (real) cost of borrowing the funds necessary to get production under way should itself have an effect on the scale of production that entrepreneurs find it worthwhile to undertake. In any event, this commonsense idea is certainly not more implausible than the notion that precisely the same type of interactions between borrowers and lenders could take place in barter-type capital markets regardless of the existence of sophisticated financial and monetary markets, and independently of the stage of evolution these institutional arrangements have reached. But the latter is what the natural rate doctrine quite clearly implies. The existence of money and financial markets literally makes no difference to the economy in these formulations.

For many economists, their heuristic understanding of what determines the natural rate of interest is no doubt conditioned by the analysis of the familiar 'loanable funds' diagram which originated with Robertson (1934). This is illustrated in Figure 6.1 in the version supplied by Leijonhufvud (1981). The vertical and horizontal axes in the figure represent, respectively, 'the' real rate of interest and the real volumes of net investment and saving. The latter are defined in terms of value magnitudes deflated by an appropriate price index. The schedule I represents the demand for new investment funds (the flow supply of bonds) and the schedule S represents the supply of saving (the flow demand for bonds). The natural rate of interest is therefore r^N, supposedly reflecting demand and supply equilibrium in the capital market. This can only be changed by subsequent shifts in the demand and supply schedules, which in the context of this diagram represent changes in the real forces of productivity and thrift, and not by any purely monetary changes.

There are, however, a number of serious logical problems with this diagrammatic analysis, as pointed out, for example, by both Rogers (1989) and Leijonhufvud (1981). One of these relates to the treatment of stock and flows, which was one of Keynes's (1936) main criticisms of the 'classical'

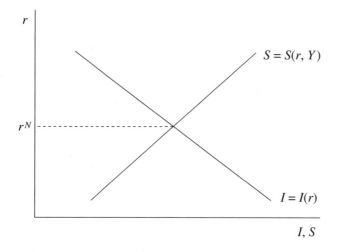

Figure 6.1

theory of interest. As drawn, the schedules I and S represent the flow supplies of, and demand for, new securities or bonds, and the natural rate of
interest is supposedly determined by these flows. However, the analysis
ignores the existence of the existing stock of securities issued in previous
periods, which have not yet reached their term to maturity. Suppose, for
example, there is reduction in the stock demand for these securities for
whatever reason (such as an increase in Keynesian 'liquidity preference'),[3]
which will reduce the price of these securities and raise interest rates. The
interest rate determined in this way may be r', for example, not r^N, and if
the forces which keep the rate of interest at this level persist, the resulting
disequilibrium would have to be eliminated in some way. The archetypal
'Keynesian' solution, as illustrated in Figure 6.2, would be a fall in real
income that shifts the savings function over to the left (Leijonhufvud,
1981). This would then 'validate' the higher real rate of interest at r', albeit
at a new lower level of income, and vitiate the idea that the 'natural' rate of
interest is somehow uniquely determined by the intersection of the original
I and S schedules.

Rogers (1989) also points out that there are still more serious logical
problems with the loanable funds analysis, relating to the fact that the supposed real investment and saving concepts in diagrams such as those in
Figures 6.1 and 6.2 are defined in value terms. In the specific example above,
they are money values deflated by some price index. The analysis therefore
immediately falls foul of the problems discussed in the 'two Cambridges'
debate about capital theory. The upshot of this debate was that, outside a

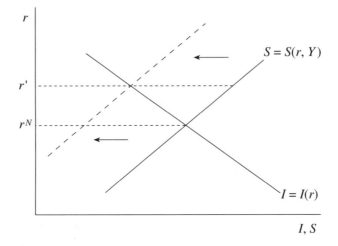

Figure 6.2

simple one-commodity world, attempts to derive an aggregative theory of
interest with reference to capital as a value magnitude collapse because of
circular reasoning. The value of capital cannot be determined until the rate
of interest is already known, and therefore cannot be used to *derive* a theory
of interest. As Rogers (1989) points out, there is therefore no way to relate
a diagram like Figure 6.1 to the underlying conception of investment and
saving being carried on 'in kind' as in the quotation from Wicksell above.
There is no necessary relation between money saving (even in 'real' terms
when deflated by a price level), and the Wicksellian conception of real
saving in the form of heterogeneous goods, and no guarantee of the existence of a monotonic downward-sloping schedule such as *I* in the diagram
relating real interest rates and the value of investment.

In spite of the logical problems associated with the loanable funds analysis, various versions of a diagram like Figure 6.1 are still current in the textbooks. It is noteworthy, however, that careful writers such as Mishkin
(2001) couch the analysis entirely in terms of stocks of existing securities
rather than flows and use only nominal magnitudes. However, as Rogers
(1989) suggests, the result of this type of procedure is simply a theory of
changes in nominal interest rates, which provides no explanation of the
underlying level of real interest rates. It is the latter, however, which the
original loanable funds theory was implicitly supposed to provide. The
theory of the rate of interest is therefore cut adrift from the underlying
forces of 'productivity and thrift', which is ironic, as this was precisely the
original criticism of Keynesian-type explanations of the rate of interest by
loanable funds theorists.

Perhaps as a result of these various logical difficulties, in practice the more formal theoretical monetary models assuming that the real rate of interest is fixed independently of monetary factors do not literally attempt to model a loanable funds capital market, but employ simplifying assumptions of one sort or another which impose fixity of the real rate of interest as one of the initial conditions.

For example, in the monetarist model there was no compunction about using a one-commodity capital-theoretic model and identifying the real rate of interest with the marginal physical product of capital. This, in turn, was taken to be essentially a constant (Friedman, 1974; Friedman and Schwartz, 1982). As pointed out by Leijonhufvud (1981) and Burstein (1963, 1988), this idea is based on the 'Chicago modification' of traditional neoclassical capital theory, which eschews the usual diminishing marginal productivity arguments to generate an effectively constant marginal product of capital. The vision is one in which there are ultimately no fixed factors, or in which technological advance may be presumed to offset whatever physical limits (for example, on land or natural resources) do exist (Smithin, 1989).

More mathematically oriented optimization models in the tradition of Sidrauski (1967), and as illustrated by Blanchard and Fischer (1989), McCallum (1991) and Walsh (1998), are able analytically to restrict the rate of return on capital to a unique long-run value via the alternative assumption of a constant rate of time preference, implying that the subjective 'discount' that economic actors apply to future versus present receipts is unchanging. In the steady state, neglecting the complications caused by depreciation and population growth, both the real rate of return on capital and the real financial rate of interest are then supposed to be equated to this constant rate of time preference, and hence are tied down by whatever the rate of time preference is. As mentioned, however, it is recognized that there is no particular theoretical justification for this assumption,[4] and its imposition simply reflects the traditional heuristic notion of the way in which the economy operates, as illustrated by the series of historical quotations reported above. The point is usually illustrated in an 'infinitely-lived representative agent model', as follows. The single agent, taken somehow to represent the entire economy, is assumed to maximize the objective function:

$$Max: \int e^{-\rho t} U(c, m) dt, \qquad U_c > 0, \ U_m > 0 \qquad (6.1)$$

subject to the following constraints:

$$da/dt = y + v - \delta k - \pi m - c \qquad (6.2)$$

$$a = k + m \qquad (6.3)$$

$$y = f(k), \qquad f_k > 0 \tag{6.4}$$

and also certain 'boundary conditions' (Intriligator, 1971; Blanchard and Fischer, 1989), which limit the overall mathematical scope of the problem. Here y stands for output, c for consumption, k for the capital stock, m for real money balances, a for total real wealth ('assets'), v for the *real* value of monetary injections or transfers (not under the control of the 'agent'), π for inflation and δ for the depreciation rate on 'capital'.[5] The symbol ρ stands for the crucial 'rate of time preference', which in turn is taken to be a constant. The first step in solving this type of problem is to form a current value Hamiltonian:

$$H = U(c, m) + \lambda[f(a - m) + v - \delta(a - m) - \pi m - c], \tag{6.5}$$

where λ is the so-called 'co-state variable'. The following will then be among the first-order conditions for a solution to the 'intertemporal dynamic optimization problem':

$$U_c(c, m) - \lambda = 0 \tag{6.6}$$

$$U_m(c, m) - \lambda(f_k - \delta + \pi) = 0 \tag{6.7}$$

$$d\lambda/dt = -\lambda(f_k - \delta - \rho) = 0 \tag{6.8}$$

It can be shown that the steady state of this type of model is a saddlepoint (Blanchard and Fischer, 1989). Therefore, relying on 'rational expectations' arguments, it is possible to assume that some mechanism will exist to land this economy on its 'stable arm', and hence ultimately for it to arrive at the steady-state equilibrium. This will be characterized by $da/dt = dm/dt = dk/dt = d\lambda/dt = dc/dt = 0$. Also (by the definition of real balances m) we will have the quantity theory result that $\pi = \mu$, where μ is the rate of growth of the nominal money supply. Hence, using equations (6.6) to (6.8) and the GDP identity, the steady-state solution will be:

$$U_m(c, m)/U_c(c, m) = f_k - \delta + \mu \tag{6.9}$$

$$f_k - \delta = \rho \tag{6.10}$$

$$c = f(k) - \delta k \tag{6.11}$$

It is equation (6.10) that is most relevant for the current argument, as this implies that the real rate of interest is uniquely determined, 'nailed down' as it were, by the assumption of a constant rate of time preference.

Economists of the 'Chicago school', in particular, seem to have taken what Burstein (1988) calls the 'nil influence' hypothesis (of money on interest rates) very seriously, and at one point Fama (1975), for example, presented empirical evidence from postwar US data, which supported a conclusion that the real rate of interest was effectively constant. However, this obviously seems much less plausible in the light of the experience of the past quarter-century and more since the end of Fama's sample period, and the work of Mishkin (1981, 1984), Dotsey and Scholl (2000) and others suggests that this result does not hold in periods other than the relatively tranquil postwar years. Of course, these later findings could always be explained in Wicksellian fashion as prior changes in the natural rate. However, with reference to several of the specific episodes involving large changes in *ex ante* real rates in recent decades. the majority of observers of the practical scene must surely concede the relevance of changes in central bank policy (Smithin, 1990a, 1990b), with the remaining debating point, once again, relating to how permanent those changes would be likely to be. In any event, recent experience, in conjunction with the logical problems of loanable funds theory, must provide at least some reason to doubt the confident assertions of the historical writers that central bank interest rate policy leaves no permanent trace on the real economy.

ALTERNATIVE CONCEPTIONS OF THE RATE OF INTEREST

In a further attempt to sort out the confusion which abounds concerning the theory of the rate of interest in the literature, it may be helpful to point out that there are at least three separate interest rate or rate of return concepts which are commonly employed (for example, in the above optimization problem) and should be sharply distinguished, but which are often confused with one another. In the world of neoclassical macroeconomic models, these are respectively the 'financial' or 'money' rate of interest, r, meaning the rate of interest charged on loans of money, the rate of time preference, ρ, relating to the subjective evaluation of present versus future satisfactions as discussed above, and finally the marginal physical productivity of capital (MPK), which in traditional notation is written as f_k. All of these concepts obviously should be thought of as real rates in the Fisher sense. For example, r is defined as:

$$r = i - \pi^e \tag{6.12}$$

where i is the nominal rate on money loans, and π^e is the expected rate of inflation.

In long-run equilibrium, neglecting complications caused by depreciation, population growth and so on, the basic idea is that all three of these
interest rate concepts must be equal. What fundamentally distinguishes the
various alternative theories of interest, however (and neglecting for the
time being the caveats to be raised about the concept of the MPK itself), is
the assumptions made about causality in the context of this three-way
equality. The authors of the historical quotations above, for example,
simply take the real rate of return to economic activity (in some sense) as
given, and assume that the financial rate of interest must ultimately adjust
to that standard. Bringing the modern analytical concept of the rate of time
preference into this picture, and if the MPK itself is supposed to stand for
'the real return to economic activity', this assumption can be expressed as:

$$r = \rho = f_k \tag{6.13}$$

where the implied direction of causality is from right to left. In other words,
both the rate of time preference and the financial rate of interest are supposed to adjust to the exogenous standard set by the MPK. As shown
above, many modern analytical models achieve a similar result to the classicals simply by postulating an exogenous rate of time preference, implying
a direction of causality:

$$r = f_k = \rho \tag{6.14}$$

But a counter-argument to both of these positions, involving 'a monetary
theory of the *real* rate of interest' (Burstein, 1995, emphasis added), would
be that, if the crucial role of the money/credit system in the financing of
production is correctly understood, it might be more sensible to think of
the chain of causality as being the following:

$$f_k = \rho = r \tag{6.15}$$

In this case, the implied argument is that rate of interest is first determined
in the financial system (hence a monetary theory of interest) and that *both*
the marginal physical product of capital and the rate of time preference
must adjust to the money rate of interest, rather than the other way around.
The MPK or its equivalent should adjust, contrary to Thornton, Ricardo,
Wicksell *et al.*, because the availability and cost of finance after all determines which projects entrepreneurs find it worthwhile to undertake and
which they do not. Projects with lower rates of return than the prevailing
cost of finance will not be undertaken. Also the rate of time preference can
change endogenously with changes in the wealth and/or consumption levels

of those making intertemporal consumption decisions (Kam, 2000). The argument is that, given the importance of money and credit in the overall system, it is the rate of interest on money, or the cost of finance, which 'rules the roost', and it is the real economy that must adjust to this rate and not vice versa. It can be argued that this is at least a more intelligible concept than that of a hypothetical natural rate of interest, which remains unchanged regardless of whether or not a sophisticated financial system exists and regardless of the state of development of that system. In fact, there is no real reason to suppose that the opportunities available to entrepreneurs remain unchanged regardless of the nature of the economic system under which they live, and regardless of the actual development of institutions, including financial institutions, within a given system. There is no reason to suppose that their opportunities remain unchanged regardless of the cost and conditions of finance that are available.

Keynes, evidently, was one major economist who believed that in real-world capitalist or market economic systems the rate of interest is determined primarily by monetary factors, and that the real economy must adjust to interest rates rather than vice versa. For example, he was explicit about the importance of his 'monetary theory of interest' in a famous letter to Hicks about Hicks's (1937) *SI/LL* (later *IS/LM*) diagram. As quoted by Moore (1988b), Keynes writes: 'I consider that the difference between myself and the classicals lies in the fact that they regard the rate of interest as a non-monetary phenomenon.' There are also numerous passages in the *General Theory* in which Keynes (1936) reverses the usual direction of causality, not directly employing the neoclassical MPK concept, but via his own concept of a subjective 'marginal efficiency of capital' (MEC). For example:

> It is true that in equilibrium the rate of interest will be equal to the marginal efficiency of capital, since it will be profitable to increase (or decrease) the current scale of investment until the point where equality has been reached. But to make this into a theory of interest . . . involves a circular argument . . . the 'marginal efficiency of capital' partly depends on the scale of current investment, and we must already know the rate of interest before we can calculate what this . . . will be . . . what the schedule of the marginal efficiency of capital tells us, is, *not* what the rate of interest is, but the point to which output of new investment will be pushed, given the rate of interest.

> It seems . . . that the *rate of interest on money* plays a peculiar part in setting a limit to the level of employment, since it sets a standard to which the marginal efficiency of a capital-asset must attain if it is to be newly produced. (Original emphasis)

As pointed out by Moore (1988b), Keynes (1936) also explicitly criticized the key passage from Ricardo, quoted above, in a way that makes the central issue quite clear:

If Ricardo had been content to present his argument solely as applying to any given quantity of money created by the monetary authority, it would still have been correct on the assumption of flexible wages . . . But if by the policy of the monetary authority we mean the terms on which it will increase or decrease the quantity of money, i.e., the rate of interest at which it will, either by a change in the volume of discounts or by open-market operations, increase or decrease its assets – which is what Ricardo expressly does mean . . . – then it is not the case . . . that the policy of the monetary authority is nugatory or that only one policy is compatible with long-period equilibrium . . . Assuming flexible money wages, the quantity of money as such is, indeed, nugatory in the long period; but the terms on which the monetary authority will change the quantity of money enters as a real determinant in the economic scheme.

A monetary theory of real interest rate, then, presents quite a different aspect than the view in which interest is assimilated into non-monetary concepts such as the rate of time preference or the marginal physical productivity of capital. There are still some problems with Keynes's MEC concept in this regard, however, primarily because of its insistence on retaining the idea of marginal equalities and similar constructs as part of its basic 'metaphysics'. The following section therefore contains some brief remarks on this issue, which prefigure the treatment in Chapter 7 below.

INTEREST AND PROFIT

The further question to be addressed, over and above that of the direction of causality between the different interest rate concepts, is whether, once the rate of interest is seen as primarily a monetary or financial concept, and also the idea of a natural rate in a barter exchange economy is rejected, there is any point in continuing to retain *any* degree of assimilation of non-monetary categories such as marginal productivity or time preference to those of interest. This is clearly the ethos of the optimization problem solved above, and of the various marginal equalities listed in equations (6.12) to (6.14). Also, even Keynes's MEC concept, albeit much clearer than neoclassical ideas on what constitutes interest and what constitutes profit, still retains something of that flavour. But, by accepting that the interest rate 'rules the roost', in Keynes's (1936) phrase, in the sense that causality goes from the financial interest rate to the real economy and not vice versa, is there any merit nonetheless in retaining the marginalist treatment of that causality? If the monetary/financial system is regarded primarily as a system of social relations, in which the money of account, banks, central banks, credit creation and so on are examples of 'collectively assigned status functions' (Searle, 1998), or 'continually reproduced interdependencies' (Lawson, 1997), which in turn enable the productive system itself to function, it would seem more coherent to consistently treat the interest rate as a *different* concept than any type of rate of return to economic activity as such. This then calls into question whether any notion of an aggregative 'rate of profit' is meaningful and, even if it exists, whether it should automatically conform to the monetary rate of interest.

In short, the argument is that interest should be regarded as a different category from that of profit and, in terms of income distribution, as competitive with it. The distinction to be made is that between the return to lending money or financial resources as such, and the reward to entrepreneurial or productive activity. Moreover, the latter is best seen as 'mark-up' or surplus generated on the cost of production (including financing costs), which corresponds to a real phenomenon in the monetary production economy, rather than as an epistemically subjective concept such as time preference or the (unobservable) marginal productivity of a physical asset. The usual argument in favour of the equalization of some notion of a profit *rate* with an interest rate on money is the idea of 'capital arbitrage' (to use a term employed by Nell, 1998).[6] In other words, capital funds might be supposed to be allocated to growth in real assets, or growth in financial assets, depending on the highest rate of return. However, in a world in which there is a clear distinction to be made between monetary/financial activity and the deployment of physical assets, any such forces must presumably be weak as between financial investments of various kinds and the activity of actually organizing production. The latter is a sociologically distinct category. 'Money' can easily be switched between alternative investments, but physical capital, once in place, cannot. From this point of view equity investment can be seen simply as another version of rentier activity (Robinson, 1956). There may therefore be arbitrage between, for example, the returns on fixed income assets and shares, but *profits* themselves are seen as simply the surplus over and above both production costs and all 'financing' costs including dividend payments. And, what is relevant is not a rate of profit *per se*, which in any event is difficult, if not impossible, to calculate on anything except a purely historical accounting basis, but the profit *share* in current income. It should be noted that the maintenance of sharp distinctions of this kind is a key feature of the model presented in Chapter 7 below.

ALTERNATIVE MONETARY THEORIES OF INTEREST: 'HORIZONTALISTS' VERSUS 'STRUCTURALISTS'

The above arguments have made the case that the rate of interest (and specifically the 'real' rate), should be regarded primarily as a monetary phenomenon. The position is complicated, however, by the fact that two competing views on the monetary determination of interest rates exist, which may or may not be compatible with one another. The first of these is Keynes's own theory of liquidity preference, from the *General Theory*, according to which the rate of interest is determined by the relative demand for a given quantity of money and the existing stock of alternative financial assets (bonds). This in turn depends on the strength of the various 'incentives to liquidity', including the 'speculative motive'. The second monetary theory of interest, which is much simpler, is just that the short rate of interest is an exogenous policy-determined variable set by the central bank (Moore, 1988a; Kaldor, 1986; Lavoie, 1984, 1992a). In this case, the money supply is demand-determined and adjusts endogenously, the money supply function being horizontal at the given interest rate. For obvious reasons, Moore (1988a) has described the economists who hold this point of view as 'horizontalists'.

Some of the horizontalist authors are critical of the original Keynesian theory on the grounds that it assumes a fixed exogenous quantity of money, in a way somewhat similar to the monetarist view (Kaldor, 1986; Lavoie, 1984; Moore, 1988a, 1988b). However, other writers, also identified as being within the 'Post Keynesian' camp, have continued to place the emphasis on liquidity preference. This group has been called the 'structuralists' (Rochon, 1999), a term originally used by Pollin (1991). There has, therefore, been some debate on the relative merits of the rival approaches and a number of authors, including Chick (1984, 1991, 2000), Dow (1996), Dow and Dow (1989), Palley (1996) and Wray (1990, 1992), have explored the possibility of reconciling the liquidity preference approach with endogenous money. A number of the issues involved have also been raised in the exchanges between Moore (1989, 1991) and Goodhart (1989, 1991).

Wray (1992), for example, argues that a 'fourth' approach to interest rate determination is required (the other three being the loanable funds theory, Keynesian liquidity preference with exogenous money, and the horizontalist theory with endogenous money), in which both the rate of interest and the money supply are determined endogenously. This approach would differ from the horizontalist theory in that the supply function of money would be upward-sloping rather than horizontal, reflecting the view that, as banks increase the supply of money in response to increases in the demand for credit, they will require higher interest rates as compensation for taking what are perceived to be more illiquid, and hence 'riskier', positions. This argument is similar to that in the earlier work of Minksy (1957). Lavoie (1992b, 1996, 1997), however, defends the horizontal supply of money function on the grounds of (a) the likely beneficial impact of a profitable increase in lending on the bank's equity position, (b) the existence of unused overdraft facilities, and (c) the distinction between the micro-economic and macroeconomic constraints on bank lending. There is a difference between the limits to profitable bank lending in the case of the individual bank and client, and the possibilities for the expansion of the system as a whole, when all the players are expanding in step. In Lavoie's view (1992b, 1996, 1997) the rising supply of money function reintroduces elements of the neoclassical scarcity analysis, and is not compatible with the endogenous money theory. Lavoie (1992b) does suggest, however, that a potential reconciliation between the liquidity preference theory and the horizontalist approach may be effected by recognizing that the effect of the former on interest rates is real, but may be best thought of as a temporary rather than a permanent phenomenon.

Hicks (1989) seems to argue that *all three* main interest rate theories, the real loanable funds theory and the two monetary theories, can be reconciled by the suggestion that each was more appropriate, or would have had the better of the argument, in a specific epoch or stage of evolution of the economic system. Having explicitly discussed Marshall's version of the barter-oriented real interest rate theory, he expresses the point in the following way: 'If Marshall was put out of date by Keynes, has not much the same thing happened to Keynes's own theory, at least in the form he gave it in his most famous book?' As between the two 'monetary' theories, Hicks's point is that the postulated choice between a given supply of non-interest-bearing money and 'bonds' as in the *General Theory* is of little relevance in the present-day environment in which the bulk of the money supply on any definition consists of the 'inside' interest-bearing liabilities of financial institutions. In the days of daily interest chequing accounts and other inno-vated financial products, the only non-interest-bearing money is small change, and as Hicks (1989) put it, at his time of writing 'we are on the way to a credit economy'. The horizontalist theory with endogenous money and exogenous interest rates then becomes the appropriate theoretical vehicle, and Hicks (1982b) has provided his own analysis of the workings of such an economy. There are some difficulties with this evolutionary approach to reconciling the different theories, however. As pointed out by Smithin (1991), whether Hicks was correct in defending Marshall's interest rate theory, even for its own time, for example is problematical. Borrowing and lending was not done 'in kind' even in the nineteenth century, if it ever was. Chick (1991) has also explored some of the difficulties with Hicks's pro-posed reconciliation of the liquidity preference and loanable funds theories.

In the end, it seems to be agreed by economists from a number of different schools of thought, including Dow and Saville (1990), Goodhart (1989, 2002), B. Friedman (2000), Lavoie (1992b, 1996) and Moore (1988a), that the endogenous money approach with policy-determined short rates does reflect the contemporary institutional realities, at least to a first approximation. Moore (1988a, 1988b) also points out that Keynes himself, both before and after the *General Theory*, also frequently made statements to this effect, in spite of his alternative explanation of interest rate determination via liquidity preference. The only remaining debating points would then be, first, whether the setting of short nominal interest rates by the central bank also has an impact on the real rate, and second, what is the relationship between those interest rates directly set by the central bank and the entire term structure of interest rates including long rates. Do monetary policy changes in short rates also ultimately influence the long rates, or is there room for an alternative principle by which interest rates other than those directly controlled by the central bank can be determined? In the latter case, it would be possible for long-lasting discrepancies between bank rate and the interest rates on other assets to emerge.

As for the first point, if the natural rate concept is dubious, it seems clear that central bank power to control nominal short rates of interest should also be thought of as power to control the real rate also. Although the monetary policy instrument is a nominal rate, central bank officials do form expectations about the inflation rate and, for any given setting of the nominal rate, will be aware of the implications for the real rate. Moreover, those expectations will be widely shared, just because they are the central bank's expectations.

As for the term structure of interest rates, one point that is often made in this connection is that so-called 'inversions' of the yield curve can and do occur. Long rates are normally higher than short rates, but situations do occur in which the reverse holds. This situation, moreover, is often regarded as the harbinger of an imminent recession. Such observations, however, are readily explained by the so-called 'expectations' theory of the term structure, and are not inconsistent with the overall pattern of rates being dictated by central bank actions. In the expectations theory, long rates are just a weighted average of expected short rates (with some adjustment for risk). Therefore an empirical observation of long rates lower than short rates would imply no more than that the rise in short rates is expected only to be temporary, or in general that there is uncertainty as to what policies will be followed in the future. This type of observation, therefore, would not negate the view that a consistent and continuing policy on short rates in one direction or the other would eventually cause an adjustment of other rates in the same direction.

Wray (1990), however, also reminds us of Keynes's scepticism, at least in the *General Theory*, that monetary policy would always be adequate to quickly impact the entire structure of rates, particularly in the downward direction. Lavoie and Seccareccia (1988) also discuss this potential 'structural asymmetry', that is, that it may be easier to raise the whole structure of rates than to lower them. As evidence of this, Wray (1990) reports data from the USA in the 1930s when the discount rate fell continuously from 5.19 per cent in 1929, to 2.60 per cent in 1933 and 1.0 per cent in 1939, but a measure of longer bond rates actually rose from 5.6 per cent to 7.76 per cent from 1929 to 1933 and was only down to 4.96 per cent by 1939. It would be agreed, presumably, that the Great Depression of the 1930s was an extreme case in many ways, but, nonetheless, particularly for the 1929–33 period, these figures can evidently be seen as indicating that some factor other than current central bank policy was at work.

One way to reconcile such observations with an underlying endogenous money framework, however, is to recall the assumed hierarchical structure of the financial system. Firstly, there is a central institution whose liabilities define the standard of value and represent the ultimate means of payment of the system, and if this institution is assumed to be always ready to make loans at a given rate of interest, using one institutional technique or another, we would have an endogenous money system in that sense. Also, however, there are a wide variety of alternate media of payment, each of which attracts its own rate of return, and these are all related to the ulti- mate base money in a pyramid of interlocking claims. Under normal circumstances, it might be hypothesized that there will be a fairly stable mark-up relationship between the interest rates set at the centre and those prevailing elsewhere, depending on such things as the costs of intermedia- tion and the perceived degree of reliability of the alternative exchange media. In this context, reliability means the degree of confidence of poten- tial holders that the asset under consideration really is a good substitute for the ultimate monetary asset. Less reliable assets, presumably, would need to offer a relatively higher yield in order to be acceptable, but there is no reason to suppose that the 'risk premium' defined in this sense would itself be a function of the *level* of the base rate. It follows that, in periods in which neither the relative perceived standings of the various claims nor the costs of intermediation are much altered, a change in interest rates at the centre will quickly affect the entire structure of rates (in either direction) as the other players also adjust their rates in line with the traditional mark-ups. However, it is also conceivable that in times of heightened uncertainty (such as the early 1930s) estimates of the perceived reliability of the alternative claims versus the central asset may well change dramatically, such that the premium for holding them increases regardless of what is happening to bank rate. Hence interest rates elsewhere in the system could rise, even if the central bank was pushing in the opposite direction, owing to 'liquidity pref- erence' in this sense.

In a genuine endogenous money system, however, there must be some sort of limit as to how long this divergence can persist. If the central bank is assumed to continue to be ready to lend sums of the basic monetary asset at a new lower rate, it must eventually occur to some arbitrageurs that profits can be made by borrowing at this rate and then acquiring assets (at first at least at the safer end of the spectrum) which temporarily yield the higher rates. This process will increase the demand for the alternative assets and make those already holding them feel somewhat more confident, thus eventually increasing the price and reducing the yield on those assets. A similar process will presumably eventually permeate the whole of the asset structure, at a greater or lesser pace, until the usual differentials are approximately restored. The key issue then is whether the central bank remains ready to lend on demand; if so, this is obviously a somewhat different situation from a panic in which there is literally 'no more money to be had', as in the conventional presentation of liquidity preference with exogenous money. In short, in an endogenous money environment, the central bank should always be able eventually to drive down the general level of interest rates if they so choose, provided they are sufficiently persistent. Lavoie (1992b) sums up generalized liquidity preference arguments along these lines by suggesting that the role of liquidity preference is limited to 'temporary rather than permanent situations'.

CONCLUSION

The most basic conclusion of this chapter would be that in the credit economy there is no natural rate of interest. Interest rates are determined in the financial sector proximately by the decision of the ultimate provider of credit, in other words the central bank. This institution also sets the pace for real interest rates, and not just nominal rates. The real interest rate (on Fisher's definition) is just the nominal rate minus expected inflation. Hence the central bank can set the real rate, if it wishes, simply by adjusting the settings of the nominal rate to offset changes in expected inflation.

The usual argument that central banks *cannot* affect the real rate is based on the assumption that there does exist a natural rate from which the financial real rate must not deviate. An alternative vision is that the central bank itself is the causal factor, through its control over the provision of credit for the whole society. In this case, rates of return on other financial instruments, and also the real economy, must adjust to what is happening in the financial sector as influenced by central bank policy, and not vice versa.

If this argument is correct, the non-neutrality of money (defined, as Keynes said, as the *terms on which* the authorities will change the quantity of money) represents a more fundamental and deep-seated economic phenomenon than the temporary effects which are usually admitted to flow from nominal rigidities and the like. The latter, however, would still continue to be important as a practical policy matter.

Meanwhile the role of traditional Keynesian liquidity preference in a credit economy can be seen as defining the relationship between the 'standard' monetary asset and the other assets that are more or less acceptable. In episodes when there has been a collapse of confidence for one reason or another, we can certainly imagine very high premia being required to persuade agents to hold the alternative assets and, in those circumstances, the ability of the central bank to affect the whole rate structure may well be temporarily restricted. Overall, however, the basic picture is that the institution or agency that controls the supply of the 'most acceptable' monetary asset also controls the basic structure of interest rates.

One task which this chapter has not achieved is to link up this discussion of the impact of monetary policy on the real economy with that of the alternative theories of money and inflation as discussed in Chapters 3, 4 and 5. An attempt to synthesize some of this material is therefore made in Chapter 7.

NOTES

1. Note that Ricardo is using the term 'market rate' in the same sense that Wicksell later used the term 'natural rate'. Wicksell's market rate is closer to what Ricardo means by 'the rate at which the bank will lend'.
2. On this issue, see also Lucas (1980), Epstein and Hynes (1983) and Fried and Howitt (1983).
3. Leijonhufvud (1981) argues that Keynes's liquidity preference theory of the *General Theory* (1936) was a retrograde step from the theory of the *Treatise on Money* (1930), which was a 'stock-flow' treatment. In terms of Figure 6.1, a stock-flow treatment would presumably allow for some influence of the *I* and *S* schedules themselves, instead of just 'drawing a line across the page'. Note, however, that Rogers (1989) shows that there are other reasons to be critical of the construction of these schedules.
4. The references cited in note 2 are also relevant at this point.
5. This is a one-commodity model, which ignores any problems of capital theory.
6. Nell (1998) is one writer who does make a clear distinction between real interest and profit.

REFERENCES

Barro, R.J. (1988), 'Interest rate smoothing', NBER Working Paper No. 2581, May.
—— (1989), 'Interest rate targeting', *Journal of Monetary Economics*, 23, 3–30.
Blanchard, O.J. and S. Fischer (1989), *Lectures on Macroeconomics*, Cambridge, MA: MIT Press.
Burstein, M.L. (1963), *Money*, Cambridge, MA: Schenckman Publishing Co.

—— (1988), 'Knut Wicksell and the closure of his system: critique and reconstruction of the cumulative process', *Studies in Banking Theory, Financial History and Vertical Control*, London: Macmillan.

—— (1995), 'Classical Macroeconomics for the Next Century', unpublished manuscript, York University, Toronto.

Chick, V. (1984), 'Monetary increases and their consequences: streams, backwaters and floods', in A. Ingham and A.M. Ulph (eds), *Demand, Equilibrium and Trade: Essays in Honour of Ivor F. Pearce*, London: Macmillan.

—— (1991), 'Hicks and Keynes on liquidity preference: a methodological approach', *Review of Political Economy*, 3, 309–19.

—— (2000), 'Money and effective demand', in J. Smithin (ed.), *What is Money?*, London: Routledge.

Dotsey, M. and B. Scholl (2000), 'The behavior of the real rate of interest over the business cycle', Federal Reserve Bank of Richmond, Working Paper No. 00-9.

Dow, A.C. and S.C. Dow (1989), 'Endogenous money creation and idle balances', in J. Pheby (ed.), *New Directions in Post Keynesian Economics*, Aldershot, UK and Brookfield, US: Edward Elgar.

Dow, J.C.R. and I.D. Saville (1990), *A Critique of Monetary Policy: Theory and British Experience*, Oxford: Clarendon Press.

Dow, S.C. (1996), 'Horizontalism: a critique', *Cambridge Journal of Economics*, 20, 497–508.

Epstein, L. and A.J. Hynes (1983), 'The rate of time preference and dynamic economic analysis', *Journal of Political Economy*, 91, 611–35.

Fama, E. (1975), 'Short-term interest rates as predictors of inflation', *American Economic Review*, 65, 269–82.

Fried, J. and P. Howitt (1983), 'The effect of inflation on real interest rates', *American Economic Review*, 73, 968–80.

Friedman, B.M. (2000), 'The role of interest rates in Federal Reserve policymaking', NBER Working Paper 8047, December.

Friedman M. (1968), 'The role of monetary policy', *American Economic Review*, 58, 1–17.

—— (1974), 'A theoretical framework for monetary analysis', in R.J. Gordon (ed.), *Milton Friedman's Monetary Framework: A Debate with his Critics*, Chicago: University of Chicago Press.

—— and A.J. Schwartz (1982), *Monetary Trends in the United States and the United Kingdom: Their Relation to Income, Prices and Interest Rates 1867–1975*, Chicago: University of Chicago Press.

Goodhart, C.A.E. (1989), 'Has Moore become too horizontal?', *Journal of Post Keynesian Economics*, 12, 29–34.

—— (1991), 'Is the concept of an equilibrium demand for money meaningful?', *Journal of Post Keynesian Economics*, 14, 134–6.

—— (2002), 'The endogeneity of money', in P. Arestis, M. Desai and S. Dow (eds), *Money, Macroeconomics and Keynes: Essays in Honour of Victoria Chick*, London: Routledge.

Hicks, J.R. (1937 [1982a]), 'Mr Keynes and the classics', reprinted in *Money, Interest and Wages: Collected Essays on Economic Theory*, vol. 2, Oxford: Basil Blackwell.

—— (1982b), 'The credit economy', *Money, Interest and Wages: Collected Essays on Economic Theory*, vol. 2, Oxford: Basil Blackwell.

—— (1989), *A Market Theory of Money*, Oxford: Oxford University Press.

Intriligator, M.D. (1971), *Mathematical Optimization and Economic Theory*, Englewood Cliffs, NJ: Prentice-Hall Inc.

Kaldor, N. (1986), *The Scourge of Monetarism*, 2nd edn, Oxford: Oxford University Press.

Kam, A.E. (2000), 'Three essays on endogenous time preference, monetary non-superneutrality and the Mundell–Tobin effect', unpublished PhD thesis, York University, Toronto.

Keynes, J.M. (1936), *The General Theory of Employment Interest and Money*, London: Macmillan.

Lavoie, M. (1984), 'The endogenous flow of credit and the Post Keynesian theory of money', *Journal of Economic Issues*, 18, 771–97.

—— (1992a), 'Jacques Le Bourva's theory of endogenous credit money', *Review of Political Economy*, 4, 436–46.

—— (1992b), *Foundations of Post-Keynesian Economic Analysis*, Aldershot, UK and Brookfield, US: Edward Elgar.

—— (1996), 'Horizontalism, structuralism, liquidity preference, and the principle of increasing risk', *Scottish Journal of Political Economy*, 43, 275–300.

—— (1997), 'Loanable funds, endogenous money, and Minsky's financial fragility hypothesis', in A.J. Cohen, H. Hagemann and J. Smithin (eds), *Money, Financial Institutions and Macroeconomics*, Boston: Kluwer Academic Publishers.

—— and M. Seccareccia (1988), 'Money, interest and rentiers: the twilight of rentier capitalism in Keynes's *General Theory*', in O.F. Hamouda and J. Smithin (eds), *Keynes and Public Policy after Fifty Years*, vol. 2, *Theories and Method*, Aldershot, UK and Brookfield, US: Edward Elgar.

Lawson, T. (1997), *Economics and Reality*, London: Routledge.

Leijonhufvud, A. (1981), 'The Wicksell connection: variations on a theme', *Information and Coordination: Essays in Macroeconomic Theory*, New York: Oxford University Press.

Lucas, R.E. Jr. (1980), 'Two illustrations of the quantity theory of money', *American Economic Review*, 70, 1005–14.

McCallum, B.T. (1991), 'Inflation: theory and evidence', NBER Reprint No. 1581, August.

Minsky, H.P. (1957), 'Central banking and money market changes', *Quarterly Journal of Economics*, 71, 171–87.

Mishkin, F.S. (1981), 'The real rate of interest: an empirical investigation', *Carnegie-Rochester Conference Series on Public Policy*, 15, 151–200.

—— (1984), 'The real interest rate: a multi-country empirical study', *Canadian Journal of Economics*, 17, 283–311.

—— (2001), *The Economics of Money, Banking and Financial Markets*, 6th edn, New York: Harper Collins.

Moore, B.J. (1988a), *Horizontalists and Verticalists: The Macroeconomics of Credit Money*, Cambridge: Cambridge University Press.

—— (1988b), 'Keynes's treatment of interest', in O.F. Hamouda and J. Smithin (eds), *Keynes and Public Policy after Fifty Years*, vol. 2, *Theories and Method*, Aldershot, UK and Brookfield, US: Edward Elgar.

—— (1989), 'A simple model of bank intermediation', *Journal of Post Keynesian Economics*, 12, 10–28.

—— (1991), 'Has the demand for money been mislaid?', *Journal of Post Keynesian Economics*, 14, 125–33.

Nell, E.J. (1998), *The General Theory of Transformational Growth: Keynes After Sraffa*, Cambridge: Cambridge University Press.

Palley, T.I. (1996), *Post Keynesian Economics: Debt. Distribution and the Macro Economy*, London: Macmillan.

Pollin, R. (1991), 'Two theories of money supply endogeneity: some empirical evidence', *Journal of Post Keynesian Economics*, 13, 366–96.

Ricardo, D. (1817 [1973]), *The Principles of Political Economy and Taxation*, London: J.M. Dent & Sons.

Robertson, D. (1934), 'Industrial fluctuations and the natural rate of interest', *Economic Journal*, 44, 650–56.

Robinson, J. (1956), *The Accumulation of Capital*, London: Macmillan.

Rochon, L-P. (1999), *Credit, Money and Production*, Cheltenham, UK and Northampton, MA, USA: Edward Elgar.

Rogers, C. (1989), *Money, Interest and Capital: A Study in the Foundations of Monetary Theory*, Cambridge: Cambridge University Press.

Searle, J.R. (1998), *Mind, Language and Society: Philosophy in the Real World*, New York: Basic Books.

Sidrauski, M. (1967), 'Rational choice and patterns of growth in a monetary economy', *American Economic Review*, 57, 534–44.

Smithin, J. (1989), 'Hicksian monetary economics and contemporary financial innovation', *Review of Political Economy*, 1, 192–207.

—— (1990a), *Macroeconomics after Thatcher and Reagan: The Conservative Policy Revolution in Retrospect*, Aldershot, UK and Brookfield, US: Edward Elgar.

—— (1990b), 'Empirical and conceptual problems in contemporary macroeconomics', *British Review of Economic Issues*, 12, 73–95.

Smithin, J. (1991), Review of Hicks' *A Market Theory of Money* (1989), *Eastern Economic Journal*, 17, 377–9.

Thornton, H. (1802 [1962]), *An Inquiry into the Nature and Effects of the Paper Credit of Great Britain*, New York: Augustus M. Kelley.

Walsh, C.E. (1998), *Monetary Theory and Policy*, Cambridge, MA: MIT Press.

Wicksell, K. (1898a [1969]), 'The influence of the rate of interest on commodity prices', reprinted in E. Lindahl (ed.) *Knut Wicksell: Selected Papers on Economic Theory*, New York: Augustus M. Kelley.

—— (1898b [1965]), *Interest and Prices*, New York: Augustus M. Kelley.

Wray, L.R. (1990), *Money and Credit in Capitalist Economies: The Endogenous Money Approach*, Aldershot, UK and Brookfield, US: Edward Elgar.

—— (1992), 'Alternative approaches to money and interest rates', *Journal of Economic Issues*, 26, 1–33.

7. An alternative monetary model of inflation and economic growth

INTRODUCTION

This chapter presents a model which combines features of what Keynes (1933) called a 'monetary production economy' and Wicksell (1898) called a 'pure credit economy'. Production takes time and is financed by loans from financial institutions or 'banks'. The nominal liabilities of the financial institutions also represent the only exchange media circulating in the system. The objective of productive activity is to realize monetary profits denominated in terms of bank liabilities. Money is created when loans are extended, and is destroyed via the 'law of reflux' when loans are repaid, thus giving rise to the characteristic problems of the monetary circuit (Graziani, 1990; Parguez, 1996). The argument follows Hicks (1982, 1989) in asserting that this structure is as least as reasonable a simplification of contemporary economic reality for theoretical purposes as (say) the assumption of a pure commodity money economy might have been in the heyday of the quantity theory.[1] As suggested in the Post Keynesian literature on endogenous money (Kaldor, 1986; Moore, 1988; Lavoie, 1992; Rochon, 1999) in such an environment a short-term rate of interest, rather than the rate of growth of an outside monetary base, is the relevant monetary control variable. Moreover, in current conditions the monetary authorities will likely attempt to target the short-term real rate rather than the nominal rate (Taylor, 1993; Lavoie, 2000; Goodhart, 2002). This they can do by continuously adjusting the administered setting of the nominal rate for expected inflation.

A crucial difference between the model presented here and those in the tradition of Wicksell is that there is no 'natural rate' of interest in this framework. In the absence of a natural rate, the implication must be that monetary policy actually sets the tone for real interest rates throughout the system. Moreover, a given setting of the short rate, if maintained consistently, also affects long rates via expectations and the term structure (Moore, 1988; Lavoie, 1996). Although it may be true that 'liquidity preference' considerations do sometimes allow for slippage between those interest rates which are directly controllable by policy and those on other assets, particularly in periods of heightened uncertainty or perceived crisis (Hicks, 1982; Wray, 1990; Dow, 1996; Lavoie, 1996; B. Friedman, 2000), nonetheless it is taken as a basic principle here that the policy actions of the central bank do ultimately set the general level of interest rates throughout the system.

As discussed in previous chapters, controversies about the impact of monetary policy have typically focused on the effects on inflation, on the one hand, and on output growth and employment, on the other. Those theories assuming the existence of natural rates of growth, interest and unemployment tend to focus on the inflationary impact of any monetary policy changes. When the link between money and inflation is the main concern, the impact of monetary policy on output growth is often ignored altogether or, at most, treated as a temporary or transitory phenomenon. We have also discussed, however, competing theories of inflation which present a picture in which these linkages are almost completely reversed. In this type of theory, inflation rather than output becomes essentially a non-monetary phenomenon, and monetary policy in turn matters primarily for the determination of output and employment. As suggested by Smithin (2002) however, in the context of a discussion and critique of Phillips curve-type explanations of the interaction between growth and inflation, these traditionally dichotomous modes of thinking may not actually be the most relevant. Any reasonably comprehensive theory of inflation and growth should be able to explain, equally convincingly, periods of low growth with high inflation, low growth with low inflation, high growth with low inflation and high growth with high inflation. All of these have occurred at various times and places. This chapter models certain suggested macroeconomic interactions in a credit economy framework that may plausibly explain some of these effects. According to our model, monetary policy-induced changes in real interest rates can and do permanently affect *both* inflation *and* output, albeit not necessarily in any clear-cut unidirectional fashion. Higher real interest rates, or 'tight money', will usually tend to reduce growth, but whether or not this will have the desired impact on inflation tends to depend on a complex of other relevant factors. A similar set of remarks might also be made about increases in aggregate demand growth, holding real interest rates constant. An increase in the rate of growth of aggregate demand will tend to increase the growth rate of real GDP in the usual 'Keynesian' fashion, but, whether or not this will be accompanied by higher inflation, no change in inflation or even a fall in inflation, is less certain. Much depends on the behaviour of both the productivity and profitability of industry.

THE FINANCING OF PRODUCTION

Consider a simple one-sector macroeconomic model of production in which a consumption good, $Y(t)$, is produced by labour inputs, $N(t)$. If the coefficient $A(t)$ represents the average product of labour we therefore have:

$$Y(t) = A(t)N(t) \qquad (7.1)$$

In this formulation, $Y(t)$ should be understood as the output of a production process that *starts* in time (t). However, a time dimension can be introduced by assuming that these goods will not actually be available for sale until the next period, $(t+1)$. This is a convenient way of introducing the notion that the overall production process takes time and, importantly, that interest charges are therefore an integral component of final product prices. This one-period production lag will define the basic unit of time in the model. The model also imposes the *ex post* equilibrium condition that aggregate demand equals aggregate supply, so that if $D(t)$ stands for real aggregate demand in time (t), and given the overall lag in the production/marketing process, we may write:

$$D(t) = Y(t-1) \qquad (7.2)$$

This does not imply, however, that 'supply creates its own demand' as the determinant of output produced in time $(t-1)$ will have been the *expected*, rather than the actual, demand for the product in (t), as this was perceived in $(t-1)$. Given the production/marketing lag, the actual level of demand in time (t) will help to determine such variables as the inflation rate and income distribution in that period, but it cannot determine the amount available for sale. This will have become a predetermined variable by the time the actual demand is realized.

The production and transactions structure of the model is a simplified version of that previously worked out by MacKinnon and Smithin (1993), and is contrived so that firms enter each period with a stock of finished goods on hand but no money balances (no claims on financial institutions). Monetary profits received in the previous period are assumed to have been distributed to the owners of the firms before the current period begins. Also the technical nature of the production process is assumed to be such that new production must be started and workers must be paid 'in advance', even before the current period goods market opens. The new nominal wage bill, $W(t)N(t)$, must therefore be financed by borrowing from banks at the prevailing nominal interest charge $i(t)$. Having borrowed the current wage bill, firms will eventually have to repay principal plus interest, which is also denominated in terms of bank liabilities. Allowing for the production lag, however, it may be presumed that the loan contracts will specify that firms do not have to repay principal and interest on the current nominal wage bill until after the goods produced have been offered for sale at the *next period's* goods market.

When loans are extended, expanding the asset side of bank balance sheets, the liabilities side of their balance sheets, and hence the money supply, will expand also. If the notation, $M(t)$, is used to stand for the *increment* to the money supply at time (t), we can therefore write:

$$M(t) = W(t)N(t) \qquad (7.3)$$

When the goods market in (t) opens, the newly created money supply, $M(t)$, will already be in the hands of the workforce in the form of current wages and will be available for expenditure on the supply of goods brought forward from the previous period. Note also that, as loans outstanding from last period have not yet been repaid, last period's increment to the money supply $M(t-1) = W(t-1)N(t-1)$ is still in circulation, in the hands of savers and recipients of other types of income, and is also available for spending as required. There are therefore always two sources of funds from which payment for current spending can be made, the money newly endogenously created in the current period *plus* money endogenously created in the previous period.

When goods market trading in the current period is completed, firms will be in possession of money balances equal to $P(t)Y(t-1)$, which they can then use to retire the principal of loans outstanding from the previous period and pay interest. The remainder will represent monetary profits to be distributed to firm owners. Firms will then be in the same position as they were to start with, that is with stocks of goods on hand but no money balances. Note also that, as the loans from last period, equal to $M(t-1)$, have now been retired, the only money balances available to be carried forward to period ($t+1$) will be the current increment to the money supply, $M(t)$, backed by current period loans. This staggered sequence of loan issue and repayment enables the model to avoid the logical difficulties sometimes associated with endogenous money models in which only the cost of production is loan-financed (Seccareccia, 1996), as discussed in Chapter 5 above. In the present environment two generations of loans are circulating in any period with only one repayment to be made, which means that there will be no problem in generating monetary profits. It is always feasible that monetary profits can be positive as long as new nominal borrowing exceeds the previous wage bill, plus any 'hoarding' of money balances, plus the interest charge inherited from the last period.

For some purposes it is useful to derive an expression for the increment to real money balances in any period as a function of the production carried out during that period. From equations (7.1) and (7.3) above, and dividing both sides by the price level $P(t)$ for period(t), this expression is:

$$M(t)/P(t) = [W(t)/P(t)][Y(t)/A(t)] \tag{7.4}$$

THE DEMAND FOR MONEY

It will be noted that the holdings of 'money' and 'wealth' are conflated in this model, which can be defended on the grounds that some such process is taking place or is already in existence in the real world. However, the formulation must therefore allow for the existence of a stock demand for money in addition to the flow demand associated with financing the wage bill. Loans taken out in period $(t-1)$, for example, will not be repaid until *after* the closing of the goods market in (t). Therefore someone must be willing to hold the associated liabilities of the banking system over the turn of the period. This is, in fact, a convenient device by which the problem of the stock demand for money can be introduced into the present framework, albeit in a rudimentary fashion.

In the present environment, one argument that might be made is that a main reason for holding money balances over to a subsequent period would be to have some additional funds on hand to be able to participate in that period's goods market. These would be held in addition to, or as a substitute for, any sums expected to be obtainable from participation in the upcoming labour market. In textbook terminology, this would be primarily a 'precautionary' demand for money. Agents hold money over the turn of the period as insurance against the possibility of not being able to obtain enough funds for their needs by participating in ongoing economic activity. A simple hypothesis, therefore, would be that the stock demand for nominal balances, deflated by next period's price level, is proportional to the expected real demand for goods next period (which in turn is equal to this period's production). In other words:

$$M(t)/P(t+1) = BY(t), \qquad 0 < B < 1 \tag{7.5}$$

Logically, there might also be expected to be some influence of the (real) interest rate on the demand for money in equation (7.5). However, as 'money' in this model consists of the interest-bearing liabilities of financial institutions, and money balances held over are the only vehicle for saving, it is clear that an increase in interest rates would have a positive rather than

a negative impact on the demand for real money balances held over the turn
of the period (MacKinnon and Smithin, 1993). This is the opposite effect
to that predicted in conventional models of money demand, which assume
a non-interest-bearing money. As the inclusion of a positive interest rate
argument in equation (7.5) would not affect the main results reported
below, it is therefore neglected for the sake of simplicity.

THE SOURCES OF INFLATIONARY PRESSURE IN AN ENDOGENOUS MONEY ENVIRONMENT

For a given level of real wages, determined, for example, by the wage bargaining process, the model sketched in the previous two sections can determine a simple expression for inflation rate of the economy without at this
stage any further reference to details of the production process. The price
level would also be determinate provided that an initial condition can be
specified on at least one of the nominal variables at some date in the past.[2]

For a given level of real wages and productivity, the underlying rate of
inflation can be obtained by lagging equations (7.4) and (7.5) by one period,
and taking logarithms of the results. This will yield the following:

$$m(t-1) - p(t-1) = [w(t-1) - p(t-1)] + y(t-1) - a(t-1) \qquad (7.6)$$

$$m(t-1) - p(t) = b + y(t-1) \qquad (7.7)$$

In these expressions, lower-case letters have been used to stand for natural
logarithms, for example $p(t) = lnP(t)$. Note also that as B (upper case) is a
fraction, b (lower case) must be a negative number. This being the case, it
will be useful in what follows to define a further variable β (where $\beta = -lnB$
$= -b$), with $\beta > 0$. Now the inflation rate can be determined by substituting (7.7) into (7.6). Taking the conventional symbol $\pi(t)$ to stand for the
inflation rate between periods $(t-1)$ and (t), we then have:

$$\pi(t) = \beta + \{[w(t-1) - p(t-1)] - a(t-1)\} \qquad (7.8)$$

The inflation rate therefore depends on a term involving a parameter, β, of
the money demand function (which is positive) and on the gap between the
(log of) lagged real wages and productivity. This view of inflation therefore
does recall various cost-push or wage-push theories of inflation that were
influential in the past. Note, however, that it is the real wage bargain rather
than the nominal wage bargain that matters. In addition, 'liquidity preference' (in some sense) affects the inflation rate. An increase in the original

parameter, B, will reduce β, and hence reduce the inflation rate, and vice versa.

PROFITS, OUTPUT GROWTH AND THE BUSINESS CYCLE

In order to model in more detail the macroeconomic interdependencies suggested above, note that, on these assumptions, a forward-looking estimate of next period's GDP, viewed from the perspective of those making decisions in the current period, will be:

$$P(t+1)\,Y(t)=[1+k(t)][1+i(t)]W(t)N(t) \qquad (7.9)$$

where $k(t)$ is the expected profit share from the sale of current production (actually realized in $t+1$). Equation (7.9) looks at matters from the point of view of those entrepreneurs involved in making the essential 'gamble' or 'bet' entailed in participating in the production process (Parguez, 1996; Rochon, 1999). Now taking logarithms and rearranging, this will yield:

$$a(t)=k(t)+r(t)+[w(t)-p(t)] \qquad (7.10)$$

where $r(t)$ is the real rate of interest prevailing in time (t). Equation (7.10) is an 'interest–wage–profit frontier' (Smithin, 2001), and is arguably the fundamental relationship on the supply side in a money-using capitalist economy. It suggests in essence that the average product of labour must resolve itself into three shares in the functional distribution: the profit share, the real rate of interest and real wages.

To derive a more complete macroeconomic model we make the following further assumptions: (i) that in keeping with the earlier discussion of the monetary framework we can think of the level of real interest rates as being determined essentially by the policy of the central bank, (ii) that real wages will tend to increase with growth, and (iii) that productivity is itself endogenous, and is positively related to the rate of growth.

As for the first assumption, clearly it is not argued that such control will always obtain with complete precision in practice, given the underlying ambiguities of the real rate concept, and the expectational element in defining it. Nonetheless, as mentioned, the view *is* taken that the policy stance of the central bank is what sets the real rate in a 'rough and ready' fashion. It is assumed that, whenever the central bank adjusts its nominal interest rate policy instrument, the majority of economic actors have a definite idea of what this change implies for real rates, as viewed by them from that point in time. We therefore have a 'monetary theory of the real rate of interest', as opposed to a 'real theory of the real rate of interest' (Burstein, 1995).

The second assumption, that real wages rise with growth, is a hypothesis about the determinants of real wages at the systemic level, rather than anything resembling a conventional labour supply function derived from the theory of labour/leisure choice. The argument is simply that the bargaining power of labour is likely to be enhanced in a fast growing economy, a view which goes back at least to Adam Smith (1776) in the *Wealth of Nations*. It is not suggested, however, that the parameters derive from microeconomic labour supply elasticities, or that the employment or unemployment pattern that emerges is necessarily a chosen position on the part of labour. For example, real wages may be determined by:

$$[w(t) - p(t)] = w_0 + hg(t), \qquad h > 0 \tag{7.11}$$

where w_0 is some base level of real wages (determined by sociological and institutional considerations), and $g(t)$ is the real economic growth rate.

The third assumption allows for the contribution of capital investment to productivity, and also for productivity enhancement through such factors as 'learning by doing' and increasing returns. A possible specification in the present context would be:

$$a(t) = a_0 + vg(t-1), \qquad v > 0 \tag{7.12}$$

This allows for exogenous 'productivity shocks', and also an endogenous component, whereby current productivity depends on past growth. As pointed out by Marterbauer (2000) this is in the spirit of 'Verdoorn's law', after Verdoorn (1949).[3] Note, however, that by making the level (rather than the rate of growth) of productivity depend upon GDP growth, the specification does impose an eventual steady state on the model for heuristic purposes, albeit not a 'fixed point' in the sense of a classical or neoclassical natural rate. Now using (7.11) and (7.12) in (7.10), and assuming that the real rate of interest is kept more or less steady at r, by monetary policy, the 'supply side' of the model becomes:

$$k(t) = a_0 + vg(t-1) - r - w_0 - hg(t) \tag{7.13}$$

The variable r has the connotation of a 'target' real interest rate, set via:

$$i(t) = r + \pi(t+1) \tag{7.14}$$

In some ways this is not dissimilar to the orthodox 'Taylor rule', after Taylor (1993), except in not allowing, for simplicity, any feedback from the employment and inflation outcomes. Also, crucially, the intercept in the monetary rule is definitely taken to be a *target* on the part of the monetary authorities rather than a predetermined Wicksellian 'natural rate', as would be the standard interpretation.[4]

AGGREGATE DEMAND CONSIDERATIONS AND THE STEADY STATE

Recall that Keynes (1936), in his classic exposition of the theory of effective demand, used the following notation:

$$D = D_1 + D_2 \tag{7.15}$$

where D_1 was identified as 'consumption', assumed to be a function of current employment, and D_2 was supposedly 'investment'. The latter however, more generally and accurately, could (should?) simply have been defined as that component of aggregate demand, whether destined for the purchase of capital goods or not, which is *not* influenced by current production/employment. If we now use the expression c to stand for the traditional propensity to consume and use explicit time subscripts, a version of (7.15) which can be integrated into the present model is:

$$D(t+1) = c Y(t) + D_2(t+1) \tag{7.16}$$

This argues that some of the income needed to pay for next period's demand for current production will be generated by that production itself, and also that, following Keynes, there is another component of expected future demand which is independent of current production. Given equation (7.1), we can write:

$$Y(t) = [1/(1-c)]D_2(t+1) \tag{7.17}$$

which is a version of Keynes's (1936) and Kahn's (1931) 'multiplier' concept. Now taking logarithms of equation (7.17), lagging the result one period, and subtracting yields:

$$y(t) - y(t-1) = d_2(t+1) - d_2(t) \tag{7.18}$$

where $y(t) - y(t-1)$ is the growth rate, $g(t)$. We might further suggest that expected demand growth will be determined by:

$$d_2(t+1) - d_2(t) = \theta + ek(t) \qquad (7.19)$$

implying that the overall 'demand side' of the model can conveniently be written as:

$$g(t) = \theta + ek(t) \qquad (7.20)$$

Here, θ is the growth of 'autonomous demand' (treated henceforth as a parameter), while the second term on the left-hand side suggests that demand growth will also increase with profitability due to the absorption of output by firms. As mentioned, however (and given equation 7.12, which already allows for ongoing changes in productivity), we still do not need to inquire in too much detail how far this expenditure by firms actually contributes to any productive 'capital stock'. This may well be the intention of some individual firms/entrepreneurs making the investments (whether they succeed or not), and there may also possibly be a discernible aggregative empirical relationship between the total of such spending and productivity.[5] Equally, however, firms may use their surplus simply to absorb goods and services for their own sake (to redecorate the boardroom, buy an executive jet, schedule a sales conference at a golf resort and so on). These types of activities add to demand, but would not be thought of as productive in any technical sense. In the 'Keynesian' tradition, therefore, the demand-creating aspects of 'investment' are taken as seriously as the technical specifications of new machines.

Equations (7.13) and (7.20) constitute a complete macro model which can be solved for the time paths of both GDP growth (the business cycle) and the profit share. The growth cycle, or business cycle, is given by:

$$g(t) = [ev/(1+eh)]g(t-1) + [1/(1+eh)]\theta + [e/(1+eh)](a_0 - r - w_0) \quad (7.21)$$

If $|ev/(1+eh)| < 1$, the system will converge, giving steady-state solutions:

$$g = \{1/[1+e(h-v)]\}\theta + \{e/[1+e(h-v)]\}(a_0 - r - w_0) \qquad (7.22)$$

$$k = \{(v-h)/[1+e(h-v)]\}\theta + \{1/[1+e(h-v)]\}(a_0 - r - w_0) \qquad (7.23)$$

Equations (7.22) and (7.23) therefore summarize the long-run determinants of the growth rate and the profit share, respectively, or at least they do so on the assumption that the original specifications were realistic and that there is no radical change in the underlying social structure over the same long run.

INTERPRETATION OF THE FORMAL RESULTS FOR GROWTH AND PROFITABILITY

The above results can be visualized in a simple graphical framework by constructing the equilibrium loci:

$$k = a_0 - r - w_0 + (v - h)g \qquad (7.24)$$

$$k = (1/e)(g - \theta) \qquad (7.25)$$

Equations (7.24) and (7.25) both illustrate relationships between the profit share and growth rate. Equation (7.25), summarizing the demand side, is upward-sloping in k,g space.[6] The slope of equation (7.24), however, relating to supply and income distribution, is ambiguous. It will be downward-sloping for $h > v$, and upward-sloping otherwise. The issue at stake is the impact of growth on the profit share. In a system which is not 'technologically progressive', and/or in which the bargaining power of labour over real wages is exceptionally strong, growth will tend to reduce profits, because real wages will increase faster than productivity. On the other hand, if growth enhances productivity by more than enough to offset any increases in real wages, the profit share can increase.

There are therefore three possible configurations which, borrowing terminology from the Post Keynesian and 'social structuralist' literature (see Epstein and Gintis, 1995), can be labelled the *profit-squeeze*,[7] *golden-age Keynesian* and *austere neoclassical* cases, respectively. The first of these, with $h > v$, is illustrated in Figure 7.1. As can be seen, in this case there will be a definite relationship between real interest rates, economic growth and profitability. A higher real rate of interest will reduce both the rate of growth and profits; vice versa for a fall in interest rates. Note, however, the specific way in which interest and profit are related in this context. There is no tendency, for example, for any *rate* of profit and the interest rate to be equal, or even for the profit share (net of interest) to move in the same direction as the interest rate. Interest and profit are two different concepts. The fact that an increase in the rate of interest tends to *reduce* the profit share does accord with commonsense notions of the likely impact on industry of monetary tightening, although it clearly differs from what has sometimes been suggested in theoretical discussions.[8] Another Keynesian-style result that seems to follow is that an increase in the (rate of growth of) autonomous demand increases the growth rate of real GDP. Moreover, this is a permanent or long-run effect, as was the interest rate result discussed above. Neither is an artifact of ephemeral short-run rigidities or misperceptions. In our 'profit sqeeze' case, interestingly, the increased growth and employment caused by

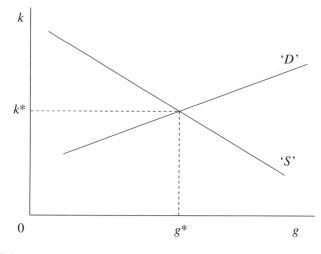

Figure 7.1

a demand expansion is accompanied by a *fall* in profit share, which is why it deserves such a label. In terms of political economy, this may go some way towards explaining the apparent hostility even of non-financial business to 'Keynesian economics' that is often observed in practice. The mechanism by which the fall in profit occurs is simply a question of increased growth improving the bargaining power of labour and hence real wages, thereby cutting into profits. This need not occur, however, in the case of growth stimulated by lower interest rates, as in that case there is space for an increase in both wages and profits.

A more harmonious regime would prevail if $v > h$, but with the slope of equation (7.26) flatter than that of equation (7.25). This is illustrated in Figure 7.2. The system is now sufficiently technically progressive for growth to stimulate an 'adequate' improvement in productivity. This allows the profit share to increase, even though there may also be an increase in real wages. The reason for calling this the 'golden-age Keynesian' case is simply a conjecture that some such conditions may have prevailed during the so-called 'golden age of capitalism' (Marglin and Schor, 1990), in the indus-trialized nations in the third quarter of the twentieth century. Something of the sort would seem to have been necessary to make the putatively Keynesian policies of the period palatable to both 'big business' and 'big labour'. The difference from the more pessimistic scenario is that, as demand growth now causes an increase in both economic growth and profitability, there is no reason for entrepreneurial capital to oppose expan-sion. As for interest rate changes, the same results as before continue to

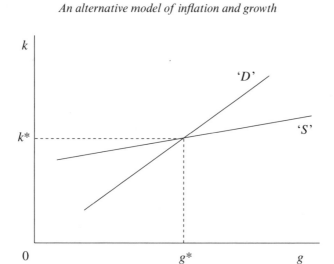

Figure 7.2

apply, so in that respect there still seem to be some potential sources of conflict between 'financial capitalists' and 'industrial capitalists'.

We now turn to changes in the parameters a_0 and w_0. As might be expected, a positive 'productivity shock' (an increase in a_0) always tends to increase both growth and profits. The opposite conclusion holds for an increase in w_0, the intercept term in the wage equation. This latter result requires careful interpretation, however. There is a positive correlation here between *actual* real wages and GDP growth, unlike the case in the much-criticized textbook Keynesian model. The latter only allows a reduction in unemployment if real wages fall. In the present case, growth itself causes the hypothesized increase in the bargaining power of labour. A change in the intercept term, however, a 'labour relations shock', seems to represent a different type of change in labour's bargaining position, that which occurs even in the absence of an increase in economic activity. This may come about, for example, through social legislation favouring labour unions or other historical/institutional changes. An improvement in labour's position in this sense tends to reduce both profitability and the growth rate. Such developments may therefore be strongly resisted by management. Some such mechanism has been suggested to explain relatively poor productivity growth in the well-documented case of Britain before the 1980s (Kilpatrick and Lawson, 1980; Lawson, 1997). Note, however, that this is a different result from those usually emerging in 'canonical' Kaleckian/Post Keynesian models (see Lavoie, 1992), which stress the positive impact of real wages on demand.[9]

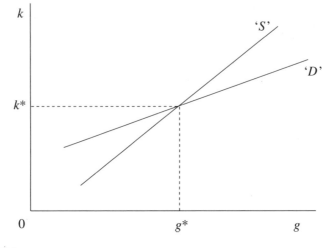

Figure 7.3

In the last of the three potential configurations, illustrated in Figure 7.3, equation (7.26) now has a steeper slope than equation (7.25). This is called the 'austere neoclassical' case because austerity-type policies as recommended by neoclassical economics now seem to work. In other words, a reduction in the demand parameter θ now *apparently* leads to an increase in both the rate of growth and the profit share. So this would be a solution in the spirit of fiscal conservatism, IMF-type policy packages and so on. However, we can also assert that this will not be a viable scenario in practice as the slopes of the schedules now violate the stability condition, $|ev/(1 + eh)| < 1$. Therefore the only two practically relevant scenarios are actually those depicted in Figures 7.1 and 7.2, respectively. Presumably, the best recipe for economic success in a capitalist-type system would be the latter, which requires that the system be technologically progressive in a particular sense.

THE COMPARATIVE STATICS OF MONETARY POLICY AND OTHER MACROECONOMIC CHANGES

From equation (7.24) the comparative static results for steady-state growth can be stated more formally as follows:

$$dg/dr = -\{e/[1 + e(h - v)]\}, \qquad (<0) \qquad (7.26)$$

$$dg/d\theta = \{1/[1+e(h-v)]\}, \qquad (>0) \qquad (7.27)$$

$$dg/da_0 = \{e/[1+e(h-v)]\}, \qquad (>0) \qquad (7.28)$$

$$dg/dw_0 = -\{e/[1+e(h-v)]\}, \qquad (<0) \qquad (7.29)$$

In other words, lower target values of the real interest rate of interest tend to lead to lower equilibrium levels of output growth and vice versa. Similarly, higher rates of growth of autonomous demand lead to higher growth, exogenous technical progress leads to higher growth, and increases in social conflict (a labour relations shock) lead to lower growth.

From the point of view of monetary policy choices, these results suggest that central banks concerned with output and employment outcomes might attempt to pursue a cheap money policy in the sense of stabilizing *real* interest rates at some fairly low level. Also, in terms of other policy options, they suggest that maintaining the pressure of aggregate demand is important for growth and not just for short-run stabilization purposes.

Meanwhile the steady-state inflation rate can also be inferred by combining equations (7.8), (7.11), (7.12) and (7.22) to yield:

$$\pi = \beta + w_0 + a_0 + (h-v)\{1/[1+e(h-v)]\}\theta + \{e/[1+e(h-v)]\}(a_0 - r - w_0) \qquad (7.30)$$

or, simplifying:

$$\pi = \beta + \{1/[1+e(h-v)]\}[w_0 - a_0] + \{e(h-v)/[1+e(h-v)]\}\theta - \{e(h-v)/[1+e(h-v)]\}r \qquad (7.31)$$

which gives rise to the following comparative static results for inflation (recalling that the stability condition $|ev/[1+eh]| < 1$, is assumed to hold):

$$d\pi/dr = -e(h-v)/[1+e(h-v)], \qquad (?) \qquad (7.32)$$

$$d\pi/d\theta = e(h-v)/[1+e(h-v)], \qquad (?) \qquad (7.33)$$

$$d\pi/da_0 = -1/[1+e(h-v)], \qquad (<0) \qquad (7.34)$$

$$d\pi/dw_0 = 1/[1+e(h-v)], \qquad (>0) \qquad (7.35)$$

Interestingly enough, the impact on inflation of a change in the real interest target, for example, will be ambiguous, depending on the sign of $(h-v)$, that is, once again on the relative 'technical progressivity' of the system. For a fall in real interest rates, it is simply a variation on a fairly standard argument current among practitioners in the financial markets to argue that this would be inflationary, even if accompanied by an increase in the growth rate as per equation (7.26) above. This case does in fact occur when we have $(h > v)$. However if, on the other hand, there is a productivity improvement as a result of the increased growth, which is greater than that of any increase in real wages, then the lower real interest rates will not actually be inflationary. There will be higher growth with *lower* inflation. Similarly, we noted that an increase in demand growth (holding real rates constant) always leads to an increase in economic growth. However, this change also may or may not be inflationary. Again, this will depend on the sign of $(h - v)$. The political economy of this latter case is particularly suggestive. For $(h > v)$ a demand expansion will certainly lead to an increase in growth, but also to higher inflation and, as discussed earlier, lower profits. It is therefore easy to see how the view that the boom is 'unsustainable' might gain ground in some quarters. Finally, note that the impact on inflation of changes in either of the parameters a_0 and w_0 is unambiguous. A fall in the former (representing an exogenous positive 'technology shock') will reduce inflation, whereas a rise in the latter will increase it.

The results from equations (7.26) to (7.30) and (7.32) to (7.35) can be conveniently summarized in Table 7.1, illustrating the complete set of steady-state comparative static (or 'comparative dynamic') results relevant to the concept of an inflation/growth trade-off.

From the above it can be noted that there is no question here of a vertical long-run Phillips curve (LRPC), which would suggest that a given steady-state growth rate (or natural growth rate) can be compatible with any inflation rate, and without reference to the other parameters of the system. Instead, in Table 7.1 there are a wide variety of alternative steady-state growth/inflation combinations, each of which could potentially occur. Many different configurations of conventional short-run Phillips curves (SRPC) may also exist, depending on such things as temporary nominal rigidities, misperceptions, and the like, but it should be stressed that the results here refer only to the more fundamental LRPC argument.

Table 7.1   Summary of comparative static results

	dr	$d\theta$	da_0	dw_0
dg	−	+	+	−
$d\pi(h>v)$	−	+	−	+
$d\pi(h<v)$	+	−	−	+

The co-movements of inflation and growth depend upon both the source of the initial 'disturbance' to the economy and the other parameters of the system. For monetary policy (interest rate) changes it is quite possible to observe a positive relation between growth and inflation but also, in some circumstances, a negative one. Similar remarks apply to autonomous changes in aggregate demand growth. For technology shocks the LRPC would always be negatively sloped (in π,g space), whereas a labour relations shock can be one of the possible causes of 'stagflation'. As suggested above, therefore, there are plausible explanations for all of the observed growth/inflation combinations that might occur.

CONCLUDING REMARKS

This chapter has essentially followed the 'horizontalist' literature as in Kaldor (1986), Moore (1988) and Lavoie (1996) in treating the rate of interest as a policy-determined variable set by the administrative decisions of the central bank. The rate of interest is determined outside the ordinary framework of demand and supply analysis, and yet it is pivotal for the behaviour of the rest of the system. Given a policy-determined interest rate, the purpose of this chapter has been to work out the consequences of interest rate changes in a simple model of a credit economy, in which production takes time and the money supply responds endogenously to the financing needs of productive firms. In particular, the focus has been on the impact of interest rate changes and other macroeconomic changes on output growth, profits and inflation. One point on which the analysis differs from some of the earlier literature is that the main channel by which interest rate changes have an impact is mainly from the supply side, via the effect on costs of production. The key relationship in the model is an 'interest–profit–wage' frontier, the characteristics of which depend on such things as the bargaining power of labour, monetary policy and technical change.

It could be argued that more conventional monetary theory such as Chicago-style monetarism, or, as shown earlier, contemporary representative agent models with constant rates of time preference, also have exogenous interest rate concepts (Tobin, 1974; Smithin, 1989), but the policy-determined interest rate discussed here should not be confused with other sources of interest rate exogeneity. In more conventional monetary theory, the real rate of interest is exogenous *to the monetary system*. It would be in the nature of a 'natural rate' supposedly determined in the barter economy solely by the forces of productivity and thrift. Monetary interest rates would then be supposed to conform to this exogenously set standard rather than vice versa. In this chapter, however, the position is reversed, the interest rate is set by the central bank *within* the monetary system, and it is the real economy that must do the adjusting.

One important conclusion that emerges is that, even though the rate of interest is clearly a monetary phenomenon in the sense described above, it still makes a difference whether the authorities seek to stabilize nominal rates or 'real' rates (defined as the rate of interest on money loans adjusted for expected inflation). In the past the usual notion of cheap money policy has been that nominal interest rates should be kept low. If the above analysis is correct, however, the notion of cheap money should be reinterpreted to mean low real rates of interest rather than low nominal rates.

One main result of the analysis is that a cheap money policy (lower real rates of interest) will tend to increase *both* the growth rate *and* the share of entrepreneurial profit. Whether or not this will lead to inflation, however, as would be the usual criticism, is ambiguous. This certainly could occur but there is also a distinct possibility that the expansion would lead to lower rather than higher inflation. In any event, there is no question of 'short-term pain for long-term gain', or vice versa. Even if the opposite policy of 'tight money' did reduce inflation as expected, in that case, to keep inflation low permanently by monetary policy means would also require a permanently depressed low-growth real economy. The model therefore implies that the most sensible policy advice to be given to central banks is that they should aim at a cheap money policy in the sense of low (but still positive) real interest rates. They should follow a 'real interest rate rule', rather than a monetary growth rule or an inflation rate rule. Although such a rule would hardly solve all the economic problems that beset every society, it might well be the least destructive task which central banks could set themselves.

An increase in the rate of growth of autonomous demand, holding real interest rates constant, will tend to increase the GDP growth rate. However, in this case, if the endogenous rate of increase in technical progress is not strong, the same expansion will also tend to reduce the profit share and increase inflation. In a more technically progressive system, the growth/profit relationship may be altered to become upward-sloping. In this case, the rate of increase in productivity is more than enough to offset improvements in the real wage caused by the improved bargaining power of labour. This would imply a more harmonious relationship between labour and entrepreneurial capital, as now both profits and real wages can increase with demand-led growth. Again the 'increasing returns' element in this case would enable there to be an economic expansion without inflation. A fortuitous (exogenous) improvement in technical progress, as in the so-called 'new economy' scenario, will also tend to increase both the growth rate and profitability in a non-inflationary environment. Hence, presumably, one of the incentives for innovation under capitalism.

A final caveat that should be mentioned is that the formal scope of this chapter has been restricted to the closed economy context. Strictly speaking, therefore, any policy advice given would apply to a hypothetical closed economy, the world economy as a whole (from the point of view, for example, of a hegemonic nationally based central bank dominating global monetary developments, or an international agency), or the situation of the leading player in a relatively self-contained trading system with fixed exchange rates. Open economy issues, including the situation of a small open economy with flexible exchange rates, are, however, taken up in Chapter 8.

NOTES

1. As pointed out by such writers as Ingham (2000), Heinsohn and Steiger (2000) and Wray (2000), however, it is doubtful if there ever actually was a time when the commodity money approach was factually correct.
2. The supposed indeterminacy of nominal prices under monetary regimes other than those involving an exogenous money supply has been much debated in the literature. It poses no problem in the framework presented here, as long as an initial condition can be specified.
3. According to evidence presented by Marterbauer (2000) for the European case, the best specification on empirical grounds would involve both lagged and contemporaneous growth terms. However, adding an extra coefficient would not affect the qualitative results worked out below.
4. See equation (5.16) above.
5. These effects and others are already implicitly included in equation (7.15).
6. On the reasons for this see, for example, the discussion of the 'social structuralist' model by Gordon (1995).
7. Smithin (2001) called this the 'pseudo-Marxist case', but this now seems misleading. In Marx there is a falling *rate* of profit, whereas here it is the profit share or aggregate mark-up that is declining. It is not really a meaningful exercise to attempt to calculate any profit rate in this framework.
8. See, for example, the discussion by Mongiovi (1996) of some of the relevant literature.
9. Recall the discussion in Chapter 5 above.

REFERENCES

Burstein, M.L. (1995), 'Classical Macroeconomics for the Next Century', unpublished manuscript, York University, Toronto.

Dow, S.C. (1996), 'Horizontalism: a critique', *Cambridge Journal of Economics*, 20, 497–508.

Epstein, G.A. and H.M. Gintis (eds) (1995), *Macroeconomic Policy after the Conservative Era*, Cambridge: Cambridge University Press.

Friedman, B.M. (2000), 'The role of interest rates in Federal Reserve policymaking', NBER Working Paper 8047, December.

Goodhart, C.A.E. (2002), 'The endogeneity of money', in P. Arestis, M. Desai and S.C. Dow (eds), *Money, Macroeconomics and Keynes: Essays in Honour of Victoria Chick*, London; Routledge.

Gordon, D.M. (1995), 'Growth, distribution and the rules of the game: social structuralist macro foundations for a democratic economic policy', in G.A. Epstein and H.M. Gintis (eds), *Macroeconomic Policy after the Conservative Era*, Cambridge: Cambridge University Press.

Graziani, A. (1990), 'The theory of the monetary circuit', *Economies et Sociétés*, 24: 7–36.

Heinsohn, G. and O. Steiger (2000), 'The property theory of interest and money', in J. Smithin (ed.), *What is Money?*, London: Routledge.

Hicks, J.R. (1982), 'The credit economy', in *Money, Interest and Wages: Collected Essays on Economic Theory*, vol. 2., Oxford: Basil Blackwell.

—— (1989), *A Market Theory of Money*, Oxford: Oxford University Press.

Ingham, G. (2000), 'Babylonian madness: on the historical and sociological origins of money', in J. Smithin (ed.), *What is Money?*, London: Routledge.

Kahn, R.F. (1931), 'The relation of home investment to unemployment', *Economic Journal*, 41, 173–98.

Kaldor, N. (1986), *The Scourge of Monetarism*, 2nd edn, Oxford: Oxford University Press.

Keynes, J.M (1933), 'The monetary theory of production', lecture series delivered at Cambridge University, Michaelmas (Fall) Term.

—— (1936), *The General Theory of Employment Interest and Money*, London: Macmillan.

Kilpatrick, A. and T. Lawson (1980), 'On the nature of industrial decline in the UK', *Cambridge Journal of Economics*, 4, 85–102.

Lavoie, M. (1992), *Foundations of Post-Keynesian Economic Analysis*, Aldershot, UK and Brookfield, US: Edward Elgar.

—— (1996), 'Horizontalism, structuralism, liquidity preference, and the principle of increasing risk', *Scottish Journal of Political Economy*, 43, 275–300.

Lavoie, M. (2000), 'A Post Keynesian view of interest parity theorems', *Journal of Post Keynesian Economics*, 23, 163–79.

Lawson, T. (1997), *Economics and Reality*, London: Routledge.

MacKinnon K.T. and J. Smithin (1993), 'An interest rate peg, inflation and output', *Journal of Macroeconomics*, 15, 769–85.

Marglin, S.A. and J.B. Schor (eds) (1990), *The Golden Age of Capitalism: Reinterpreting the Post-War Experience*, Oxford: Clarendon Press.

Marterbauer, M. (2000), 'Economic growth and unemployment in Europe: old questions, some new answers', mimeo, York University, Toronto.

Mongiovi, G. (1996), 'Some critical observations on Post Keynesian macroeconomics', in S. Pressman (ed.), *Interactions in Political Economy: Malvern after Ten Years*, London: Routledge.

Moore, B.J. (1988), *Horizontalists and Verticalists: The Macroeconomics of Credit Money*, Cambridge, Cambridge University Press.

Parguez, A. (1996), 'Beyond scarcity: a reappraisal of the theory of the monetary circuit', in E.J. Nell and G. Deleplace (eds), *Money in Motion: The Post Keynesian and Circulation Approaches*, London: Macmillan.

Rochon, L-P. (1999), *Credit, Money and Production*, Cheltenham, UK and Northampton, MA, USA: Edward Elgar.

Seccareccia, M. (1996), 'Post Keynesian fundism and monetary circulation', in E.J. Nell and H. Deleplace (eds), *Money in Motion: The Post Keynesian and Circulation Approaches*, London: Macmillan.

Smith, A. (1776 [1981]), *An Inquiry into the Nature and Causes of the Wealth of Nations*, Indianapolis: Liberty Fund.

Smithin, J. (1989), 'Hicksian monetary economics and contemporary financial innovation', *Review of Political Economy*, 1, 192–207.

—— (2001), 'Profit, the rate of interest, and "entrepreneurship" in contemporary capitalism', *Kurswechsel*, 2/01, 89–99.

—— (2002), 'Phillips curve', in B. Snowdon and H.R. Vane (eds), *An Encyclopedia of Macroeconomics*, Cheltenham, UK and Northampton, MA, USA: Edward Elgar.

Taylor, J.B. (1993), 'Discretion versus policy rules in practice', *Carnegie-Rochester Conference Series on Public Policy*, 39, 195–214.

Tobin, J. (1974), 'Friedman's theoretical framework', in R.J. Gordon (ed.), *Milton Friedman's Monetary Framework: A Debate with his Critics*, Chicago: University of Chicago Press.

Verdoorn, P.J. (1949), 'Fattori che regolano sviluppo della produttiva del lavaro', *L'Industria*, 1, S.3–10.

Wicksell, K. (1898 [1965]), *Interest and Prices*, New York: Augustus M. Kelley.

Wray, L.R. (1990), *Money and Credit in Capitalist Economies: The Endogenous Money Approach*, Aldershot, UK and Brookfield, US: Edward Elgar.

—— (2000), 'Modern money', in J Smithin (ed.), *What is Money?*, London: Routledge.

8. The international economy and alternative exchange rate regimes

INTRODUCTION

Up to this point the discussion has assumed the existence of a single self-contained monetary network dominated by a central bank-type institution whose liabilities represent both the standard of value (unit of account) and the agreed ultimate means of payment (medium of settlement) of the system. The liabilities of this institution are the base of an inverted pyramid of other financial assets which may have heterogeneous risk characteristics, but which are generally acceptable as alternate exchange media on varying terms. The interest rate policy of the central bank sets the tone for the structure of interest rates throughout the system.

In the present chapter, however, the closed economy assumption of a single financial network will be dropped, and the focus of the discussion will be the coexistence of a number of competing financial networks, each with a different standard of value and a different financial centre. This then immediately raises issues involving the interaction of the competing centres, the rates of exchange between the different standards of value, and contradictions between the interest rate policies prevailing in each bloc.

FINANCIAL NETWORKS AND NATIONAL ECONOMIES

Historically, the competing networks have been identified with the boundaries of nation states, for the simple reason that the coercive power of the state, including such devices as the power of taxation and legal tender laws, has made state-owned or state-dominated central banks the natural candidates for the role of the financial centre in each jurisdiction. In many cases, therefore, discussion of the interaction between competing financial centres has been coextensive with the discussion of the problems of the international economy and rates of exchange between national currencies.

It is true that the use of a particular standard of value need not be restricted to the residents of a given national jurisdiction. This is illustrated, for example, by the phenomenon of the growth of 'offshore' financial markets. In this situation, residents of one jurisdiction have more confidence in promises to pay denominated in the unit of account set by the central bank of some other network than in those expressed in the standard nominally prevalent in their own geographical area. This does not imply, however, that the interest rate policy of the central institution whose promises to pay are the focus of any considerable offshore market is any the less significant. Offshore markets are obviously not subject to detailed national regulation, but claims arising in such markets are still ultimately promises to pay in terms of the standard defined by the central institution, and interest rates charged by the centre will affect interest rates throughout both the domestic and offshore networks for that reason. In cases where there is a significant offshore market, therefore, the relevant economic space may be better defined by the use of a particular currency rather than the national boundaries *per se*. Nonetheless, the 'international' issues involving the relationship between the competing financial networks, and the policies of the competing central institutions, arise with as much force in the one case as in the other, the difference being that, when offshore markets exist, the spillover effect of changing financial policies on the real economy will be more widely diffused geographically.

Another situation in which a given currency is widely used across what are theoretically international boundaries would be the adoption of a 'common currency', such as the Euro, currently used among the majority of member states of the European Union (EU). It should be stressed, however, that this kind of development is evidently a politically driven rather than an economic process. It involves essentially a redefinition of the political settlement itself, and ultimately the constituents of state power. It is therefore by no means analogous to the Mengerian concept of a single monetary standard emerging from some kind of market process (Goodhart, 1998). From the point of view of monetary economics, a common currency area, such as the 'Euro-zone', will itself become the relevant economic unit. Similar remarks apply to instances of 'official dollarization', currency board arrangements and so forth, in other parts of the globe.

A 'HEGEMONIC' SYSTEM

Referring again to the historical experience, the world economy has in practice often been dominated by a 'hegemonic' system of relationships between the international financial networks (Eichengreen, 1989; Gray, 1992). This is a situation in which, for example, the national central bank of one player dominates the others and effectively sets the tone for world monetary policy as well as domestic monetary policy. This institution becomes effectively the 'world' central bank and its liabilities become the world standard of value and ultimate means of payment. Obvious examples would be the role of the Bank of England and the pound sterling in the nineteenth and early twentieth centuries, and that of the Federal Reserve Board and the US dollar in the mid-twentieth century, particularly during the Bretton Woods era of 'fixed but adjustable' exchange rates from 1944–1971. In more recent times, the dominance of the German Bundesbank over the European Monetary System (EMS), before the advent of the single currency in 1999, also provides a typical example of a concentric system at more restricted (regional) level.

Evidently, the rise of such a hegemon to dominate either the global financial system or a regional system is a similar phenomenon in some sense (albeit on an international scale) to the rise to prominence of an individual central bank on the national scale. Extraordinary financial power accrues to the institution whose liabilities come to be regarded as more reliable and trustworthy than those of its competitors, and eventually come to be taken as representing the standard of value and ultimate means of payment in themselves. It is interesting to note, moreover, that the occurrence of this phenomenon at the international or regional level seems to illustrate that the centralizing tendencies in monetary systems are not only (or rather not exclusively) a result of legal restrictions and acceptability in the payment of taxes, even though the latter do explain why state institutions rather than private institutions have typically performed the central banking function in actual economies. More generally, 'money is a social relation' (Ingham, 1996, 2000, 2001) in both the national and international arenas, as pointed out in Chapter 2 above.

Experience seems to show that the emergence of world or regional 'monocentres', to appropriate a term used by Hicks (1982, 1989), is based on fairly crude indicators of national economic success. Basically, a national economy seems to be able to claim a leading position for its national central bank if it has built up a large excess of net credits of outside nations on which it could potentially draw if necessary. In practice, these claims may well be denominated in the currency of the monocentre itself. Their ultimate significance, however, is that they represent substantive claims (accepted as such) against the real resources of other nations, presumably built up over time by a record of current account surpluses reflected in capital outflow. Once a large credit position has been achieved, the promises to pay of the creditor are apparently seen as more trustworthy and acceptable than those of its rivals, and status as a world or regional monocentre, with concomitant power over interest rates, would then follow.

It has sometimes been suggested, in fact, that such a hegemonic system for the international economy actually turns out to be a more stable and desirable system than one in which there are several players, each with an independent degree of 'market power'. In the latter case the policies of the different players may work at cross-purposes with one another, and they may each deliberately employ so-called 'beggar-thy-neighbour' policies in the struggle for global market share. On this view the hegemon can impose discipline on the international financial system and, by a judicious use of monetary policy in its capacity as international lender of last resort can supposedly steer the international economy between the extremes of inflation and deflation and promote international trade. If one accepts this point of view, this would also support the case for the establishment of some kind of international financial institution (IFI), by political treaty or agreement, which could deliberately play this role of a 'world central bank' (Smithin and Wolf, 1999). This might perhaps be on the model of Keynes's famous international clearing union (ICU) plan during World War II (HM Treasury, 1943), or some new modification or variant of the Bretton Woods system itself (Davidson, 1991, 1994; Grieve-Smith, 1999). Such a system, however, whether it arises by evolution or by deliberate design, will evidently concentrate international financial power in an obvious way, and hence introduce the problem of ensuring that the powerful central IFI always pursues a sensible and stable monetary policy at the global level. This is basically the same problem as that of ensuring that national central banks will always pursue such policies domestically, but 'writ large'.

In effect, the existence of a strong central player means that the performance of the global or regional system will be as dependent on the policy shifts of that key player as the domestic economy is on the policy of the domestic central bank. An inflationary policy pursued by the central player will spread inflation through the global system, and a deflationary policy will cause system-wide economic distress. In the situation where a national central bank of a powerful nation performs the central role, it is frequently also the case that the perceived domestic policy interests of the major player will clash with what seems to be required for the good of the system as a whole, and sometimes with disastrous results. Clear examples of this historically would be the period between the two world wars, when the Bank of England was no longer sufficiently powerful to act as central banker to the world economy and the only feasible alternative centre (the US Federal Reserve Board) was reluctant to assume the role. The inexperienced 'Fed' was arguably responsible for spreading a massive deflation around the world during the Great Depression. Later central bank and general US government policy was arguably largely responsible for the break-up of the Bretton Woods system of fixed exchange rates in 1971–3, apparently as a result of the inflation financing of the Vietnam War. A still more recent example would be the role of the tight-money high-interest rate policy of the German Bundesbank (pursued for domestic policy reasons relating to German unification) in precipitating the crises in the exchange rate mechanism (ERM) of the European Monetary System (EMS) in the early 1990s. In short, the policy of the major player determines the fate of the whole system in both positive and negative directions.

FIXED AND FLOATING EXCHANGE RATES AND CURRENCY UNIONS

The policy debate about the relationship between the competing international financial networks has often revolved around the issue of whether rates of exchange between the alternative standards of value should be 'floating' or 'fixed'. In the case of floating or 'flexible' rates, the exchange rate between any two currencies is determined proximately by relative supply and demand on the international financial markets. In the fixed exchange rate case, the relationship between national currencies is kept within narrow limits according to some international agreement or convention, and domestic central banks must stand ready to take whatever action is appropriate to force the value of the currency to remain within preset bounds. This would include intervention in the foreign exchange markets to buy or sell as large a volume of the currency as required, and also changes in interest rates.

As well as the extremes of fixed and floating rates there have also been advocates of some compromise between the two in the form of a 'managed float'. This is a situation in which exchange rates are floating in principle, but the monetary authorities do take a view about what the appropriate value of the exchange rate should be (against one or all of its competitors) at any point in time, and periodically take action to achieve this. Frequently also, some view would be taken as to the correct speed of the appreciation or depreciation of the currency, if not the absolute level.

As mentioned, another point of view would be to push the concept of fixed exchange rates to its logical conclusion and question whether there is any merit in the different political jurisdictions having a separate currency at all. In other words, there are many who advocate a single currency or a currency union between several states. Even if there are probably very few advocates of a single world currency at this point in time, this has come to pass in the narrower context of the EU. The political developments of the late 1980s and early 1990s (which also had much deeper roots relating to the overall European political crisis of the twentieth century),[1] led to ambitious plans for a single currency in Europe, as embodied in the recommendations of the 1989 *Delors Report* and the 1991 *Maastricht Treaty* (Delors, 1990; Kenen, 1992). These were implemented in the 1999–2002 period.

IMPLICATIONS OF ALTERNATIVE EXCHANGE RATE REGIMES

In terms of the relationship of the other players to some powerful international financial centre, debate about the nature of the exchange rate regime would not actually make much sense if the central institution was genuinely all-powerful and there was therefore no scope at all, under any circumstances, for any of the other centres to pursue an independent monetary policy. More realistically, given that promises to pay denominated in different currencies can never be exactly perfect substitutes, there will usually exist some centres whose promises to pay do independently attract some degree of trust and confidence and therefore in principle have some freedom to manoeuvre to a greater or lesser extent. For such centres, the choice of the exchange rate regime is a matter of great significance. In the case where the monetary system based on a particular financial centre is associated with a traditional nation state, the choice effectively determines whether or not it will be possible to retain even a modest degree of national sovereignty in economic policy making.

Evidently, at one extreme a single currency solution would in principle make the global economy (if applied at that level) or the regional economy (in a more modest experiment) behave much like the individual closed economies discussed in previous chapters. Power over monetary and interest policy would devolve to the single central banking institution that issues the asset representing the ultimate standard of value in the system. As discussed, the economic performance of the entire system would then depend to a considerable extent on the policies, sensible or otherwise, of this all-powerful institution. In practice, there may also be additional difficulties in imposing a common currency solution on jurisdictions which were not previously fully integrated economically, politically and culturally, because of the residual barriers to the mobility of the factors of production that this implies.

A less extreme choice would be a fixed exchange rate regime between jurisdictions which nevertheless retain some degree of political and economic independence. This still implies a voluntary relinquishing of power over monetary policy for most of the jurisdictions concerned. In entering a fixed exchange rate arrangement, these players are essentially agreeing to allow the international centre to set monetary policy for the system as a whole, and they give up whatever independent influence over interest rates would otherwise remain. Once again, the economic performance of the entire system depends on the policy of the central institution, although obviously less unequivocally or permanently so than in the case of a common currency.

Finally, on the assumption that some jurisdictions, which could conceivably pursue an independent policy, continue to exist, either a managed float or, literally, a 'freely floating' exchange rate are solutions that allow them to exercise this option.

At the time of writing, it is probably fair to say that a majority of academics and practitioners, and certainly the financial press in many countries, tend to favour either a fixed exchange rate regime among the major currencies or such arrangements as the common currency in the EU. There seem to be a number of reasons for this. First, and most obvious, is the *apparent* failure of the so-called 'dirty float', which has been in place since the breakdown of the post-war Bretton Woods system. In particular, over the period of the last quarter of the twentieth century and into the twenty-first, fluctuations in the real exchange values of currencies were often extreme, and numerous severe 'misalignments' occurred, to the point where excessive currency movements were widely seen as interfering with the growth of international trade and rational planning decisions at the individual firm level. The straightforward view of business executives is simply that fixed exchange rates or a common currency would simplify the planning task and make life much easier from their point of view. The points rarely seem to be made, however, that perhaps the fluctuations of which they complain were themselves caused by bad policy decisions on the part of the major players (which therefore should be the true focus of complaint), or that they might find that the interest rate volatility, which may be required to stabilize exchange rates in many cases, could be more onerous that the exchange rate fluctuations themselves.

Secondly, there is also a vague sense that structural changes in the world economy at the turn of the twentieth and twenty-first centuries, the much discussed but disparate developments which are often lumped together under the heading of 'globalization', have somehow (mysteriously) made the notion of flexible exchange rates, separate currencies and independent national monetary policies either anachronistic or unviable. In this type of argument, particular stress is laid on recent technological and regulatory changes in financial markets, which have vastly increased and facilitated international capital movements. According to some proponents, these trends have effectively established a global capital market, which supposedly undermines attempts by any individual jurisdiction at an independent policy. It is not usually made clear, however, just who is supposed to set monetary policy and interest rates in this framework, other than worldwide 'market forces'.

Thirdly, and in keeping with the basic arguments put forward in this book, it might be suggested that another important influence on the willingness of academics, politicians, business leaders and even the general public in various jurisdictions to support either a fixed exchange rate or common currency solution is simply the widespread acceptance of an economy theory which asserts that 'money does not matter' for real economic outcomes. If money does not matter, except in transitional periods and for the determination of nominal variables and the inflation rate, there can easily be a perception that control of monetary policy is simply a technical issue, which can easily be turned over to the central bank of a hegemonic power or some supranational bureaucracy with a mandate to reduce inflation. From this point of view, given the other pressures pushing the international community towards increased integration, it might seem that little is lost and much is gained by an increasing centralization and concentration of power over monetary policy. If money does 'matter' however, as argued in different ways in the preceding chapters, it would seem logical that control over monetary policy should 'matter' also.

THE BALANCE OF PAYMENTS AND INTERNATIONAL FLOWS OF FUNDS

As for the implications of greater capital mobility in the modern era, one interesting point to be made is that, in practice, the growth of the global capital market has patently not equalized real interest rates across jurisdictions with different currencies (Lavoie, 2000). Furthermore, it has coincided with a period in which central bank policy over interest rates in the separate jurisdictions has (apparently) been more decisive than ever in its impact on their respective economies. What the changes in capital markets *have* done, of course, is to greatly increase the responsiveness of capital movements to changes in interest rates and other policy indicators, and to ensure that in effect it is developments in the capital account which are the driving force for the evolution of the national balance of payments experience, rather than the current account.

In the broadest possible terms, the overall balance of payments of the domestic economy consists of the balance across the current and capital accounts. The latter reflects new international borrowing and lending and equity investment, and the former comprises the balance of trade in goods and services plus net interest and dividend payments on past capital transactions. In symbolic terms:

$$BP = CA + KA \qquad (8.1)$$

where *BP* stands for 'balance of payments', *CA* for 'current account' and *KA* for 'capital account'. In a fixed exchange rate system, it is possible for an overall surplus or deficit on the balance to occur and this will be reflected in changes in the level of foreign exchange reserves held by the domestic central bank. This can be termed 'official financing' or *OF*. When there is a balance of payments surplus, official holdings of foreign exchange reserves will increase, and they will decrease if there is a balance of payments deficit. In other words:

$$OF = BP = CA + KA \qquad (8.2)$$

In a pure floating rate system, however, the domestic authorities will not intervene in the foreign exchange markets, and overall deficits or surpluses in the balance of payments will not emerge (as they are always eliminated by exchange rate changes). Hence there will be no change in the official holdings of foreign exchange rate reserves. In this case:

$$OF = BP = 0 \qquad (8.3)$$

This situation rarely occurs in practice, because there is never a 'pure' float. Floating rate regimes are almost always 'managed floats' or 'dirty floats'. However, the theoretical case of the pure float, in which equation (8.3) holds, does unambiguously establish the general principle embodied in the next expression, which is obtained from equations (8.2) and (8.3) combined:

$$CA = -KA \qquad (8.4)$$

The general principle is simply that the current account usually moves in the opposite direction to the capital account. This will also be true even outside the case of the pure float, up to a correction for changes in the volume of official financing. Moreover, the latter will typically not be large enough to upset the basic relationship. The main point in making this observation is that in former years many economists implicitly visualized the direction of causality in the balance of payments flowing from the current account to the capital account. An improvement in 'competitiveness' would lead to a current account surplus. Roughly speaking, exports would be greater than imports, and the nation as a whole would be 'earning' more than it was spending. It would then be natural to find outlets to invest these surplus funds abroad, causing capital outflow. A nation 'living beyond its means', on the other hand, with a negative current account, would be forced to borrow abroad to make up the difference, thus causing capital inflow. This is the standard way of looking at the process. One of the results of the increased international mobility of capital in recent years, however, has been to make it clear that, if anything, the causality now apparently flows the other way. Capital account developments dominate the current account, rather than the other way around, and the trade performance of the nation seems to emerge almost as a side-effect of what is happening on the capital account. This may be an undesirable and uncomfortable development for all sorts of reasons, but, on the other hand, it is not clear that this points to the conclusion that the national economies should respond by giving up whatever control over monetary policy they still possess. Paradoxically, the scenario outlined here may imply that domestic monetary policy becomes more powerful rather than less. An increase in domestic real interest rates, for example, would cause rapid capital inflow and a real appreciation of the currency, and hence do further damage to the export and import-competing industries over and above that caused by the rise in interest rates in the first place. This result would logically seem to be an argument for careful thought about what a sensible monetary policy might be in the new environment, rather than for abandoning the control of the remaining monetary levers to the central bank of some other powerful nation, or to an international bureaucracy.

The balance of payments numbers discussed above can be linked up with the standard macroeconomic national accounts framework by noting the following definition of gross domestic product (GDP):

$$GDP = Y = C + I + G + (X - IM) \tag{8.5}$$

where C stands for consumption, I for investment spending, G for government spending and $(X - IM)$ for 'net exports'. For an open economy, however, it is important to distinguish between gross national product (GNP) and GDP, as follows:

$$GNP = Y + R \tag{8.6}$$

where R is 'foreign investment income', identified above as one of the two main components of the current account, which can be positive or negative depending on whether the domestic economy is a net creditor or net debtor nation. The point is that in the open economy 'national income' can be either greater or less than what is produced domestically, depending on the foreign credit position. Finally, by definition:

$$GNP = C + Sv + T \tag{8.7}$$

where Sv is saving,[2] and T is total tax collection.

Using equations (8.5), (8.6) and (8.7), cancelling the 'C's, and rearranging, we arrive at the following familiar expression:

$$(G - T) + (I - Sv) = (IM - X) - R \qquad (8.8)$$

or:

$$(G - T) + (I - Sv) = -CA \qquad (8.9)$$

where $G - T$ is the government budget deficit, $I - Sv$ is the domestic investment/savings balance and CA, as before, is the current account. This identity was the basis for the so-called 'twin deficits' argument, popular in the USA during the 1980s. This was the suggestion that a government budget deficit must inevitably lead to a current account deficit on the balance of payments. If $G - T$ stands for the government budget deficit and it is a positive number (government expenditures greater than taxation), and if we can also assume that $I = Sv$, or close to it, then there must be a positive number on the left-hand side of the equation. But this is the *negative* of the current account, so that the current account itself must be in deficit. Hence a government budget deficit 'leads to' a current account deficit. The flaw in the argument, however, is blatantly obvious (which did not stop it from being highly influential towards the end of the twentieth century), as there is no warrant for the $I = Sv$ assumption on which it depends. Evidently, a government budget deficit can be associated with a current account deficit, a current account surplus or a neutral position on current account, depending on the sign and magnitude of $I - Sv$.

Possibly, therefore, a more meaningful version of equation (8.9) would be:

$$[(G - T) + I] - Sv = KA - OF \qquad (8.10)$$

This now says, reasonably enough (at least as far as the algebra is concerned), that, if domestic saving is not enough to finance *both* the budget deficit *and* domestic investment, the funds must either be borrowed from abroad (positive capital inflow) or obtained from sales of foreign exchange reserves, with the latter again necessarily small in magnitude. These relationships are sometimes expressed by saying that 'net national dissaving' must be financed either by capital inflow or by sales of foreign exchange reserves. Again, this way of describing things puts the emphasis on the capital account as the active element in balance of payments developments. Net national dissaving will lead to capital inflow, which in turn leads to a current account deficit (presumably via exchange rate changes).

INTEREST RATES, EXCHANGE RATES AND CAPITAL MOBILITY

The usual starting point for a more detailed discussion of the relationship between monetary policy, the exchange rate regime and international capital flows is the so-called 'covered interest parity' (CIP) condition:

$$i(t) - i^*(t) = [F(t+1) - S(t)]/S(t) = f(t+1) - s(t) \qquad (8.11)$$

where $S(t)$ is the nominal 'spot' exchange rate at time (t), defined as the domestic currency price of one unit of foreign exchange, $F(t+1)$ is the forward exchange rate quoted for delivery of foreign exchange at time $(t+1)$ (defined symmetrically) and $i^*(t)$ is the foreign or 'world' nominal interest rate prevailing at time (t). Lower-case letters stand for the logarithm of the corresponding upper case variable. A rather stronger condition would be 'uncovered interest parity' (UIP), or:

$$i(t) - i^*(t) = s'(t+1) - s(t) \qquad (8.12)$$

where $s'(t+1)$ is the expected future spot rate (that is, the spot rate, which, as of time t, is expected to prevail in $t+1$). Note that, if CIP and UIP are both supposed to hold, then by definition it must be true that:

$$f(t+1) = s'(t+1) \qquad (8.13)$$

This would be a result consistent with rational expectations or efficient markets theory, and would indicate that the forward exchange rate corresponds exactly to the market's 'best guess' of what the future spot rate will turn out to be.

Another key element in the orthodox or 'neoclassical' approach to the foreign exchanges is the concept of 'purchasing power parity' (PPP), which dates back at least to the work of Marshall and Cassel more than a century ago (Pressman, 1999). This has to do with the *real* exchange rate between any two different currencies, which is defined as:

$$Q(t) = S(t)P^*(t)/P(t) \qquad (8.14)$$

where $P(t)$ and $P^*(t)$ are the aggregate price levels prevailing in the domestic economy and the rest of the world, respectively. Taking logarithms, the log of the real exchange rate will be:

$$q(t) = s(t) + p^*(t) - p(t) \qquad (8.15)$$

The purchasing power parity doctrine asserts, symmetrically with other elements of orthodox monetary theory as discussed in previous chapters, that the relative price of foreign and domestic goods $q(t)$ is indeed a 'real' variable corresponding to the terms of trade derived from a barter-oriented international trade model. Hence, as with the case of the natural rate of interest discussed earlier, by assumption it cannot permanently be changed by purely monetary factors. Two versions of PPP are usually mentioned in the textbooks, 'absolute PPP' and 'relative PPP'. In absolute PPP, which is also known as the 'law of one price', the value of the real exchange rate is taken to be $Q=1$ (or $q=0$), which implies that price should literally be equal in the different jurisdictions when adjusted for exchange rates. The concept of relative PPP is (somewhat) more realistic, in the sense that it simply asserts that Q is a constant rather than being identically equal to one. This then supposedly allows for any 'genuine' reasons why the real price of goods would differ in one jurisdiction versus another, which would include transportation costs, the presence of non-traded goods and so forth. But, again, the point is that monetary policy *per se* is not supposed to affect these underlying relative prices. In what follows, it will obviously be most convenient to identity the orthodox model with $Q=1$, but note that this makes no difference to the basic argument. Therefore, letting $Q=1$ and $q=0$, the spot exchange rate must be given by:

$$s(t)=p(t)-p^*(t) \tag{8.16}$$

Now recall the definition of the nominal interest rate as the real interest rate plus expected inflation:

$$i(t)=r(t)+[p'(t+1)-p(t)] \tag{8.17}$$

A symmetrical definition must also apply to the foreign nominal interest rate. Therefore, using these definitions in equation (8.12), we can derive:

$$\{r(t)+[p'(t+1)-p(t)]\} - \{r^*(t)+[p^{*\prime}(t+1)-p^*(t)]\} =s'(t+1)-s(t) \tag{8.18}$$

and, using (8.16) the PPP condition, to define both $s(t)$ and $s'(t+1)$, this will reduce to:

$$r(t)=r^*(t) \tag{8.19}$$

This is the condition of *real interest rate parity* (RIP) which, in effect, transfers the doctrine of the 'natural rate of interest' to the international setting.

On these assumptions, for any jurisdiction but a hegemonic centre as described above there is no possibility of any independent control over the real rate of interest. Interest rates in the small open economy must conform to interest rates established in 'world markets' or by some world central bank.

A CRITIQUE OF INTEREST PARITY AND PURCHASING POWER PARITY ASSUMPTIONS

If the condition of real interest parity holds, this would seem to preclude the domestic central bank from having any influence over the real rate of interest in its own jurisdiction, and hence render any analysis of monetary policy worked out in the closed economy context (as in Chapter 7 above) redundant. However, and as has been seen elsewhere in our discussion of alternative visions of the monetary economy, such a conclusion is based in an essential way on the sequence of progressively stronger assumptions which are needed to derive it. If any of those assumptions can be challenged and is questionable, the final conclusion may be subject to a decisive challenge also.

In the present case, it seems to be generally conceded on all sides that the CIP assumption embodied in equation (8.12) is accurate. One argument is that this is simply the logical consequence of 'perfect capital mobility' in the current global economy. If there are few political or technological barriers to the movement of financial capital around the world, a simple arbitrage argument suffices to establish that rates of return on assets of similar risk characteristics and maturities should be equal when covered by a forward contract. Lavoie (2000) however, on the contrary, argues that the CIP condition is simply a consequence of 'mark-up pricing' in the international as well as the domestic arena. This is based on the 'cambist' approach to the forward exchanges put forward by Coulbois and Prissert (1974). According to these authors, interest rates are not endogenous variables but, as in the Post Keynesian horizontalist view, are determined by the monetary authorities in the respective jurisdiction. This then dictates what the forward premium should be. The commercial banks charge their customers on forward market a mark-up over the spot rate, which reflects the interest differential, plus a small 'turn' on the buying and selling quotes for forward exchange for their own profit. In this case, equation (8.12) might better be rewritten to read:

$$f(t+1) - s(t) = i(t) - i^*(t) \tag{8.20}$$

which is obviously not different in substance from equation (8.12), but is nonetheless important from an interpretive point of view.

Where the orthodox model is on weaker ground, however, is not in the assumption that CIP always holds, but in the additional assumption that UIP always holds also. This implies that rates of return in different centres can be equal even when *not* covered by a forward contract, or, equivalently, that the forward exchange rate and the consensus expectation of the future spot rate are always equal. But there seems to be no good reason to argue this. In practice, even in conditions in which financial capital is completely mobile in a technical sense, this condition can only hold up to the inclusion of what is usually called a 'currency risk premium' (Frankel, 1992), which is required by foreign investors if they are to hold assets denominated in the domestic currency. Even if financial capital can cross borders electronically 'at the push of a button', it must still be the case that assets denominated in different currencies, and whose exchange rates are liable to change, are still not perfect substitutes. Even given 'perfect capital mobility' there need not be 'perfect asset substitutability'. It continues to matter, in other words, precisely whose promises to pay the investor holds at any given moment (US dollars, Canadian dollars, Mexican pesos, Euros or yen). Following this line of thought, if $z(t)$ is the currency risk premium we therefore have:

$$i(t) - i^*(t) = s'(t+1) - s(t) + z(t) \tag{8.21}$$

or (consistent with equation 8.20):

$$s'(t+1) - s(t) + z(t) = i(t) - i^*(t) \tag{8.22}$$

These equations state that domestic interest rates can deviate from foreign interest rates by an amount equal to the expected depreciation or appreciation of the currency plus the risk premium.

The other dubious assumption in arriving at the RIP result above was the concept of purchasing power parity itself. Empirically, it is well known that exchange rates more often deviate from the supposed PPP levels (absolute or relative) than not (Lavoie, 2000). Consistent with the arguments developed elsewhere in this volume, to explain this it can be argued that, in a *monetary* international economy, the real exchange rate $q(t)$ must itself be a monetary variable rather than a 'real' variable determined by the barter terms of trade. In other words, the real exchange rate is itself an endogenous variable, and must therefore in principle be subject to manipulation by public policy. The barter terms of trade must conform to the real exchange rate, rather than the other way around. Therefore (because equilibrium q is not a constant) there is no meaning in the PPP theorem in its usual sense.

Substituting the simple definitions of both the current and expected future real exchange rate, and of domestic and foreign real interest rates into equation (8.21), it can be shown that real interest rate parity generally does not hold. The real interest differential will be:

$$r(t) - r^*(t) = q'(t+1) - q(t) + z(t) \tag{8.23}$$

or again, if the interest rates are taken to be the independent variables:

$$q'(t+1) - q(t) + z(t) = r(t) - r^*(t) \tag{8.24}$$

In other words, real interest rates in the domestic economy can deviate from those elsewhere by an amount equal to the expected *real* appreciation or depreciation of the currency and the risk premium. So we cannot rule out *a priori* a monetary policy that aims at different real interest rates than those prevailing in the rest of the world, as long as separate currency systems continue to exist and exchange rates (at least potentially) are free to move.

CAPITAL OUTFLOW OR 'CAPITAL FLIGHT'?

The above argument further suggests that the real question about the effects of increased international capital mobility in modern times is the issue of whether or not, in the new environment, a concerted attempt to lower domestic real interest rates relative to those elsewhere will always lead to instability. Does equation (8.23) or (8.24) mean that it is only possible to keep real rates lower than those elsewhere if the real exchange rate (as defined) is expected to fall continuously? This would mean a continuous expected real appreciation of the currency, which might well be regarded as implausible in the circumstances.

However, Paraskevopoulos *et al.* (1996) and Paschakis and Smithin (1998) have shown that, if an individual national economy does succeed in depressing real interest rates to a lower level than prevails elsewhere, although the final result is certainly a permanent real depreciation of the currency and an increase in the real net foreign credit position, the process is *not* necessarily unstable. Moreover, this conclusion holds precisely in the conditions under discussion here, that is in the modern environment with few or no barriers to capital mobility except the basic condition that promises to pay denominated in different currencies are not perfect substitutes. The point is that the increase in the foreign credit position may actually have a beneficial impact on the risk premium demanded by foreign investors to hold assets denominated in the domestic currency (see also Branson,

1988), and this enables the gap between foreign and domestic real interest rates to be maintained.

In what follows, let $D(t)$ stand for the real net foreign debt of the domestic economy,[3] that is, the opposite of the foreign credit position. A positive capital account (increased net foreign borrowing) will obviously increase $D(t)$. In terms of our previous notation, this implies that equation (8.4) can now be rewritten as:

$$D(t) - D(t-1) = -CA \qquad (8.25)$$

This states that capital inflow (an increase in the foreign debt) will be associated with a deficit on current account, and vice versa.

What was suggested above is that the risk premium is a negative function of the real net foreign credit position of the domestic economy, and hence a positive function of the real net foreign debt position. This might be defended, for example, on the straightforward grounds that a greater degree of trust and confidence attaches to promises to pay denominated in the currency of a creditor nation than in that of a debtor nation. In other words:

$$z(t) = z[D(t)]. \qquad z_D > 0 \qquad (8.26)$$

In this case, given a stable solution to the system, such that $q'(t+1) - q(t) = D(t) - D(t-1) = 0$ in equilibrium, in other words if the real exchange rate does not appreciate or depreciate indefinitely after a shock, domestic interest rates can permanently differ from foreign interest rates according to:

$$z(D) = r - r^* \qquad (8.27)$$

where D (with no time subscript) is the equilibrium net foreign debt position.

Lower domestic real interest rates will certainly lead to capital outflow and a real depreciation of the currency as the usual arguments suggest, but the reason why the process need not be unstable is that the negative impact on the capital account is not necessarily a 'bad thing' from the point of view of the credit rating of the domestic economy. In the first place, the current account will improve, as suggested above. Moreover, it should also be recalled that another name for capital outflow, after all, is 'foreign investment'. If this does not become actual 'capital flight' in which both the capitalists and their funds decamp, the domestic country experiencing capital outflow is building up a net credit position with the rest of the world which will generate a future flow of interest and dividend income to domestic residents. To the extent that the promises to pay of creditor nations are regarded as relatively more trustworthy and reliable than those of debtor nations, this may improve the international status of the currency rather than damage it. If low real interest rates are also good for output and employment, there may therefore be a 'virtuous cycle' in nations with low (but still positive) real rates of interest.

To take account of the case where there *is* a danger of capital flight, and of 'international liquidity preference' considerations (Dow, 1999) more generally, note that Paschakis (1993) suggests a simple linear functional form to characterize $z(t)$, as below:

$$z(t) = z_0 + z_1 D(t) \tag{8.28}$$

which in equilibrium would yield:

$$z(D) = z_0 + z_1 D \tag{8.29}$$

So changes in the parameter z_0 could be used to capture (heuristically at least) any dramatic changes in the reputation of a currency for non-economic reasons.

FIXED EXCHANGE RATES AND THE DOMESTIC RATE OF INTEREST

We should note that, in a 'credible' fixed exchange rate regime, it remains true that the domestic monetary authorities do lose control of the domestic rate of interest. In such an environment, the nominal exchange rate is not expected to change so that $s'(t+1) - s(t) = 0$. Also, if the regime really is credible, in the sense that is confidently expected to hold without reservation, then by definition $z(t) = 0$ also. Therefore, from equation (8.21) or (8.22), it would be the case that:

$$i(t) = i^*(t) \tag{8.30}$$

In this situation the domestic nominal interest cannot deviate from the 'world' rate (or, in the case of a currency union, the rate set by the supranational central bank) and there is no domestic control over monetary policy. This is actually a traditional conclusion of the literature on fixed exchange rates. However, the definition of a credible fixed exchange rate regime used here is, of course, very strong, and in the case where there is some doubt about the permanence of the regime, or if periodic adjustments are allowed, the conclusion is softened. There would now be some scope for a forward market and a currency risk premium. Suppose, for example, that the exchange rate is not actually expected to change, but there is some residual doubt about this. In such a case:

$$z(t) = i(t) - i^*(t) \qquad (8.31)$$

However, to achieve this degree of policy independence under fixed exchange rates implies that the regime itself must be less than perfect in some sense. There must be an 'escape clause' or some doubt about the authorities' willingness to make a permanent commitment. Therefore, in either an irrevocable fixed exchange rate regime or a currency union, nominal interest rates will be the same in all jurisdictions. Real interest rates could still fortuitously differ if there were any residual inflation differentials (Marterbauer and Smithin, 2000), but (by definition again) in that case there would still be no scope for domestic monetary policy to influence either the inflation rate or domestic real rates. In general, in the absence of such residual inflation differentials, we would have $q'(t) = q(t)$, and hence, from equation (8.23) or (8.24):

$$r(t) = r^*(t) \qquad (8.32)$$

The conclusion is therefore that the more binding is the fixed exchange rate regime, the more this robs the domestic economy of the ability to conduct an independent policy. But note that the arguments often advanced in favour of currency unions, dollarization, unilateral exchange rate pegs or a global fixed exchange rate regime tend to be highly disingenuous in this respect. If seems frequently to be argued that *because of* globalization, capital liberalization and so on in the contemporary world, the individual jurisdictions already have little or no room to manoeuvre as far as monetary policy is concerned, and so it would seem that little is lost from the domestic policy point of view by accession to such arrangements. As shown above, however, quite the opposite is true: it is the currency arrangements themselves which are decisive, even in the modern world of 'perfect capital mobility'. In fact, this conclusion is only logical in the context of monetary economies in which money does 'matter'.

CONCLUSION

The premise of this chapter, as throughout the book, is that the conduct of monetary policy, specifically control over interest rates, is one of the most important determinants of real economic outcomes such as the level of output and employment. Therefore (even, it can be argued, in the context of supranational trading organizations such as the EU) it follows that those national economic authorities which retain political accountability for the economic well-being of their citizens might be well advised to retain control of monetary policy in so far as this is possible.

There is obviously no guarantee that in any individual case the performance of a national authority would always be an improvement on that of a supranational central bank in a currency union or the leading player (the key currency nation) in a fixed exchange rate system. However, the retention of separate national currencies, which either float or are at least subject to periodic revaluations, does at least allow for a possible escape route from the straitjacket that a centralized monetary policy could become. It is difficult to believe that the point will never arrive in the development of trading relationships at the global or regional level at which the priorities of the national unit will differ from those of policy makers at the centre. It also seems to be an important consideration that a *national* central bank may be at least somewhat more responsive to the political will of those directly affected by their policies. Although it is often suggested that one of the advantages of a supranational institution is that it is far more removed from the political process (and therefore, presumably, from the perspective of orthodox economics, free to impart a *deflationary* bias to its policies), the opposite point of view can also be taken on the grounds of basic democratic principles.

It is not suggested that either central banks or international organizations should be unconcerned with inflation.[4] However, there is an implied judgment in these remarks that in the recent past central bankers have tended to overemphasize the role of the monetary authorities in controlling inflation and to neglect the real impact of their policies. In the contemporary environment, these tendencies would likely be reinforced in fixed exchange rate regimes or by the setting up of supranational monetary authorities remote from the political process. The popular opinions that the benefits of free trade arrangements and the like cannot be obtained without monetary integration, and/or that an independent national monetary policy is impossible in the current global environment, have not been subject to proper critical scrutiny. Similarly, those who fear that the substantial exchange rate misalignments are an inevitable consequence of moving away from rigidly fixed exchange rate regimes essentially misinterpret what have often been the policy-driven causes of those misalignments.

It would certainly be true, on the other hand, that commitments by trading partners each to pursue stable macroeconomic policies leading to prosperity and full employment would themselves prevent dramatic fluctuations in exchange rates. And, frequently, such a commitment might well dictate very much the same policy responses regardless of the nature of the exchange rate regime. However, if it is important for economic prosperity that real interest rate fluctuations be kept within reasonable bounds, it is precisely this that may be impossible in a completely integrated system in which the views of the policy makers at the centre dictate otherwise. Existing nation states therefore (unlike many of those in contemporary Europe) may be well advised to retain whatever monetary sovereignty they can, so that interest rates can be set as far as possible with domestic policy priorities in mind. This would seem to be an increasingly important requirement in the face of the structural changes that are currently driving the world economy, rather than the reverse.

NOTES

1. See, for example, the discussion by Parguez (2000).
2. We use Sv to stand for saving in this chapter, as the previous symbol, S (from Chapter 5), will now stand for the 'spot exchange rate'.
3. Again, there is a change in notation to be reported here. In chapter 7 above, D was used for a different concept, namely real aggregate demand.
4. But see Chapters 7 and 9 for a more nuanced interpretation of the role played by inflation under capitalism.

REFERENCES

Branson, W.H. (1988), 'Sources of misalignment in the 1980s', in R.C. Marston (ed.), *Misalignment of Exchange Rates: Effects on Trade and Industry*, Chicago: University of Chicago Press.

Coulbois, P. and P. Prissert (1974), 'Forward exchange, short term capital flows and monetary policy', *De Economist*, 122, 283–62.

Davidson, P. (1991), 'What international payments scheme would Keynes have suggested for the twenty-first century?', in P. Davidson and J. Kregel (eds), *Economic Problems of the 1990s: Europe, the Developing Countries and the United States*, Aldershot, UK and Brookfield, US: Edward Elgar.

—— (1994), *Post Keynesian Macroeconomic Theory: A Foundation for Successful Economic Policies for the Twenty-First Century*, Aldershot, UK and Brookfield, US: Edward Elgar.

Delors, J. (1990), 'Economic and monetary union at the start of stage one', *The Journal of International Securities Markets*, Autumn.

Dow, S.C. (1999), 'International liquidity preference and endogenous credit', in J. Deprez and J.T. Harvey (eds), *Foundations of International Economics: Post Keynesian Perspectives*, London: Routledge.

Eichengreen, B. (1989), 'Hegemonic stability theories of the international monetary system', in R.N. Cooper (ed.), *Can Nations Agree?*, Washington, DC: The Brookings Institution.

Frankel, J.A. (1992), 'International capital mobility: a review', *American Economic Review*, 82, 197–202.

Goodhart, C.A.E. (1998), 'The two concepts of money: implications for the analysis of optimal currency areas', *European Journal of Political Economy*, 14, 407–32.

Gray, H.P. (1992), 'Why a hegemonic system works better?', mimeo, Rensselaer Polytechnic Institute, New York.

Grieve-Smith, J. (1999), 'A new Bretton Woods: reforming the global financial system', in J. Michie and J. Grieve-Smith (eds), *Global Instability: The Political Economy of World Economic Governance*, London: Routledge.

Hicks, J.R. (1982), 'The credit economy', in *Money, Interest and Wages: Collected Essays on Economic Theory*, vol. 2., Oxford: Basil Blackwell.

—— (1989), *A Market Theory of Money*, Oxford: Oxford University Press.

H.M. Treasury (1943), *Proposals for an International Clearing Union*, Cmd. 6437, London: HMSO.

Ingham, G. (1996), 'Money is a social relation', *Review of Social Economy*, 54, 243–75.

—— (2000), 'Babylonian madness: on the historical and sociological origins of money', in J. Smithin (ed.), *What is Money?*, London: Routledge.

—— (2001), 'New monetary spaces?', paper presented at the OECD conference 'The Future of Money', Luxemburg, July.

Kenen, P.B. (1992), *EMU after Maastricht*, Washington, DC: Group of Thirty.

Lavoie, M. (2000), 'A Post Keynesian view of interest parity theorems', *Journal of Post Keynesian Economics*, 23, 163–79.

Marterbauer, M. and J. Smithin (2000), 'Fiscal policy in the small open economy within the framework of monetary union', WIFO Working Paper No. 137, Vienna, November.

Paraskevopoulos, C.C., J. Paschakis and J. Smithin (1996), 'Is monetary sovereignty an option for the small open economy?', *North American Journal of Economics and Finance*, 7, 4–18.

Parguez, A. (2000), 'For whom tolls the monetary union: The three lessons of European monetary union', paper presented at the conference 'The Political Economy of Monetary Union', University of Ottawa, October.

Paschakis, J. (1993), 'Real Interest Rate Control and the Choice of an Exchange Rate System', unpublished PhD. thesis in economics, York University.

—— and J. Smithin (1998), 'Exchange risk and the supply-side effects of real interest rate changes', *Journal of Macroeconomics*, 20, 703–20.

Pressman, S. (1999), *Fifty Major Economists*, London: Routledge.

Smithin, J. and B.M. Wolf (1999), 'A world central bank?', in J. Michie and J. Grieve-Smith (eds), *Global Instability: The Political Economy of World Economic Governance*, London: Routledge.

9. Inflation and the economy

INTRODUCTION

As will be obvious from the discussion in the preceding chapters, one of the persistent themes in monetary economics has been the idea that inflation is a major social problem. Given also that the majority of monetary theories, particularly in the quantity theory tradition, have stressed the link between money and prices, the corollary has usually been that the primary objective of monetary policy should be to reduce or eliminate inflation. Yet at the same time most of these schools of thought have usually also admitted that monetary policy has at least *some* impact on real economic variables such as output and employment, while disputing whether this is of a temporary or permanent nature. Obviously, therefore, difficult issues of political economy can and do arise in situations where choices must apparently be made between competing monetary policy objectives.

This being the case, it might have been thought that one of the main tasks which monetary economists should have performed is to provide a clear and persuasive analysis of just why high (or these days even moderately high) inflation rates are seen as so damaging to the economy that the mere threat of inflation is enough to justify severe corrective action. Yet, remarkably, this is the one thing that the economics profession has conspicuously failed to do. This is not to deny that a certain amount of fairly sophisticated analysis along these lines has been attempted. However, most of the costs of inflation which have been suggested by the technical analysis have turned out to be unpersuasive, to say the least, from the practical political point of view. It is unlikely that the various technical points that have been raised can account for what seems to be almost a fear of inflation (whether genuine or induced), which does sometimes seem to motivate political electorates. The absence of any really convincing economic arguments might also seem to suggest that the instinctive dislike of inflation, which many economists themselves profess, is not really based on anything more solid than the various notions that influence the general public.

Standard economic theory faces a basic and obvious problem in dealing with inflation. This is simply that economists are taught to think always in 'real' rather than 'nominal' terms. What supposedly matters in not the 20 nominal dollars, Euros or yen in the consumer's pocket, but what those 20 dollars, Euros or yen can buy in terms of goods and services. But, once this lesson is learnt, it is then hard to see why a general inflation, in which most nominal prices and incomes are going up by roughly the same amount, should matter very much in terms of the real goods and services which can be purchased. There are numerous rhetorical devices by which the problem can be sidestepped, for example by statements to the effect that *rates of change* of nominal variables are themselves 'real' variables. These statements are meaningless, however, unless it is also explained exactly why it is that the rates of change themselves matter.

One pragmatic response to questions about the costs of inflation would be that, in practice, even in a general inflation, we cannot be sure that everyone's incomes and prices will be adjusted at the same time and in precisely the same amounts. Such an observation, which was favoured for example by such a notable economist as Hicks (1982), may well explain in a commonsense way why inflation *per se* is often unpopular with the public, even if the argument is not solidly grounded in 'economic theory'. There remains, however, the further question of why this type of actual or anticipated distributional injustice could not be dealt with more effectively by other measures (such as indexation) rather than by the 'blunt instrument' of macroeconomic policy actions which may also have a serious impact on real output and employment.

This chapter will attempt to summarize and evaluate the various arguments that have been put forward as to why inflation should be an overriding concern.[1]

THE TRADE-OFF BETWEEN INFLATION AND UNEMPLOYMENT

Clearly, the premises of the original Phillips curve literature arising from the work of Phillips (1958) were that both inflation and unemployment (or low growth) are 'bad' in some sense, but also that, given the idea of a permanent trade-off, each society would be able to make some assessment of the relative costs of inflation and unemployment and choose some 'optimal' cost-minimizing mix of the two.

The later concept of the 'expectations-augmented' Phillips curve, however, as discussed in Chapter 4 above, suggested that such trade-offs only apply in the short run. In the long run, it came to be believed that any inflation rate at all was compatible with the so-called 'natural rate of unemployment'. This general framework obviously changes the consensus evaluation of the relative costs of inflation and unemployment. It might be recognized, for example, that the cost of reducing inflation will normally be

a recession, but if the benefits of lower inflation are expected to be permanent, and the recession will only be temporary, it might well be argued that
the cost is not too onerous relative to the benefits. In fact, it is not too much
to claim that the frequent monetary policy-induced recessions, which
occurred in many jurisdictions from the 1980s onwards, were deliberately
provoked by monetary authorities whose actions were based on arguments
of this kind. The overriding objective was to cure inflation and the resulting recessions were seen as simply an undesirable but explicitly temporary
side-effect of the pursuit of this policy. In the case of the 'monetarist experiments' (Smithin, 1990) of the 1979–82 period, it was even the case
that rational expectations *policy irrelevance* arguments, advanced by such
authors as Lucas (1972), Sargent and Wallace (1975) and Barro (1976), had
convinced some economists that a deflationary policy could be pursued
without any short-run output effects, as long as the actions of the central
bank were pre-announced and 'credible'. A deliberate disinflationary
policy would then carry no costs at all. Events since this period, however,
have obviously not borne out this extreme view.

Contrary to the conventional wisdom as it stood around that time, more
recent events must if anything have somewhat rehabilitated the notion of an
inflation/unemployment trade-off, if not in the textbooks, at least in terms of
realpolitik. Experience seems to show that the pain of the recessionary
periods required for disinflation is severe, and more long-lasting than the
expression 'short-term' would suggest. As discussed earlier, the concept of
hysteresis, suggesting that the time path of an economic variable depends on
its own history then comes into play (Blanchard and Summers, 1986;
Wyplosz, 1987; Setterfield, 1993; Ball, 1999). To recognize these issues of
path dependency does not restore a precise quantitative notion of a trade-off
between inflation and unemployment, as in the original Phillips curve, but at
least puts the longer-term real effects of monetary policy back on the table.

The opposite view that the long-run Phillips curve (LRPC), if not vertical, is positively sloped (that is, that the longer-run association between
inflation and growth is negative, at least for positive rates of inflation) has
also been influential. This idea was originally floated by Friedman (1977)
in his Nobel Prize lecture, and theoretical support is provided by some of
the 'cash in advance' (CIA) literature (Stockman, 1981; Abel, 1985), which
treats inflation as a tax on economic activity. Similar arguments are also
used informally by those advocating practical policies to reduce or eliminate inflation, as in Howitt (1990). Nonetheless, it would be fair to say that
there is little evidence for this position comparable to that originally accumulated by Phillips (Barro, 1995; Temple, 2000). Moreover, as shown by
Kam (2000), and previously by MacKinnon and Smithin (1993), it is a
straightforward matter to devise models with an LRPC going the other

way, and which are equally 'rigorous' from the viewpoint of having neoclassical 'microfoundations'. (See also Smithin, forthcoming, for a general critique of this methodology.) A negatively sloped LRPC would be a revival of the 'Mundell–Tobin effect' (Mundell, 1963; Tobin, 1965), whereby inflation stimulates growth by discouraging the holding of financial assets in favour of 'real capital', which in turn is similar to the earlier 'forced saving' arguments of classical economics (Hayek, 1932).

Finally, recall the analytical results presented in Chapter 7 above, which indicated a far more complex set of potential interactions between inflation and growth than anything suggested in the Phillips curve literature. In the face of this complexity, identifying the precise costs of inflation (if any) will always remain high on the economist's agenda.

THE SUGGESTED COSTS OF INFLATION

The reasons which economists have given over the years for inflation imposing costs on society fall into four main categories. The first and most basic of these is what Hicks (1982) has called the 'oldest argument'. This suggests that, as the basis of the market economic system is the principle of contract expressed in nominal or money terms, instability in the value of money will threaten the system itself. In a serious inflation people will become wary of entering into money contracts and the system could break down. A second set of arguments has been based on the general presumption, whether justified or not, that the medium of exchange cannot itself be indexed against inflation. This would be most obvious if money consisted only of notes and coins, for example, rather than interest-bearing bank deposits. In such circumstances inflation, even if it does not lead to the catastrophic consequences of a complete breakdown of the system, will nonetheless lead society to economize on the use of such non-indexed money. This, in turn, is presumed to be a 'bad thing' if the services provided by money are useful. The third broad category of anti-inflation arguments concentrates on the literal resource costs of frequent price changes, such as the need to print new catalogues or price lists. For obvious reasons, these have been dubbed 'menu costs' in the current literature. Finally, a fourth class of arguments would focus on the perceived unfair distributional consequences of inflation. In practice, inflation does not affect all income earners and asset holders equally, and this would certainly be viewed by potential losers as a sufficient reason to be opposed to inflationary policies. There might also be a broad social consensus against inflation even if it was not clear beforehand who the potential winners and losers might be. In this case, even the *ex post* winners might be opposed to inflation *ex ante*.

There have been many variations on all of these themes both in the professional and popular literature over many years and the dividing lines between them are not watertight. However, in what follows some order will be imposed on the discussion by looking at examples of the arguments made under each of these headings in turn.

INFLATION AND THE MONETARY SYSTEM OF PRODUCTION

On the argument that inflation threatens the monetary system of production based on nominal contracts, Hicks (1982) quotes Dennis Robertson, writing in the 1920s, as follows:

> Our economic order is largely based upon the institution of contract – on the fact, that is, that people enter into binding agreements with one another to perform certain actions at a future date, for a remuneration which is fixed here and now in terms of money. A violent or prolonged change in the value of money saps the confidence with which people accept or make undertakings of this nature.

Hicks points out that it was natural for Robertson, at his time of writing, to think in these terms. At that juncture the great inflations of World War I and its aftermath were fresh in the memory, and these had followed a century and more of near price stability during the nineteenth and early twentieth centuries. In such circumstances, Robertson's comments are perfectly understandable. Hicks continues by saying, however, that, viewed as a more general proposition, what Robertson's argument seems to require is not so much price stability *per se* but *predictability*. If the inflation rate was consistently around 10 per cent, say, and this was expected to continue, there would be no problem in entering into nominal contracts that take this into account.

Indeed, as Hicks also notes, in a situation where inflation has become entrenched, Robertson's point could be used to make an equally powerful case against deflation. For example, the argument could have been applied *against* the explicit policies of 'disinflation' which were a prominent feature of the early 1980s when Hicks himself was writing. In a situation where inflation has become entrenched, a large proportion of contracts and economic planning generally will be based on the assumption that the inflation is going to continue. When disinflationary initiatives take place, therefore, they can cause great disruption. In particular, a great deal of borrowing that had been undertaken on the assumption of continuing inflation will suddenly become unviable. It could be argued, for example, that this was one of the important elements in the much-discussed debt crisis of the LDCs (less developed countries) towards the end of the twentieth century. Hence Robertson's argument is not valid against inflation as such, but only against unpredictability and variability in the inflation rate.

THE COSTS OF A PERFECTLY ANTICIPATED INFLATION WHEN MONEY PAYS NO INTEREST

There is an alternative argument, however, associated with the 'Chicago school' of economists, to the effect that there would be costs even to a 'steady-state' inflation which was perfectly anticipated. For many years this was the standard theoretical case of the economists against inflation. The classic exposition is to be found in an article published by Bailey (1956). Bailey's original argument, it will be recalled, was based on the twin assumptions that 'money' does not bear an explicit interest rate, and that the holding of real money balances involves a utility or 'convenience' yield. The demand curve for real balances is interpreted as a marginal utility curve of money, with the area under the curve measuring the total utility of any particular holding. If the schedule is drawn against the nominal rate of interest (because of the assumption that money itself does not attract interest), a higher expected rate of inflation (equal to the actual inflation rate in the steady state) will lead to a lower level of real balances held. This occurs via the 'Fisher effect' of inflation on the nominal interest rate. The suggested welfare cost is the utility yield forgone by the reduction in real money holdings. In a simple graphical depiction this would show up as an area of lost consumer surplus under the demand curve, analogous to the well-known 'Harberger triangles' of public finance.[2]

The argument is ingenious, but it is fair to point out that, as an attempt to buttress the view that inflation imposes serious social costs, it has tended to meet with scepticism in many quarters. This is not only because attempts to put a dollar figure on these losses for moderate rates of inflation have tended to come up with fairly small numbers (Feldstein, 1979). More seriously, it is difficult to motivate the actual source of these losses in everyday terms. Textbook discussions of the issue tend to refer to the so-called 'shoe-leather' costs of inflation, meaning, for example, the extra time and trouble involved in additional trips to the bank when less ready cash is on hand. This line of argument however, particularly in the modern era of Internet banking, does not seem to be a very convincing explanation for the prospect of inflation engendering such panic amongst policy makers. It may be imagined that it is a great disappointment to intermediate-level students in macroeconomics and monetary economics to learn that the tremendous problems caused by inflation, which the newspapers and electronic media insist should be avoided at all costs, really come down only to this.

In an article very much in keeping with the anti-inflationary temper of the times of the late twentieth century, Feldstein (1979) extended Bailey's static argument to the dynamic case, in an attempt to demonstrate that the issue should be taken more seriously. Feldstein's contribution was to present a revised estimate of the quantitative importance of Bailey's analysis. He pointed out that, as the welfare loss is associated with the change from one permanent rate of inflation to another, it is itself permanent. We should therefore consider not just the current welfare loss, but also the present value of the sum of that loss and all analogous losses in the future. On the one hand, the total must be discounted at an appropriate rate but, on the other, the annual loss must be growing through time as the economy grows. If the chosen discount rate is *less* than the rate at which the loss is growing, the relevant present value integral will not converge to a finite value, and the loss is infinite. As Feldstein also presented a number of arguments for a relatively low discount rate being applied, the upshot is a drastic upward revision of the usual suggested magnitude of 'shoe-leather' costs. In the context of a natural rate model of unemployment, the analysis would imply that *any* reduction in inflation is beneficial, regardless of the cost in terms of unemployment. In a natural rate model any increase in unemployment is bound to be temporary. Even if adjustment is very slow, full employment will be restored in a finite time, so that the costs of unemployment are never infinite, while those of inflation may be. The argument clearly did not consider any possible hysteresis effects, as discussed above.

The argument that inflation should be reduced at any cost may have suited the mood of the time, but in the longer term it may be suggested that Feldstein's argument did not really succeed in rehabilitating the notion of the shoe-leather costs of inflation. By the end of the twentieth century, the idea seemed to have fallen out of favour. As discussed by Smithin (1983), there are a number of technical criticisms that can be made, but on a commonsense level it seems to be obvious that in practice people must be applying a fairly high discount rate to the sum of all future inflation costs. In logic, the type of argument put forward by Feldstein must apply to any type of monetary loss. If a hundred-dollar bill is lost through a crack in the sidewalk, for example, it can be argued that this could have been invested to earn a rate of interest roughly corresponding to the growth rate of the economy in perpetuity. If we apply a sufficiently low discount rate, the loss is infinite and the person losing the hundred dollars should be suicidal. As we do not observe such extreme reactions in practice, it must be presumed that the discount rates actually applied are much higher than those in Feldstein's calculations.[3]

Probably even more significant in the demise of the shoe-leather costs argument, however, has been the pace of financial innovation in recent times. This has undermined the credibility of the crucial underlying assumption that money does not bear interest. Deregulation and other innovations mean that interest-bearing chequing accounts are now commonplace and, to the extent that the nominal interest rates on these accounts keep pace with the rate of inflation, money itself is 'indexed' (Smithin, 1984). On a theoretical level the response might be made that as long as *some* non-interest bearing money continues to exist the point continues to be relevant. However, if the purpose of the argument is to convince the public that inflation really is a serious social problem, it is apparent that for practical purposes the existence of an interest-bearing medium of exchange, and computerized banking itself, makes the notion of 'shoe-leather costs' less and less compelling. Reflecting this reality, the shoe-leather cost of a perfectly anticipated inflation no longer seems to be the main argument of those who argue that there is a significant welfare cost of inflation. Note, also, however, that similar criticisms could be made of *any* argument about the costs of inflation that similarly relies on the notion of money as hand-to-hand currency, which bears no interest. For example, the literature which views inflation as a tax on transactions in the presence of a 'cash in advance' constraint (Stockman, 1981; see also Walsh, 1998), also seems to rest on the anachronistic assumption that money bears no interest.

THE MENU COSTS OF INFLATION

By way of contrast to the old-fashioned shoe-leather arguments, the literal 'menu costs' of inflation did apparently receive more attention in the late twentieth-century literature (Mankiw, 1985; Ball *et al.*, 1988), but actually not so much in the context of the welfare cost of inflation as that of a potential explanation of nominal price rigidity at the microeconomic level of price-setting oligopolistic or monopolistic firms. The major purpose of this literature was, in fact, to provide support for the so-called 'new Keynesian' view of the macroeconomy, in the tradition that identifies Keynesianism with nominal rigidities in the setting of prices and wages. Less attention seems to have been paid to the original role of menu costs as a supporting argument in the case against inflation.

As for being convincing in the latter sphere, the idea of menu costs would seem to suffer from the same type of credibility problem as shoe-leather costs. That is, it is hard to see how these costs could really be all that significant. It is difficult to imagine, in other words, that this type of consideration would be sufficient to cause the 'fear of inflation' on the scale that seems to exist at the political level. In the literature on price rigidity it is actually taken for granted that menu costs are 'small' (Mankiw, 1985). This is not a problem in that context, because it can be shown that relatively minor menu costs at the microeconomic level may lead to large non-neutralities for the macroeconomy (Ball *et al.*, 1988). Small menu costs obviously are a problem, however, if the point is to argue that there are significant direct resource costs of inflation. Moreover, the specific types of menu costs that are often suggested also seem to arise mainly in the context of variable and unpredictable inflation (as with Robertson's systemic costs) rather than that of simply high inflation rates. Items such as the costs of reprinting menus and price lists, and customer ill will, may well be less burdensome in the case where inflation is confidently predicted than when it is a surprise (Smith, 1987). It is certainly the case, moreover, that the technical literature on menu costs presupposes that what is at issue is the stochastic variability of the aggregate price level, rather than its drift. Hence we seem to be coming back to the point, made above, that it is variability and unpredictability in the inflation rate which supposedly cause the most problems.

DISTRIBUTIONAL ISSUES

The final set of problems that are suggested as potential costs of inflation relates explicitly to an inflation that is not perfectly anticipated. The consequences of such an inflation will be distributional, in the sense that the real rewards of economic activity will be distributed differently from those that would have occurred if there had been no inflation. This will be regarded as unfair by those who lose, and as a windfall by those who gain. The mere fact that the outcome is different than expected is bound to increase social tensions, even if there are as many winners as losers. The redistribution of income will also have important effects on economic incentives.

One of the best accounts of the distributional consequences of an unanticipated inflation, after 80 years, is still that provided by Keynes (1923) in the first chapter of his *Tract on Monetary Reform*. This is somewhat ironic in view of the reputation Keynes would later have in monetarist circles. In the *Tract*, Keynes examined the effects of an unanticipated inflation on three classes of society, the 'investing class' (rentiers or financial capitalists), the 'business class' (entrepreneurs, manufacturers and merchants) and the 'earner' (workers). Anticipating the obvious neoclassical objection that the threefold class division of income does not necessarily correspond to the personal distribution of income, Keynes conceded that 'the same individual may earn, deal and invest', but nonetheless suggested that there was something to be learned by investigating the effect of inflation on the three different income sources, particularly in terms of the effects on the incentives to engage in each type of activity. We might also agree that, as applied to individuals in contemporary society, the class divisions suggested by Keynes may well be obsolete, with the role of the investing class, for example, played by the pension funds and other institutional investors, and that of the business class by large corporations. Nonetheless, we can still follow Keynes's argument on the effects of inflation on the incentives for the provision of financial capital, the organization of productive activity and the supply of work effort, respectively. This remains the crucially important issue.

Keynes's major point was the familiar one that an unanticipated inflation redistributes income and wealth from creditors to debtors. If outstanding debts are denominated in terms of nominal dollars or pounds, an inflation reduces the real capital value of the debt, and for a given nominal yield on the debt instrument the real value of interest payments on the debt is reduced also. Both of these effects obviously benefit the debtor. Keynes could see some benefits for society as a whole (obviously not for the creditors) in such a transfer, in the sense that debtors tend to be the 'active' part of the community (for example, farmers, merchants or manufacturers) who have borrowed to set the productive process in motion. On the other hand, creditors are 'inactive'. Nonetheless, he felt that inflation as such was an inefficient way of achieving this transfer and that there should be 'other ways [of adjusting] the redistribution of national wealth, if, in course of time, the laws of inheritance and the rate of accumulation have drained too great a proportion of the income of the active classes into the spending control of the inactive'. The main worry which Keynes had (in 1923) about a redistribution away from the investing class was that it would remove the incentives for saving and capital accumulation, which he felt had been the cornerstone of Victorian prosperity. Needless to say, this was a view held by Keynes well before he published the *General Theory* (1936). The later Keynes would have had investment leading to savings, rather than the other way around, and would therefore presumably have been more sanguine about anything that weakened the motives for saving.

The effects of the unanticipated inflation on Keynes's other two classes are much more benign. The business class of entrepreneurs actually benefit, not only because the real value of their outstanding debt decreases (assuming them to be typically the debtor class), but also from the fact that the rise in prices makes it easy to make profits, as their stocks of goods in process appreciate on their hands.[4] Keynes felt that wage-earners also do not suffer very much from inflation, as the labour unions are usually able to secure rises in nominal wages, which at least compensate for the inflation. During an inflationary period there is little resistance on the part of employers, whose profits are rising anyway, to nominal wage increases.

However, in addition to the point about the disincentive effects on capital accumulation, Keynes also felt that, even if inflation does not actually reduce the real wages of labour, it will nonetheless cause social stress because of perceived injustices. Hence, in spite of any temporary stimulus to output that an unanticipated inflation may cause, Keynes essentially made the case that price stability was the most sensible goal for public policy to aim at. As with the position of Robertson, however, it must be borne in mind that this argument was made in the context of the 1920s. At that point in history, the impact of both inflation and deflation in the aftermath of World War I, coming immediately after the Victorian/Edwardian era of price stability, was obviously much more of a shock to contemporaries than the inflationary experience of the later twentieth century could be.

In addition to those suggested by Keynes, many other examples of the distributional effects of inflation can be given. For example, and as noted in Chapter 2 above, governments also are frequently debtors and historically this has been one of the main motives for them to pursue inflationary finance, the so-called 'inflation tax'. The idea here is that government is extracting resources from the holders of real money balances via the inflation tax, and redistributing them to other constituencies in the course of the various spending and transfer programmes. We are not concerned here with arguments as to the 'optimal' size of the deficit (see Smithin, 2002b), but simply with the observation that, as with all redistributional programmes, this is objectionable to those who are taxed and less so to those who are the recipients of the largesse. A related set of complaints involves the distortions to the regular tax system, which occur when income brackets, exemptions and allowances are defined in nominal terms and not adjusted for inflation. This so-called 'bracket creep' also represents a redistribution of real income from taxpayers to the government. Another problem that is often brought up during inflationary periods is the effect of unanticipated inflation on the living standards of people whose incomes are fixed in nominal terms. For example, this would include persons living on pensions whose nominal value was fixed in a previous non-inflationary period. These observations apply mainly to private sector pensions, as state pensions tend to be formally or informally indexed to some measure of inflation, as the result of political pressure. Hicks (1982) has pointed out that the impact of inflation on wage relativities represents another distributional and distorting effect. It is impossible in practice for all nominal wages to be adjusted smoothly and simultaneously when an inflation occurs, and, because of the sense of unfairness created by this situation, damage may be done to the system of industrial relations.

INDEXATION

One fairly general response to many of the possible difficulties discussed above, including, in particular, those caused by the distributional effects of inflation, is to suggest that they can be dealt with rather simply by indexation. This means that contracts should be expressed in real terms. In the case of a future delivery of some quantity of goods, the promise to pay should include whatever is now agreed in current dollars, yen or Euros, plus an adjustment for some measure of inflation. For example, the parties may agree to adjust the final purchase price of the goods by the amount of any change in the consumer price index or retail price index.

A general adoption of indexation, it may be argued, would be a much simpler solution to the problems of inflation than an enforced period of recession or depression in the real economy. Interestingly enough, however, indexation has not proved to be a popular solution amongst economists, and actually much less so than the alternative remedy of periodic 'planned recessions' to reduce inflationary pressures. There are apparently two sets of reasons for this. The first is a concern that indexation will itself tend to perpetuate or institutionalize inflation through an inertial process. The second is that indexation will tend to freeze the pre-existing set of relative prices and, even if it succeeds in protecting incomes from the ravages of inflation, will prevent necessary adjustments of relative prices from taking place. This will damage the efficiency of the price system. Although these typical arguments are frequently heard, neither of them is particularly convincing. The first seems to rely on a theory of the causes of inflation which is different to that of any of the major schools of economic thought discussed above, while the second assumes the inability of the parties to contracts to distinguish between the *real* wage or price bargain which is being entered into and that which needs to be adjusted to take inflation into account. As far as the latter is concerned, there seems to be no reason, in principle, why indexed contracts could not be written to allow for changes in relative prices also.

It is a 'stylized fact', nonetheless, that at least in those fairly moderate inflations which have occurred in the industrialized world, the actual indexation of contracts is much less of a phenomenon in practice than *a priori* reasoning would seem to suggest. Under moderate inflations, that is to say, people seem to persist in writing contracts in nominal terms in spite of the obvious incentives not to do so. Only when hyperinflations occur does indexation seem to become a matter of urgency. The conclusion that some economists have drawn from this is that the inflations occurring in the industrialized world in the recent past have simply not been sufficiently disruptive to make general indexation worth the trouble (McCallum, 1986). If so, however, this would surely also undermine the case that it is necessary to have severe recessions every few years to reduce inflation rates from these moderate levels. The fact remains that almost all of the reasons that have been put forward for inflation being a major problem could arguably be dealt with by using appropriate indexation schemes. Moreover, such an approach could hardly be more troublesome the alternative inflation 'cures', with detrimental effects on the real economy, that have been tried in practice. This is one more instance of the mystery of why inflation *as such* is regarded with such distaste.

ALTERNATIVE INFLATION NORMS

For many years the preferred monetary policy option of those who regarded inflation as the major economic problem was one variant or another of the proposal put forward by Friedman (1960) to the effect that the rate of growth of the nominal money supply should be held constant at some low level. According to traditional monetarist ideas, this would deliver a low and stable inflation rate on average (Friedman, 1983). As suggested above, stability and predictability of the inflation rate seemed to be regarded as particularly important, on the argument that this would avoid any impact on real economics outcomes of confused price signals. Low inflation rates were also regarded as desirable, either on the basis of shoe-leather types of arguments, or simply because it was felt that higher average rates would be inherently more unstable. Monetary policies loosely based on the monetarist prescription were, of course, put into practice in many jurisdictions in the late twentieth century. They came to grief not because they failed in promoting disinflation, but because the identification and control of the real- world counterparts to the theoretical concept of the money supply seemed to be increasingly difficult, given the wave of financial innovation and deregulation which was proceeding at the same time. But, also, the cost of disinflation, in terms of severe recessions and lost output and employment, seemed to many to be unacceptably high.

Even so, a still harder-line attitude to inflation subsequently became popular in some policy-making and academic circles. It was now argued that so-called 'zero-inflation' or literal price stability should become the exclusive target of monetary policy. This was taken very seriously in some jurisdictions. It was the explicit policy of the Bank of Canada in the 1988–93 period, for example (Lipsey, 1990; Laidler, 1990a; Freedman, 1991; Selody, 1990), and Dowd (1992) points out that a zero inflation target was actually written into the Reserve Bank Act of 1990 in New Zealand. In practice, it is recognized that 'zero inflation' probably means inflation in the

0–2 per cent range for an imprecise indicator such as the consumer price index (Laidler, 1990b), but the acceptance of the general objective of price stability in the zero inflation literature is clear. The monetary means by which zero inflation could be achieved tended to be less clearly spelt out in this later literature than in earlier monetarist contributions, precisely because of the practical problems involved in defining and controlling any particular statistical monetary aggregate. In practice, the pursuit of zero inflation entails driving up real interest rates to slow down the economy sufficiently for inflationary pressures to be reduced to the desired level (see Chapter 7 above).

In terms of the various costs of inflation as discussed, it seems to be as difficult to come up with a genuine theoretical rationale for a target inflation rate of zero as it is for any other particular number. As mentioned, the most plausible arguments for inflation doing serious damage to the monetary system of production relate to variable and uncertain inflation rates. This, however, would imply that inflation should simply be stabilized at some arbitrary level, not necessarily zero. The shoe-leather costs argument might possibly apply in a system in which most of the exchange media consist of non-interest-bearing notes and coins, but that is far from the case in the modern environment. Also, as mentioned, most of the distributional issues that arise under inflation could in principle be dealt with fairly easily by some appropriate indexation scheme. The argument in favour of zero inflation, therefore, must rest on the sense that zero is in some respects a 'magic number', and that it is somehow easier to achieve, and more credible, that the inflation rate could be stabilized at zero than (say) 5 per cent or 10 per cent. Indeed, Scarth (1990) quotes the then governor of the Bank of Canada as claiming that the zero inflation target is the only one which possesses 'inherent consistency and credibility'. It seems, however, that this type of judgment is based essentially on assumptions about the psychological impact of the number zero rather than any purely economic analysis of the costs and benefits of alternative possible targets.

Dowd (1992), who advocates a zero inflation target, points out that there are at least two other inflation 'norms', which might be attractive to supporters of 'hard money'. These are, respectively, the optimal *deflation* rate implied by Friedman's (1969) 'optimum quantity of money' result, and the so-called 'productivity norm', which was important in the history of economic thought and has been revived by Selgin (1990, 1991). Dowd, however, concludes that both are inferior to price stability from the point of view of those already committed to the view that restraining inflation should be the primary objective of monetary policy.

Friedman's argument about the optimum quantity of money was based on the assumptions that money consisted of non-interest-bearing fiat money, and was essentially costless to produce. According to the standard arguments of welfare economics, a social optimum would entail agents increasing their holdings of this currency up to the point where the social and private opportunity costs of holding the currency are the same. As the social opportunity cost of holding money is zero (if there are no production costs), and the private opportunity cost is equal to the nominal interest forgone, this entails that the nominal interest rate be reduced to zero. If the real interest rate is assumed to be determined by forces *outside* the monetary system (that is, determined by the 'natural rate' of interest, as discussed in detail above), the social optimum therefore requires that the inflation rate should actually be negative. Prices should fall at a rate equal to the given real rate of interest. It should be noted that the monetarists themselves always seemed to treat this result as being of purely theoretical interest, rather than as a practical policy proposition. The practical policy actually advocated by Friedman, for example, was simply a constant rate of monetary growth, on the grounds of both feasibility and political viability. Clearly also, from the point of view of anyone who might have doubts about a zero inflation target in terms of the costs of achieving this goal, a proposal to move to actual *deflation* on a persistent basis would be treated with even greater scepticism. Dowd's (1992) critique, from the point of view of a zero inflation advocate, stresses the point that the optimal deflation result was derived under assumptions of full information and perfect foresight, and does not necessarily carry over into a situation where information problems exist. If the main problem is the variability and unpredictability of the inflation rate, the zero inflation rule dominates one which deliberately introduces deflation into an environment in which, in any event, it is not clear to all agents what the 'correct' inflation rate is.

The alternative productivity norm rule would allow for departures from zero inflation in both directions. Prices would remain constant if the productivity growth was zero, but would be allowed to fall with an increase in productivity and rise in the case of a negative productivity shock. The main arguments in favour of this are that it would promote a more 'equitable' distribution of the gains from improvements in productivity (or losses from productivity reductions), and that such a rule would be more conducive to short-run macroeconomic stability. As Dowd (1992) points out, however, the distributional argument implies that all existing holders of nominal claims should share in either the benefits of an improvement in productivity or the losses involved in a negative productivity shock, even if they are not directly connected with the current production process. It is not clear that this notion of equity would be generally accepted, or that it promotes economic efficiency. The macroeconomic stability argument is also criticized by Dowd, on the grounds that it seems to rest on the assumption that the nature of nominal wage contracts remains unchanged regardless of the underlying nature of the monetary regime. For example, in the case of a negative shock, the argument is that real wage cuts might be easier to achieve if prices are allowed to rise in the face of fixed nominal wages than if the same agents are asked to accept nominal wages cuts with stable prices in the same situation. As Dowd points out, arguments of this kind are not usually accepted as valid in neoclassical economics, so it is hard to see why an exception should be made in this case. The main criticism from the point of view of zero inflation advocates, however, would again presumably be that any rule which allows deflation and inflation to occur in some circumstances immediately injects an additional element of uncertainty into the situation, which would not be present under zero inflation. The 'right' amount of inflation or deflation, even under very simple rules that would approximate the productivity norm by stabilizing per capita nominal income, will not be obvious to economic actors *ex ante* and uncertainty over this will be a factor in their economic decision making.

Therefore, as Dowd suggests, it seems that the zero inflation rule, or literal price stability, is the natural choice for those who are predisposed to argue that inflation is the major economic problem. What such arguments do not address, however, is whether the costs of achieving and maintaining zero inflation outweigh whatever benefits are gained by following this rule. As discussed above, it is not adequate to dismiss these concerns on the grounds that the old-fashioned Phillips curve has been discredited, as in turn there are both theoretical and practical reasons to question the general validity of economic models with 'natural rates' of both output and interest rates.

INFLATION, DISTRIBUTION AND REAL INTEREST RATES

Smithin (1996) has suggested that, if the debate over the determination of *real* interest rates is taken seriously in the context of a monetary economy (in other words if it is not simply assumed that there exists some natural rate to which the money rate must conform), then the debate over inflation, and for that matter over other 'nominal' variables such as the nominal size of budget deficits or the nominal exchange rate, may actually be a proxy for a deeper form of distributional conflict, namely that over the real shares in income distribution. We can begin to see how this might work by referring back to some of the analytical results derived in Chapter 7 above, where the distributional question was precisely a matter of the division of the real GDP between real wages, the real rate of interest and the profit share. The behaviour of the inflation rate itself was also correlated with the distributional changes, although not necessarily in a causal fashion. For example, in the case where profits were 'squeezed' by a demand expansion, which raises real wages, this was accompanied by an increase in inflation. Hence firms/entrepreneurs might well support a call for reductions in aggregate demand at this point, not because of an actual causal connection between inflation and profitability but because in these circumstances lower inflation will be associated with a rise in profitability, even if economic growth slows down.

Returning now to Keynes's original discussion of the three social groups or 'classes', we can also see that the impact of inflation on each in that context is in fact closely intertwined with that of changes in the real rate of return on financial assets. These must occur as part and parcel of the attempts to change the rate of inflation in either direction by monetary policy. Recall, for example, that Keynes's business class, or industrial capital, was thought not to be *directly* adversely affected by inflation as such, because in an inflation their goods in process appreciate on their hands. Logically, though, they should have a keen interest in the real rate of interest at which they can finance their activities. For there to be any genuine profiteering from inflation, the real rate of interest must actually fall. Otherwise, in a continuing production process, refinancing next period's production at the new higher prices will eat up whatever nominal profits are gained from selling today's finished goods at similarly high prices. A high real rate of interest, on the other hand, which may be the by-product of any attempt to bring inflation down by monetary means, will be to the disadvantage of this group, for two main reasons. Firstly, an increase in real interest rates directly increases their financing costs, prohibitively so for marginal projects. Secondly, the impact of higher real interest rates on economic conditions generally, causing a downturn in overall economic activity, will in this case adversely affect profitability. Labour, also, it was suggested, can cope reasonably well with inflation itself, but will suffer from attempts to reduce it via deliberately created economic downturns caused by high real interest rates. In those cases, there will be *both* unemployment *and* lower real wages.

On the face of it, therefore, there may a divergence of views on monetary policy between labour and industrial capital on the one hand and financial capital or the rentiers on the other (Palley, 1997). The former groups have no real problems with moderate inflation, and require relatively low real rates of interest in order to prosper. The rentiers or financial capitalists, however, do seem to have economic interests which may be directly opposed to those of the other two classes in this respect, but again not over inflation *per se*. For this group, as long as the real rate of return on financial assets is positive, even an economic actor who has maintained the bulk of his/her wealth in assets denominated in terms of money is effectively indexed for inflation. Very few individuals or institutions, after all, really do keep a substantial quantity of the proverbial 'banknotes under the mattress'. They would doubtless always prefer a higher real rate to a lower, but as long as real rates remain positive by even a small margin, then at least the accumulated real value of financial assets is maintained. A major problem for the rentier, however, is when real rates of return on financial assets become negative. In this case there is literally no way to maintain the value of accumulated wealth by financial investments. In relatively recent history, during the stagflationary 1970s, negative real rates of interest did become a reality, or a serious threat, for many investors. And by making this point we immediately gain a deeper level of insight into the political economy of that decade than just by focusing on inflation alone. Not only was there inflation, there was also little protection from inflation for an influential and powerful group within the society. It is not really surprising, in retrospect, that there would then emerge powerful political forces for change.

Having made the point about the possibly divergent goals of entrepreneurs versus financiers, however, one potentially puzzling issue is that, although in the public arena the representatives of business or 'industrial capital' do frequently protest about the negative effects of the impact of high interest rate policies on the economy, they are also sometimes found to be onside with the financial agenda of low inflation, austerity measures, currency union and balanced budgets. This might be explained by a simple lack of rationality on the part of the spokespersons involved, but it can also reflect the fact that, as we have seen, recessions and unemployment are not always entirely unwelcome from the business point of view. A recession may discipline the workforce, make workers less likely to push for real wage increases, and so on. This does occur in our 'profit squeeze' case from Chapter 7, for example, as discussed. The goal of 'disciplining the workforce', however, can in other circumstances be a self-defeating strategy if what is required to do this is a serious recession in which profits also fall. There therefore remains an element of ambiguity on this question. As Palley (1997) explains the point, the preferences of labour regarding growth and inflation are likely to be at one extreme, and those of finance at the other, with those of business somewhere in the middle. Thus, according to Palley (1997), 'The fact that financial capital has a stronger interest in low inflation and high unemployment than does industrial capital, means that these two interest groups can part ways, leaving open the possibility of an alliance between labor and industrial capital.'

According to the Chapter 7 model, this parting of the ways is most likely to occur in circumstances where high interest rates (monetary policy) are the preferred means for reducing inflation. This will directly cut into both wages and profits on the road to lower inflation.

MONEY, INFLATION AND CAPITALISM

The most salient feature of the capitalist economic process, which seems to be lost in the current focus on the supposedly damaging effects even of a moderate inflation, is that the most progressive and dynamic elements in the economy at any point in time, those on whom future growth depends, tend to be those firms and individuals who have not already acquired substantial financial resources, and hence are 'hungry for success'.

A budding entrepreneur, for example, who has a bright idea for some new product or service but little initial capital, will need to borrow from a bank or other financial institution to pay for the wage bill, capital equipment and raw materials. Success will depend on the price of the final product being high enough not only to repay principal and interest on the initial loan but also to yield some reasonable level of profit. The entrepreneur has to worry not only about the rate of interest that is charged, but also the price that is eventually received. If prices in general are falling over time, even if this is desirable from the point of view of those who already have money, entrepreneurship obviously becomes a rather dubious proposition. Even if prices are only rather flat, which is actually the goal of 'zero inflation' policies, it seems that the life of the entrepreneur will still be something of a struggle. At the other extreme, when there is positive inflation, and more importantly if the interest rate which is charged is not enough to compensate lenders for the increases in prices that are occurring (that is, if real rates are negative), what is actually happening is that the existing rich are being dispossessed of their fortunes for the benefit of the up-and-coming generation. This is unfair to the former group, but the latter might argue that they, after all, are the ones on whose activities current economic progress is most likely to depend.

At some points in history, indeed, this second type of logic has been pushed to extremes, with populist or revolutionary governments (of various political stripes) deliberately using hyperinflation as a weapon to wipe out the resources of the middle class. In a functioning and democratic market economy, though, there must be obvious limits to an inflation-led redistribution of wealth, if only for the reason that the ultimate objective of today's penniless but dynamic entrepreneur is also eventually to become as rich as the previous generation. If the redistribution process becomes blatant, the incentive system itself breaks down and there will be no point in the new participants entering the capitalist struggle, even on initially very advantageous terms, if they themselves are also destined eventually to be 'expropriated'. The opposite extreme of vigorous anti-inflation policies, on the other hand, requiring very high real rates of interest, also seems not consistent with a smoothly functioning capitalism. In essence, these policies simply foster the process of the rich getting richer. They tend to shut the real economy down, prevent the new generation from getting started, and tip the balance too far in the direction of 'the dead hand of the past' (Keynes, 1923). The most reasonable conclusion to draw, then, is that it would be better to strike some kind of balance, which preserves existing wealth, but at the same time does allow scope for new economic activity and for new sources of wealth to develop. What this seems to entail, as previously argued by Smithin (1990, 1996), is not so much a focus on inflation *per se* as on the level of real interest rates. These should be 'low but still positive'. If real rates are positive they do serve the requirement of preserving existing wealth, whereas if they are reasonably low they provide no disincentive to borrowing and economic growth through entrepreneurship.

CONCLUDING REMARKS

When all is said and done on the subject of inflation, the fact remains that economists have failed to make a satisfactory case, in terms of pure theory, for inflation in itself being considered as serious a problem as many appear to believe. The most plausible theoretical arguments about the costs of inflation seem to relate to an inflation rate that is variable and unpredictable, but these would provide as strong a case against a disruptive policy of disinflation as they would for measures to prevent inflation rates increasing from whatever are their current levels. On the other hand, it cannot be denied that inflation is frequently considered a serious problem in the political arena, and may genuinely be feared by electorates. As Dornbusch (1986) has put the point: 'Even if economists cannot identify any catastrophic costs of inflation, politicians certainly can.' The basis of these fears is probably quite simply that to the general public the notion of a steady-state inflation is an abstraction. From the point of view of the public, the salient characteristics of inflation are precisely its variability and unpredictability, and hence its arbitrary distributional consequences. Even if a perfect indexation scheme could be designed as a theoretical exercise, the public is rightly sceptical that such a scheme would ever be implemented in practice. Also the potential distributional consequences of inflation may be of concern even to those who turn out to be winners *ex post*. They have no guarantee *ex ante* that this will be the case. This presumed attitude of the public is quite consistent with the observation that the most convincing of the more technical economic arguments against inflation are those that stress the disruptive effects of unanticipated inflation.

The fact that high inflation rates are regarded with more suspicion than lower ones must presumably reflect the sense that high rates are somehow automatically more variable than low rates. This may *not* actually be a feature of the most widely used theoretical models, but to many it may seem a reasonable commonsense proposition. In addition, there must also be an underlying fear that, once inflation rates have begun to creep up to what in reality are still moderate levels, the authorities will somehow lose control of the process and a genuine hyperinflation will ensue. The popularity of zero inflation as a policy goal among some academics and policy makers presumably reflects these types of sentiment, justified or not.

Given that the popular distaste for inflation is at least a political reality, it would obviously be impossible for governments and central banks to entirely ignore inflationary problems. Reducing the discussion to the above terms, however, does illustrate that the debate about the relative costs of inflation and unemployment is fundamentally a question of political economy rather than pure economic theory, and also that the focus of the discussion on inflation as such may be largely 'totemic' in nature. That is to say that it may be a proxy for the more fundamental questions of income distribution, which are really at issue. Arguably, both the political process and the prosperity of the economy would be further ahead if the latter set of questions were openly and explicitly discussed, rather than hidden behind the smokescreen of 'inflation concerns'.

As illustrated by such episodes as the implementation of the monetarist experiments of the 1980s, however, and the later enthusiasm for 'zero inflation', policy makers in recent decades seem usually to have been far more concerned about inflation than they have been about real economic outcomes such as the rate of growth of output, or unemployment rates. They have been supported in this attitude by an economics establishment which has both emphasized dubious arguments to the effect that inflation *per se* is costly and adopted an economic theory which minimizes the connections between the monetary policy actions believed to be necessary to reduce inflation and the impact on output and unemployment. There are, however, several reasons to question whether either emphasis is justified, not the least of these being the poor economic performance of many of the jurisdictions in which these ideas have been influential.

NOTES

1. Some of the arguments put forward in this chapter draw on an earlier discussion by Smithin (1990).
2. Though they were not actually triangular in shape in Bailey's original paper, because of an assumed vertical supply curve of money.
3. I am indebted to Professor Syed Ahmed of McMaster University who originally suggested this analogy some years ago.
4. As pointed out below, a rise in the nominal prices of inventories of goods on hand will only result in real profits if the nominal interest does not fully adjust. In the context of Keynes's argument, however, this condition is assured by the original argument that the inflation is unanticipated.

REFERENCES

Abel, A.B. (1985), 'Dynamic behavior of capital accumulation in a cash-in-advance model', *Journal of Monetary Economics*, 16, 55–71.
Bailey, M.J. (1956), 'The welfare cost of inflationary finance', *Journal of Political Economy*, 64, 93–110.
Ball. L. (1999), 'Aggregate demand and long-term unemployment', *Brookings Papers on Economic Activity*, II, 189–236.
——, N.G. Mankiw and D. Romer (1988), 'The new Keynesian economics and the output–inflation trade-off', *Brookings Papers on Economic Activity*, II, 1–65.
Barro, R. (1976), 'Rational expectations and the role of monetary policy', *Journal of Monetary Economics*, 2, 1–32.
—— (1995), 'Inflation and economic growth', *Bank of England Quarterly Bulletin*, May, 39–52.
Blanchard, O.J. and L. Summers (1986), 'Hysteresis and the European unemployment problem', in S. Fischer (ed.), *NBER Macroeconomics Annual*, Cambridge, MA: MIT Press.
Dornbusch, R. (1986), 'Unemployment: Europe's challenge of the 1980s', *Challenge*, September–October.
Dowd, K. (1992), 'Deflating deflation', mimeo, University of Nottingham.
Feldstein, M.S. (1979), 'The welfare cost of permanent inflation and optimal short-run economic policy', *Journal of Political Economy*, 87, 749–68.
Freedman, C. (1991), 'The goal of price stability: the debate in Canada', *Journal of Money, Credit, and Banking*, 23, 613–18.
Friedman, M. (1960), *A Program for Monetary Stability*, New York: Fordham University Press.
—— (1969), 'The optimum quantity of money', *The Optimum Quantity of Money and Other Essays*, Chicago: Aldine.
—— (1977), 'Inflation and unemployment', *Journal of Political Economy*, 85, 451–72.
—— (1983), 'Monetarism in rhetoric and in practice', *Bank of Japan Monetary and Economic Studies*, 1, 1–14.
Hayek, F.A. (1932), 'A note on the development of the doctrine of forced saving', *Quarterly Journal of Economics*, 47, 123–33.
Hicks, J.R. (1982), 'The costs of inflation', *Collected Essays on Economic Theory*, vol. 2, *Money, Interest and Wages*, Oxford: Basil Blackwell.

Howitt, P. (1990), 'Zero Inflation as a long-term target', in R.G. Lipsey (ed.), *Zero Inflation: The Goal of Price Stability*, Toronto: C.D. Howe Institute.

Kam, A.E. (2000), 'Three essays on endogenous time preference, monetary non-superneutrality and the Mundell-Tobin effect', unpublished PhD thesis, York University, Toronto.

Keynes, J.M. (1923), *A Tract on Monetary Reform*, London: Macmillan.

—— (1936), *The General Theory of Employment Interest and Money*, London: Macmillan.

Laidler, D.E.W. (1990a), 'Rapporteur's comments', in R.C. York (ed.), *Taking Aim: The Debate on Zero Inflation*, Toronto: C.D. Howe Institute.

—— (1990b), 'The zero-inflation target: an overview of the economic issues', in R.G. Lipsey (ed.), *Zero Inflation: The Goal of Price Stability*, Toronto: C.D. Howe Institute.

Lipsey, R.G. (1990), 'The political economy of inflation control', in R.G. Lipsey (ed.), *Zero Inflation: The Goal of Price Stability*, Toronto: C.D. Howe Institute.

Lucas, R.E. Jr. (1972), 'Expectations and the neutrality of money', *Journal of Economic Theory*, 4, 103–24.

MacKinnon, K.T. and J. Smithin (1993), 'An interest rate peg, inflation and output', *Journal of Macroeconomics*, 15, 769–85.

Mankiw, N.G. (1985), 'Small menu costs and large business cycles: a macroeconomic model of monopoly', *Quarterly Journal of Economics*, 100, 529–37.

McCallum, B.T. (1986), 'On "real" and "sticky-price" theories of the business cycle', *Journal of Money, Credit, and Banking*, 18, 379–414.

Mundell, R. (1963), 'Inflation and real interest', *Journal of Political Economy*, 71, 280–83.

Palley, T.I. (1997), 'The institutionalization of deflationary monetary policy', in A.J. Cohen, H. Hagemann and J. Smithin (eds), *Money, Financial Institutions and Macroeconomics*, Boston: Kluwer Academic Publishers.

Phillips, A.W. (1958), 'The relation between unemployment and the rate of change of money wages in the United Kingdom, 1861–1957', *Economica*, 25, 283–300.

Sargent, T.J. and N. Wallace (1975), 'Rational expectations, the optimal monetary policy instrument, and the optimal money supply rule', *Journal of Political Economy*, 83, 241–54.

Scarth, W. (1990), 'Fighting inflation: are the costs of getting to zero too high?', in R.C. York (ed.), *Taking Aim: The Debate on Zero Inflation*, Toronto: C.D. Howe Institute.

Selgin, G.A. (1990), 'Monetary equilibrium and the productivity norm of price-level policy', *Cato Journal*, 10, 265–87.

—— (1991), 'The "productivity norm" vs. zero inflation in the history of economic thought', mimeo, University of Georgia.

Selody, J. (1990), 'The goal of price stability: a review of the issues', Bank of Canada Technical Report No. 54.

Setterfield, M. (1993), 'Towards a long-run theory of effective demand: modeling macroeconomic systems with hysteresis', *Journal of Post Keynesian Economics*, 15, 347–64.

Smith, G.W. (1987), 'Endogenous conditional heteroskedasticity and tests of menu-cost pricing theory', paper presented at the annual meetings of the Canadian Economics Association, Hamilton, Ontario, June.

Smithin, J. (1983), 'A note on the welfare cost of perfectly anticipated inflation', *Bulletin of Economic Research*, 35, 63–9.

—— (1984), 'Financial innovation and monetary theory', *Three Banks Review*, 144, 26–38.

—— (1990), *Macroeconomics after Thatcher and Reagan: The Conservative Policy Revolution in Retrospect*, Aldershot, UK and Brookfield, US: Edward Elgar.

—— (1996), *Macroeconomic Policy and the Future of Capitalism: The Revenge of the Rentiers and the Threat to Prosperity*, Cheltenham, UK and Brookfield, US: Edward Elgar.

—— (forthcoming), 'Macroeconomic theory, (critical) realism and capitalism', in P.A. Lewis (ed.), *Transforming Economics: Perspectives on the Critical Realist Project*, London: Routledge.

—— (forthcoming), 'Can we afford to pay for social programs?', *Studies in Political Economy*.

Stockman, A.C. (1981), 'Anticipated inflation and the capital stock in a cash-in-advance economy', *Journal of Monetary Economics*, 8, 387–93.

Temple, J. (2000), 'Inflation and growth: stories short and tall', *Journal of Economic Surveys*, 14, 395–426.

Tobin, J. (1965), 'Money and economic growth', *Econometrica*, 33, 671–84.

Walsh, C.E. (1998), *Monetary Theory and Policy*, Cambridge, MA: MIT Press.

Wyplosz, C. (1987), 'Comment', in R. Layard and L. Calmfors (eds), *The Fight Against Unemployment*, Cambridge, MA: MIT Press.

10. Concluding remarks

THE QUANTITY THEORY OF MONEY

As we have seen, the most straightforward way to approach monetary policy issues, if not necessarily the most historically accurate, is to think of money as being simply commodity money, such as full-bodied coins minted from precious metals. This immediately leads on to a comparison between the total quantity of such a commodity money in existence at any point in time and the volume of goods and services traded in the economy over some convenient accounting period. In other words, it leads directly to the characteristic modes of thought associated with the quantity theory of money. With money measured in an arbitrary unit of denomination, and making allowance for the concept of the velocity of circulation, the simplest possible theory of the determination of money prices then follows. As illustrated by the passage from Hume (1752) quoted in Chapter 4 above, this approach was already more or less fully developed by the mid-eighteenth century. It can plausibly be argued that recent refinements have really added very little except mathematical sophistication. For example, the logic can be easily transferred from a commodity-based system to a regime with an inconvertible paper currency, as shown by the monetarists.

It is doubtful, however, that this general theoretical framework was entirely appropriate as a description of the reality of the market economy even at Hume's time of writing. Hicks's (1989) view that even the most basic monetary transaction has an underlying credit element was mentioned in Chapter 2. It is obvious, in fact, that the recognition of even the most rudimentary concept of trade credit would immediately call into question the notion of a completely inelastic money supply.

THE CREDIT ECONOMY AND THE NATURAL RATE OF INTEREST

The next logical (again, as opposed to strictly chronological) stage in the development of thinking about the monetary system is therefore the notion of a 'credit economy' in which the money supply consists primarily of the liabilities of financial institutions such as banks. In this environment the money supply will expand when bank lending increases, and contract when loans are repaid. Now the seemingly most natural way of thinking about monetary issues is in terms of a comparison between the interest rate charged by the banking system for money loans and (some notion of) the rate of return to be earned by employing borrowed funds in various types of productive activity. This differential will provide the incentive or disincentive for other economic actors to become indebted to the banking system, and hence the impetus for the money supply to expand or contract. Reflecting traditional attitudes, the convertibility of bank liabilities into commodity money may well continue to be regarded as a desirable feature of such a system, providing a notional linkage between the credit money system and the commodity money system. Clearly, however, as illustrated by the example of the modern technologically innovated system and also many historical instances (such as the Bank Restriction period in Britain from 1797 to 1821), it is obvious that a pure credit economy is a perfectly viable monetary system, with the liabilities of the central institution themselves becoming the effective base money of the system.

In the history of economic thought, the analysis of the credit money system has been associated particularly with the work of Thornton (1802) and Wicksell (1898), in contributions published almost a century apart. Both made monetary analysis hinge on a comparison between the interest rate charged by the bank and the rate of return to be earned in productive activity, with bank lending (and bank liabilities) adjusting endogenously. The key assumption made by both Thornton and Wicksell, however, and by many subsequent writers down to the present day, was the existence of what Wicksell was to call a 'natural rate' of interest. This was a rate of interest supposedly determined in principle in barter capital markets, and which could not be changed by monetary manipulation. Any attempt to set the bank rate different from the natural rate could therefore only lead to inflation or deflation. Because of this assumption, this type of analysis, even when allowing for the existence of a sophisticated money/credit system, will nonetheless ultimately arrive at a view of monetary policy which is not all that much different from that derived from a simple quantity theory with commodity money.

THE MESSAGE OF KEYNES

On the other hand, as discussed in detail in Chapter 6 above, the assumption of a natural rate of interest is not particularly plausible in a genuine credit economy or monetary production economy. It amounts to assuming that a unique real rate of interest is determined on barter capital markets

in which savings are (somehow) embodied in heterogeneous concrete physical commodities and can be traded to investors for use as capital goods in
specific production processes, and, furthermore, that this already unrealistic picture is in no way altered by the development of monetary payments
systems and sophisticated credit facilities. On the contrary, an apparently
much more reasonable conception for the monetary production economy
would be that the rate of interest is determined in the first instance in the
monetary or financial sector and that, if anything, rates of return elsewhere
must adjust, rather than vice versa. The argument is that, in a monetary
economy, both the type and volume of projects undertaken are fundamentally determined by the cost and availability of finance, which must be
obtained before production can commence. If the latter view is accepted,
the next step in the development of monetary theory is obviously to question the doctrine of the natural rate of interest. In the absence of a natural
rate, the keystone of the doctrine of neutral money would be removed.

It was suggested above that Keynes (1936) was one major economist who
did attempt to take this next step and abandon the natural rate of interest.
According to Keynes, interest rates were a monetary phenomenon determined by so-called 'liquidity preference', and the direction of causality
between the monetary economy and the real economy was explicitly
reversed. However, if this critique of the accepted theory of interest rates
was one of Keynes's main intended messages, it is obvious that the
'Keynesian revolution' did not succeed. Most economists today believe that
Keynes's main argument was that nominal wages can be 'sticky', and pay
no attention at all to Keynesian interest rate theory. More substantively, as
argued by both Moore (1988) and Kaldor (1986), in developing the specific
version of the liquidity preference theory of 1936, Keynes also seemed to
step back from his previous analysis of the credit economy and the monetary circuit, and return to the notion of a fixed quantity of money, similar
to that of the quantity theory and later monetarism.

CONTEMPORARY MAINSTREAM THEORY

The mainstream monetary economics that developed in the second half of
the twentieth century also seemed to return to earlier and simpler concepts,
in spite of supposedly increasing mathematical sophistication. As suggested in Chapter 3, the original achievement of the monetarists was to
restore the discussion of money and monetary issues to the economic
agenda at a time when they were being neglected by the majority of economists owing to various misinterpretations of Keynes. However, fundamentally, the monetarist model was simply an updated version of the

ancient quantity theory of money. Also the concept of the natural rate of interest was emphatically reasserted and explicitly linked with the new concept of a 'natural rate' of unemployment (Friedman, 1968).

Meanwhile, 'formal models of monetary economics' (Hoover, 1988, 1996) were occupied with the essentially hopeless task of finding some method of inserting money into otherwise primarily Walrasian economic models. The various devices which have been suggested, such as 'money in the utility function', 'cash in advance', 'overlapping generations', and so on (Walsh, 1998), may each be claimed to have provided some analytical insights. Ultimately, however, the essence of a Walrasian barter model is precisely that money is *not* needed either to effect exchange transactions or to initiate production (Laidler, 1990). Hence, almost by definition, modern formal models of monetary economics do not provide a viable basis for a realistic discussion of the monetary production economy. It is therefore not very surprising that the course frequently taken by economists with a commitment to barter-oriented 'choice theory' is to develop, for example, 'real' theories of the business cycle, or non-monetary growth theories, which purport to explain important macroeconomic phenomena with no need for any reference to the monetary system. The difficulty with such an approach, however, is that it ignores many of the important episodes of economic history in which monetary factors apparently did play a significant role, not to mention a substantial proportion of the classic literature of the history of economic thought.

Walrasian-type ideas may have reached their apotheosis with the 'new monetary economics' (NME) of the 1980s and 1990s (Cowen and Kroszner, 1994; Hoover, 1988) which seemed to suggest that technological change may soon advance to the point where money *per se* is no longer required in the economic system, and that trading really can be carried on via 'sophisticated barter systems' in which various heterogeneous assets are acceptable in exchange for goods and services. It was suggested in Chapter 2, however, that this view ignores the actual role of money in a real economy, related to the need to develop trustworthy credit relations in a situation in which production is carried on in an environment of genuine uncertainty.

It was argued that the logic of a system of monetary production dictates the need for an asset, which both fixes the standard of value and unambiguously represents final payment of debt. As stressed by the chartalist and neo-chartalist schools (Knapp, 1924; Keynes, 1930; Goodhart, 1998; Wray, 1998), historically the state has played a major role in defining the basic monetary asset via the power of taxation, financial legislation, legal tender laws and so on. In modern practice, the basic monetary asset in each society consists of the nominal liabilities of state-owned or state-sanctioned central banks. This remains true in spite of financial innovation and deregulation, and technical change. The physical form of these liabilities, whether they consist of paper notes, written entries in a ledger or electronic impulses in a computer, is not in itself a matter of much significance.

It would be a mistake, then, to think that the dominance of state central banks is purely a question of 'government interference'. The argument is rather that the logic of the monetary economy, based on trust and confidence, *requires* the development of a heirachical system. It is more a question of political and other pressures compelling the state to assume a central position in a system that could hardly exist otherwise. Therefore, throughout this book, decentralized *laissez-faire* scenarios devoid of power relations, such as those put forward by the NME school and modern 'free bankers', have been regarded as unrealistic.

ENDOGENOUS MONEY AND EXOGENOUS INTEREST RATES

If the mainstream monetary economics of the second half of the twentieth century reverted to the traditional concepts of the quantity theory of money and the natural rate of interest, it can be argued that the contributions of the Post Keynesian horizontalists (Kaldor, 1986; Moore, 1988; Lavoie, 1992), those of the circuit school (Graziani, 1990; Nell and Deleplace, 1996; Parguez, 1996; Parguez and Seccareccia, 2000) and in the later work of Hicks (1982, 1989), do represent a new development of monetary theory in the line identified earlier. These authors have returned to the notions of the credit economy, endogenous money and the monetary circuit, from which Keynes had retreated, but at the same time have followed Keynes in abandoning the idea of an artificial natural rate of interest.

In the horizontalist literature, for example, the money supply adjusts endogenously to changes in the demand for credit, and central banks are obliged to provide the necessary reserves to support a monetary expansion because of their commitment to preserve the liquidity of the system. However, they can control the price at which loans of base money are made available, that is, the short-term money rate of interest. The 'supply of money' function therefore becomes a horizontal line at the administratively determined short-term nominal interest rate, as opposed to the vertical supply function of the quantity theory. Economists with some knowledge of the institutional realities have usually confirmed that this is a reasonable description of the way in which real-world central banks operate (Goodhart, 1989, 2002; B. Friedman, 2000). Also it was suggested in Chapter 6 that the 'horizontalists' among the Post Keynesians are essentially correct in the intramural dispute with their 'structuralist' colleagues (see Dow, 1996; Lavoie, 1996; Rochon, 1999; Chick, 2000) in ruling out an inevitably rising supply curve of money (rather than a horizontal supply function at the administered interest rate) at the macroeconomic level. There may be limits to bank lending, reflected in higher interest charges or credit rationing, at the microeconomic level of the individual bank or individual client, but the same restrictions do not apply to the overall system expanding in concert.

Even granted central bank control over short term interest rates, however this still leaves plenty of room for debate as to how extensive central bank control over the whole structure of interest rates might be, and what would be the effect of interest rate changes on other key economic variables, such as output and employment, exchange rates and the inflation rate. If there is no natural rate of interest, and if the central bank can control the short rate of interest because of its monopoly in the provision of the basic monetary asset, the possibility immediately arises that monetary policy will be profoundly non-neutral. However, the full implications of this may still be resisted by many economists, on the grounds that even if there is no natural rate *per se* there must still be some 'fundamentals', operating at the level either of the domestic economy or of the international economy, which put limits on the extent to which central bank manipulation of interest rates is feasible. In this book, however, the emphasis has been on the power that central banks apparently possess, rather than its limitations.

THE ROLE OF THE CENTRAL BANK

It was suggested above that in contemporary conditions central bank power to control interest rates should be thought of, not only as control over nominal interest rates, but in a meaningful way over real interest rates also. Although the monetary policy instrument must obviously be changes in the nominal rate of interest, central bank officials do form expectations about the inflation rate and, for any given setting of the nominal rate, must be aware of the implications for the real rate. Moreover, in the absence of a natural rate of interest, it is hard to see what the real rate of interest *on money* can be, other than the structure of nominal rates, determined ultimately by the monetary authority, compared to a consensus of inflation expectations shared by the key actors in the system.

According to the expectations theory of the term structure, the long rate of interest is simply a reflection of the expected future time path of short rates. In practice, this does obviously allow for a wide range of outcomes for the yield curve, depending on what expectations actually are. If long rates stay low when short rates rise, for example, or vice versa, this may simply reflect the fact that the change in short rates is only expected to be temporary. Keynesian 'liquidity preference' then does play a role in inserting a 'wedge' between those rates of interest that are more or less directly under central bank control and rates elsewhere in the system. Nonetheless, the implication of our argument is that, in principle, a sufficiently determined and consistent policy by the central bank regarding real interest rates will eventually achieve its objective, whatever that happens to be. Eventually, the real economy must adjust to the policy-determined interest rate, rather than vice versa. This is therefore the precise opposite of the natural rate doctrine.

The reason why 'central banks' (given current institutional arrangements) do possess a high degree of economic power seems inherent in the logic of a system of monetary production. This system must generate for itself a unique monetary asset to fix values and unambiguously represent final payment. Otherwise, the 'social relations' of 'capitalist credit money' (Ingham, 1999) could not exist, and economic activity could only be carried on by an implausible barter mechanism. Inevitably, however, these requirements do confer power on the institution that comes to be responsible for issuing the key monetary asset, regardless of whether the central position is achieved by government legislation or otherwise. Essentially, this central institution dictates the terms on which production is permitted to expand. It is important, therefore, that this power be exercised responsibly.

INTEREST RATE CHANGES, OUTPUT, INFLATION AND EMPLOYMENT

Throughout this book it has been taken for granted that high real interest rates are bad for the economy, as they cause a reduction in output and employment, and that lower real rates are conducive to prosperity in the sense of a higher rate of growth. A simple model with this property, based on a one-period production lag, was discussed in Chapter 7.

In this model, higher real interest rates lead to lower growth, lower real wages and a lower profit share for non-financial business, and vice versa for lower rates. Moreover, these monetary policy effects are in principle permanent, not temporary: they would only change if the policy stance were to change, and not 'automatically' via market forces. The usual justification for higher interest rates is to cure inflation, but interestingly enough the impact of higher interest rates on inflation turned out to be ambiguous. The 'standard case' perhaps, would work out in the usual way, but if the damage done to productivity more than offsets the fall in real wages during an interest rate-induced slump, inflation could actually increase as a result of tight money policy.

The same model also produced interesting results on other potential macroeconomic changes. An increase in aggregate demand growth (holding real interest rates constant) always seems to increase output growth (in Keynesian fashion), but the impact on inflation and the profit share will depend on how 'technologically progressive' the system happens to be. If the demand growth stimulates an increase in productivity by more than enough to offset the inevitable rise in real wages, inflation may actually fall and the profit share may increase. If this is not the case, however, although demand growth will always lead to GDP growth, this will be accompanied by rising inflation and a lower profit share. This latter circumstance may well explain more about the overall political economy of macroeconomic policy making than simply focusing on inflation alone. A positive 'supply shock' meanwhile (meaning by this an exogenous improvement in productivity), will always tend to improve the growth rate and the profit share and reduce the inflation rate. Therefore the 'new economy' scenario, much discussed at the end of the 1990s, is at least a theoretical possibility in an endogenous money environment, whether or not it was a reality in practice. A 'labour relations shock', that is, an increase in industrial conflict, will have the opposite effects to an autonomous improvement in productivity.

We should note that all of these additional theoretical results also have implications for monetary policy, and should consider how the central bank might respond to the various economic events that may occur. Suppose, for example, that there is a negative productivity shock (the opposite of the new economy scenario). According to our model, this will lead to lower growth, higher inflation and reduced profitability. But the classic monetary response to higher inflation is to raise (real) interest rates. This may reduce the inflation, but at the same time it will slow growth, increase unemployment, and reduce real wages and profitability still further. It may not, in fact, even reduce the inflation rate, depending on the conditions discussed earlier. So this does give pause in thinking about what the appropriate role for monetary policy might be. As mentioned earlier, it seems important that interest rates should be kept fairly low, in order to provide incentives for borrowing and economic growth, but also that real rates should at least be positive, in order to preserve the value of accumulated financial capital and the longer-term incentive structure. What does seem unrealistic, in a credit economy in which money is one of the most important of the social relations, is the idea that the interest rate is simply the product of market forces, that whatever level it reaches is therefore 'correct', and that no-one needs to think any further about it, or its impact on income distribution. In short, the relation between money and power is more or less what our intuition tells us it is likely to be.

COMPETING MONETARY NETWORKS IN THE INTERNATIONAL ECONOMY

If the logic of a system of monetary production does suggest that power tends to accrue to the institution or institutions responsible for the provision of the basic monetary asset, one implication that seems to follow is that in the international sphere it may be sensible to defuse that power as far as is practical. This would be an argument that militates against such solutions as fixed exchange rate regimes, or a supranational common currency area (as in the contemporary EU), whose inevitable tendency is to concentrate power still further.

The international economy can be seen as the interaction of a number of competing monetary networks (often but not necessarily confined to the boundaries of political nation states), each centred on a particular central bank. The central banks set interest rates, provide reserves and generally dictate the terms on which monetary production can be undertaken within each network. In general, each central bank has at least some degree of independent power or 'credit', if only because promises to pay denominated in different currencies will never be perfect substitutes. The degree of independent power each central bank possesses will vary, and it was suggested in Chapter 8 that there will be a hierarchy of central banks in the international sphere, just as there is between financial institutions *within* a given monetary network. However, whatever degree of independence there is in each case, this will clearly be abandoned if there is commitment either to join a fixed exchange rate regime (particularly one dominated by a strong 'hegemonic' player) or a common currency area.

It cannot be plausibly maintained that the performance of any particular national central bank would *necessarily* be an improvement over that of either a hegemonic centre dominating a fixed exchange rate regime or a supranational bureaucracy setting monetary policy for a common currency area. Individual national central banks operating in a floating exchange rate environment can drive up real interest rates (in this case, real exchange rates also) and provoke unemployment, frequently with just as much enthusiasm as their internationally powerful counterparts. The case for the individual networks to retain as much independence as possible, in a regime of 'managed' floating exchange rates, rests rather on the idea that this may at least provide an escape route from deflationary pressures imposed from the outside. Also, in terms of basic democratic theory that there should be some correspondence between the definition of political jurisdictions and the accountability of those responsible for economic policy. Only in this case would there be much scope for effective political pressure to be imposed on the policy makers by those affected by their policies. In the case of EMU in Europe, for example, which is much discussed at the time of writing, it seems axiomatic that, if this is to 'work' in both the political and economic dimensions, there must be an eventual move towards a genuine European state.

Given the policy prescription that individual national central banks should attempt to stabilize real interest rates at some low but still positive level, this clearly could not be achieved unless the bank was willing to allow the currency of the domestic country to depreciate (if necessary) in real terms against that of rivals pursuing a different policy. Alternatively, the objective in a managed floating regime might be expressed in terms of a target real exchange rate designed, for example, to achieve a certain volume of exports. This in turn would require a specific policy on real interest rates. Although a very common argument today is that the power of individual central banks to set interest rates in their own jurisdictions is limited by increasing international capital mobility and globalization, reasons were given in Chapter 8 for questioning this view. It was argued above that the main impact of increased international capital mobility in the modern world is that capital account movements drive the current account rather than vice versa. If this is so, however, it becomes more important than ever to pursue a coherent policy on domestic interest rates, which in turn (relative to what is occurring elsewhere) drive the capital account.

CONCLUSION

In a monetary production economy, money is non-neutral almost by definition. Monetary policy, in the sense of central bank control over real financial interest rates, is an important determinant of the terms on which production can be undertaken.

A sensible monetary policy rule for the state central bank would be to stabilize real interest rates at low but still positive levels. This would represent a more viable policy option than many which have been suggested in the past, including both quantitative rules over the rate of growth of base money and the attempted pegging of nominal interest rates.

In order for central banks in separate political jurisdictions to retain some independent control over interest rate policy, there would have to be a 'managed' or 'dirty' floating regime for exchange rates. It clearly would be necessary to avoid international commitments such as a rigidly fixed exchange rate regime or a currency union which, by definition, allow real interest rates to be determined elsewhere.

REFERENCES

Chick, V. (2000), 'Money and effective demand', in J. Smithin (ed.), *What is Money?*, London: Routledge.

Cowen, T. and R. Kroszner (1994), *Explorations in the New Monetary Economics*, Oxford: Basil Blackwell.

Dow, S.C. (1996), 'Horizontalism: a critique', *Cambridge Journal of Economics*, 20, 497–508.

Friedman, B.M. (2000), 'The role of interest rates in Federal Reserve policymaking', NBER Working Paper 8047, December.

Friedman, M. (1968), 'The role of monetary policy', *American Economic Review*, 58, 1–17.

Goodhart, C.A.E. (1989), 'Monetary base', in J. Eatwell, M. Milgate and P. Newman (eds), *The New Palgrave: Money*, London: Macmillan.

—— (1998), 'The two concepts of money: implications for the analysis of optimal currency areas', *European Journal of Political Economy*, 14, 407–32.

—— (2002), 'The endogeneity of money', in P. Arestis, M. Desai and S. Dow (eds), *Money, Macroeconomics and Keynes: Essays in Honour of Victoria Chick*, London; Routledge.

Graziani, A. (1990), 'The theory of the monetary circuit', *Economies et Sociétés*, 24, 7–36.

Hicks, J.R. (1982), 'The credit economy', *Money, Interest and Wages: Collected Essays on Economic Theory*, vol. 2, Oxford: Basil Blackwell.

—— (1989), *A Market Theory of Money*, Oxford: Oxford University Press.

Hoover, K.D. (1988), *The New Classical Macroeconomics: A Sceptical Inquiry*, Oxford: Basil Blackwell.

—— (1996), 'Some suggestions for complicating the theory of money', in S. Pressman (ed.), *Interactions in Political Economy: Malvern After Ten Years*, London: Routledge.

Hume, D. (1752 [1987]), 'Of money', in *Essays Moral, Political and Literary*, ed. E.F. Miller, Indianapolis: Liberty Classics.

Ingham, G. (1999), 'Money is a social relation', in S. Fleetwood (ed.), *Critical Realism in Economics: Development and Debate*, London: Routledge.

Kaldor, N. (1986), *The Scourge of Monetarism*, 2nd edn, Oxford: Oxford University Press.

Keynes, J.M. (1930), *A Treatise on Money* (2 vols), London: Macmillan.

—— (1936), *The General Theory of Employment Interest and Money*, London: Macmillan.

Knapp, G.F. (1924 [1973]), *The State Theory of Money*, New York: Augustus M. Kelley.

Laidler, D.E.W. (1990), *Taking Money Seriously and Other Essays*, London: Philip Allan.

Lavoie, M. (1992), *Foundations of Post-Keynesian Economic Analysis*, Aldershot, UK and Brookfield, US: Edward Elgar.

—— (1996), 'Horizontalism, structuralism, liquidity preference, and the principle of increasing risk', *Scottish Journal of Political Economy*, 43, 275–300.

Moore, B.J. (1988), *Horizontalists and Verticalists: The Macroeconomics of Credit Money*, Cambridge: Cambridge University Press.

Nell, E.J. and G. Deleplace (eds) (1996), *Money in Motion: The Post Keynesian and Circulation Approaches*, London: Macmillan.

Parguez, A. (1996), 'Beyond scarcity: a reappraisal of the theory of the monetary circuit', in Nell, E.J. and G. Deleplace (eds), *Money in Motion: The Post Keynesian and Circulation Approaches*, London: Macmillan.

Parguez, A. and M. Seccareccia (2000), 'The credit theory of money: the monetary approach', in J. Smithin (ed.), *What is Money?*, London: Routledge.

Thornton, H. (1802 [1962]), *An Inquiry into the Nature and Effects of the Paper Credit of Great Britain*, New York: Augustus M. Kelley.

Walsh, L.E. (1998), *Monetary Theory and Policy*, Cambridge, MA: MIT Press.

Wicksell, K. (1898 [1965]), *Interest and Prices*, New York: Augustus M. Kelley.

Wray, L.R. (1998), *Understanding Modern Money: The Key to Full Employment and Price Stability*, Cheltenham, UK: Edward Elgar.

Index